Opium
Inc.

Opium Inc.

HOW A GLOBAL DRUG TRADE FUNDED THE BRITISH EMPIRE

THOMAS MANUEL

HarperCollins *Publishers* India

First published in India in 2021 by
HarperCollins *Publishers*
A-75, Sector 57, Noida, Uttar Pradesh 201301, India
www.harpercollins.co.in

2 4 6 8 10 9 7 5 3 1

Copyright © Thomas Manuel 2021

P-ISBN: 978-93-5422-927-5
E-ISBN: 978-93-5422-836-0

Typeset in 11/15.2 ITC Galliard at
Manipal Technologies Limited, Manipal

Printed and bound at
Replika Press Pvt. Ltd.

Contents

Prologue
The Great Opium Triangle

In late February 1793, the *Hindostan*, an East India Company ship, came to anchor off the coastal town of Anyer on the island of Java in current-day Indonesia. Outside the Dutch fort at Anyer, there was a small plaque commemorating Charles Allan Cathcart, the former British ambassador to China. Cathcart had died five years earlier, just off the coast of Sumatra, and so his embassy never even reached its destination. The anchored *Hindostan* was waiting for the arrival of the current British ambassador to China, George Macartney.

Macartney was en route on the *HMS Lion*, a sixty-four-gun ship that had set off with the *Hindostan* from England in September 1792. Despite having the same appointment, Macartney was a very different man from Cathcart. He wasn't born a noble, only gaining aristocratic titles later in life. When Cathcart got his appointment, he was only twenty-eight. Macartney had his first foreign posting at a similar age, representing Britain at the

Russian court. But he was now fifty-five and a long and illustrious career trailed behind him.

Macartney had even been the governor of Madras for a few years in the early 1780s. Cathcart had been in India during that time as well and had fought at the Battle of Cuddalore, which marked the beginning of the Second Anglo-Mysore War. Macartney, to some extent, negotiated the end of that war. Macartney's right-hand man George Staunton would become a baronet for his contribution to the peace negotiations. Now, in 1793, Staunton accompanied Macartney on this fateful embassy to China. He was the official ambassadorial replacement in case Macartney went the same way as Cathcart and died on the way. After his tenure at Madras was over, Macartney was offered the position of governor general of Bengal and he turned it down. He wanted to go back to England. But within a few years, here he was again, at the other end of the world, on a vital mission for king and country. The mission was to officially wish the Chinese emperor a happy eighty-third birthday on behalf of King George III of England. And, alongside that little birthday greeting, Macartney was to negotiate the small matter of free (or at least freer) trade between Britain and China. Currently, the British were limited to one port: the city of Canton (now known as Guangzhou). British traders were not allowed to land anywhere else in China and they chafed at this forced bottleneck. The Chinese had their reasons, of course. They had learned what Europeans were doing elsewhere in the world and had no plans of becoming another colony.

This expedition was trying to change their minds and so no expense was spared. It employed almost a hundred people and cost around £78,000 – which would be around Rs 90 crores today. But the East India Company had agreed to sponsor all of it. They knew the fortunes to be made if the embassy went well.

Even back then, in the eighteenth century, many in England saw China as 'the most extensive market in the world'.[1] It only had to open (or be opened) for business. To impress the emperor with British science and manufacturing, Macartney had brought a fortune in gifts. Cathcart's embassy had carried gifts but Macartney's embassy overflowed with offerings – more than six times as valuable as Cathcart's cargo.

When they reached China, the Macartney embassy got special permission to land close to Peking on account of their gifts being so delicate. Ninety wagons, forty barrows, 200 horses and 3000 workers were used to carry all of the various objects into the capital city of the Chinese empire.[2] There were telescopes and barometers, clocks and hot-air balloons, swords and pistols, textiles and stationery. The largest and most elaborate present for the emperor was a planetarium, built in Germany but embellished in England, which cost more than £1200 – more than Rs 1 crore in today's terms. This elaborate glass-encased machine contained a celestial globe that purported to show the Milky Way as well as separate mechanisms for the orbits of Earth, Jupiter and Saturn. It had three clocks that displayed various scriptural schedules that proudly proclaimed the end of time (and the world) was coming in 1836! One notable item that Macartney didn't take was an example of the recently invented steam engine because he felt it wouldn't be worth the trouble. A strange decision when he was packing such a complicated oddity as this planetarium.

But the Chinese ruler, the Qianlong emperor, was not impressed. When the British walked through his palace, they found it full of clocks, machines and other automata that the Chinese court had accumulated through the years, mostly from other European nations. The British were hoping to dazzle the Chinese with their engineering and technology but the

Chinese were far from dazzled. The emperor did indeed have a fascination for clockwork automata but it was a fascination that had been regularly indulged. And from there, things got worse. As Macartney was led to the emperor, court etiquette was explained to him – but as orders were translated, confusion broke out.

Words were slung back and forth. The exchange grew heated. Macartney was to prostrate himself with his forehead touching the floor as was traditional when meeting the emperor – but the gentleman refused. As far as he was concerned, he did not kowtow to his own king; how could he do so for a foreign emperor! Historians aren't sure how the impasse of etiquette was finally negotiated. Chinese sources tend to say he eventually kowtowed while British sources tend to deny it. What we do know is that in the end, the Qianlong emperor refused all of the requests made. The embassy was a complete failure. The emperor was emphatic that China had no need for British goods. Within a few months, Macartney was forced to get back on his ship and sail sadly back to England.

This was a disaster for Britain. They needed this trade deal more than the casual reader might imagine. The country was heading towards an economic flashpoint, what we refer to now as a balance of payments crisis, where imports were so much higher than exports that the country was literally running out of physical money to pay for their purchases. At the centre of this economic tornado was the humble, calming cup of tea.

For most of history, the Chinese mainland monopolized the cultivation of *Camellia sinensis*, more commonly known as tea. In most languages, the word for tea either starts with a 't' sound or a 'ch' sound (as in 'chai') depending on whether it first arrived there by land or sea, that is, from the western or eastern part of China respectively. When the English first discovered tea, they fell in love with it. It became a national obsession, and there seemed to be no end to the British citizenry's capacity to consume this exciting new beverage. At its peak, at the beginning of the nineteenth century, the duty on tea accounted for 10 per cent of Britain's total revenue – an extraordinary situation. To put it in context, in 2018, the total receipts from taxing corporations came to 9 per cent of the country's revenue!

But the only way to get tea was from China. And as had been made clear, the Chinese had no particular interest in British manufacturing goods or their cloth. So even as tea imports to Britain surged, there was nothing they could sell to China that could balance the equation. China would only accept silver – the equivalent of asking for cold, hard cash. But as the eighteenth century drew on, the British empire's treasury was looking bare; they were running out of silver. They didn't have enough cold, hard cash to pay for their tea habit. It became imperative for them to find something the Chinese wanted as much as they, the British, wanted tea.

Simultaneously, the British had another problem: their new colony in India wasn't as profitable as they had hoped it would be. Ever since the battles of Plassey and Buxar in the mid eighteenth century, the British had shifted from controlling a network of trading posts in India to becoming an imperial power. They governed land and raised money through taxes. It was the era of Company Raj. But as imperial wars to conquer more and more land (so they could earn more and more money) dragged on, they found they were spending an increasing share of their newly gotten money on the wars themselves. They needed a new way to make money off this hard-won colony.

And then, somewhere in the mechanical mind of the British empire, a cog clicked and fell into place. Two problems became one solution. They put their colony to work to produce something that the Chinese would buy even if they didn't want it: opium. Opium, the sticky gum harvested from the poppy plant, is a powerful narcotic. You can drink it, eat it, smoke it. It gets you high – and it is addictive. After a while, it becomes hard to stop using it. And there is nothing better for a seller than a product you can't stop buying. Over the eighteenth and nineteenth centuries, the British transformed entire farming economies in Bengal and Bihar into opium-producing machines. And their agents smuggled the drug illegally into China, exchanging it for tea.

Suddenly, the balance of trade leaned the other way. Silver started flowing back out of China into British hands. Slowly, this new equation solidified into a stable system: the Great Opium Triangle. To paraphrase the historian Tan Chung: the Chinese got opium, the British got tea, and the Indians got colonialism.[3] It was a neat formulation that belied what was really going on: the British were enabling the longest-running drug deal in the history of the world. They were knowingly getting millions of people addicted for profit, not just in China, but in India as well. Even as they passed laws against opium at home, they produced it in India and sold it in China.

At its peak, opium was the third-highest source of revenue for the British in India, after land and salt. This makes the Honourable East India Company a drug cartel masquerading as a joint stock corporation masquerading as a government. The British Raj in the nineteenth century was a narco-state – a country sustained by trade in an illegal drug.

This book is the story of opium and its place in history. This is a story about the banality of evil, the birth of megacorporations, and the foundation of empires.

In the first chapter, 'The Poppy Pioneers', the tale of opium unfolds from antiquity all the way up till the nineteenth century. From the cults of ancient Greece to the doctors of the Islamic world, opium is just one plant among many used for ritual, recreation and medicine. In the Indian subcontinent, the opium poppy was an ordinary crop. And while individuals from emperors to holy men may have consumed the extract, it was never a major item of trade. Europeans changed that. In the 1600s, the Portuguese and the English began trading in opium with India for the first time. The English were mostly importing it back home. The Portuguese started selling it to China. But it was the Dutch East India Company that first filled entire ships with chests of the dark, sticky substance. Following in their footsteps, the English East India Company officially entered the trade in the 1700s.

But in 1729, the emperor in Peking was fed up with the growing ubiquity of opium smoking among his people. He instituted a complete and total ban. However, his empire's power was waning and his prohibition had almost no effect on the trade. The British obeyed the letter of the law. They stopped exporting the drug on official Company ships and let private vessels carry on the trade under the guise of 'smuggling'. On the other end of the deal, merchants in Canton saw no reason to quit either. The only merchants who had license to trade with Europeans were called the Hong and becoming a member of the Hong involved paying serious bribes to government officials. These bribes were investments and the Hong expected to earn their money back. So these merchants were happy about the opium trade – even if it meant breaking the law. Their bribes were often called 'tea money' after the reason the British ships kept coming back.

In the second chapter, 'From Calcutta to Canton', the path between two cities becomes well-worn as opium becomes central to trade. To paraphrase historian Michael Greenberg, the East

India Company became masters of owning opium in India and disowning it in China.[4] Throughout the eighteenth and most of the nineteenth centuries, trade from Calcutta grew exponentially – taking it from shanty town to bustling capital. With their chokehold on Bengal, the East India Company instituted a large and complicated bureaucracy to manage opium production over one of the most fertile provinces in the subcontinent. Thousands of farmers cultivated and harvested the milk of the poppy – sometimes freely, often coerced, always trapped in cycles of indebtedness. From farms, it was sent to factories where it was tested, standardized and packaged in chests of mango wood. These factories employed a small army of children to crawl over ceiling-high scaffolding and painstakingly maintain the precious drug till it was ready to be shipped. From there, it travelled to Calcutta where it was auctioned to chummy millionaires who financed the ships' journeys to China.[5]

In the third chapter, 'Smugglers from Malwa', the East India Company's self-declared monopoly on opium is violated when a rival trade begins on the western coast. In central India, in the kingdoms of the Maratha Confederacy, enterprising Indian traders were financing their own opium production and shipping it to Canton themselves. This 'Malwa opium' became immensely popular in China. It was less consistent but offered greater potency. At first, the Company tried to clamp down on these 'smugglers' but to no avail. But luckily for them, the demand for opium was growing so fast that the Calcutta trade was booming as well. So in the spirit of 'if you can't beat them, buy them', the Company decided to simply start buying up the opium from Malwa in the free market. Instead of gaining control over the market, they simply succeeded in driving up the prices. They tried to close ports but the smugglers always found another way, such as Portuguese-controlled Daman. They negotiated political treaties with generous terms but opium production only increased.

Finally, in 1830, the Company threw up its hands and gave up on its dream of being a monopoly in western India. It began to allow any merchant to export opium from Bombay as long as they paid a transit duty. As paying the duty was cheaper than smuggling, the smugglers made the savvy economic choice. As a result, Bombay exploded into life.

In the fourth chapter, 'The Bombay Boom', the city goes from a handful of unwanted, malarial islands to a cosmopolitan centre of commerce. At first, Parsi traders dominated the commerce. Jamsetjee Jejeebhoy was one of them. Working with the largest opium traders at the time, Jardine and Matheson, Jejeebhoy became one of the richest men in the country. With this new wealth, he would launch a philanthropic campaign that would mark the face of Bombay forever. Apart from roads and waterworks, he would fund JJ Hospital and the JJ School of Arts, which would later birth the modernist art movement led by people like M.F. Hussain. In return, Queen Victoria named him the first baronet of Bombay. In the nineteenth century, many members of the Parsi community moved to the cotton industry. The opium trade came to be almost monopolized by a Baghdadi Jewish family, the Sassoons, who also left their legacy writ large through the docks that bear their name and other institutions they supported.

In the fifth chapter, 'The Opium Wars', the British empire goes to war for their universal rights, national dignity and the right to traffic in drugs. In 1839, in the midst of the raging opium trade, a Chinese commissioner named Lin Zexu was sent by the ruling emperor to Canton to handle the opium problem. After decades of flip-flopping on how to tackle the opium crisis, the emperor set aside his indecision and finally took a stand –

possibly because one of his sons was caught smoking in a temple in the Forbidden City. Lin Zexu was a hardliner when it came to opium. He was also honest and unwavering in a way that spelled trouble for the Hong merchants. He had first-hand experience of the perils of addiction because his tiny village was one of the first places where opium smoking was introduced. Lin considered opium a 'life-destroying drug threatening to degrade the entire Chinese people to a level with reptiles, dogs and swine'.[6]

Within two months of arriving at Canton, Lin Zexu had arrested 1600 people. He even sent a letter to the queen of England politely explaining why her people were a plague upon the earth. Soon, he was besieging the warehouses of foreign merchants, demanding they give up their stocks of opium. It took one and a half months, but eventually the merchants surrendered. Lin confiscated 21,000 chests of opium – worth more than the GDP of a small country at the time. And then he burned it. It took days for the entire stock to turn to ash and be flushed into the sea. This was an economic disaster that rippled outward through the entire global economy. Whole fortunes had been destroyed. In Bombay, several Parsi merchants committed suicide when they heard the news. The British representative in Canton, Charles Elliott, promised the howling merchants that the government would reimburse them for their lost stock. This pacified them but enraged Elliot's employers in London. The government had no desire to start indemnifying private traders. Especially because they didn't have the money!

Ever since the Macartney embassy, a popular narrative had emerged in Britain that the Chinese emperor was a pompous fool who had rejected British manufactured goods out of short-sightedness and arrogance. The drums of war, thanks in no small part to opium barons like Jardine and Matheson, had been beating for years. The entire mercantile class of British society knew the potential for profit if China became a captive market. Soon enough, the British navy was deployed.

The British won what came to be called the First Opium War in 1842 and forced China to sign the humiliating Treaty of Nanjing. Under this treaty, four new ports would be opened to Europeans, including Shanghai, which soon became the funnel for more than half of the total opium brought into China. China was also compelled to pay huge war reparations, as partial compensation for the cost of the war and all the opium that Lin had destroyed. In addition, the British annexed the island of Hong Kong. Notably, the treaty did not make opium trafficking legal. That would only happen after the British went to war for a second time. Regardless of the true reasons behind these wars, in 1879, the opium trade peaked at around £15 million – more than $1 billion today.[7]

In the sixth chapter, 'Anti-opium Crusades', the aftermath of the two wars sees public opinion in Britain slowly shift against the opium trade. Throughout the nineteenth century, various groups in England fought for the abolition of the entire industry. The most famous was the Society for the Suppression of the Opium Trade, which was started in 1874 and had attempted four separate times to introduce resolutions that would abolish the trade. Many of the original members were Quakers, a pacifist Christian group with a long history of political activism that includes winning the Nobel Peace Prize in 1947.

Around 1894, the Society for the Suppression of the Opium Trade convinced British Prime Minister Gladstone into constituting a Royal Commission to look into the opium problem. While the Commission was initially received with enthusiasm, it was soon apparent that it was compromised from its inception. It only looked at India, ignoring all effects of the trade in China. Most of the members chosen were already sympathetic to the cause of the British government in India. In the end, despite numerous interviews and a long and methodical review of the facts, the Commission endorsed the continuation of opium production. There was only one dissenting voice! Both the Indian members, and even one of the Society's nominees, sided with the Commission's judgment.

In the seventh chapter, 'Opium and Independence', the Indian nationalist movement gains steam. But opium became a tricky topic for the leaders of the freedom struggle who found themselves having to choose between the economic interests of the nation and the humanitarian costs of the trade. Most of them refused to criticize opium – despite stridently criticizing alcohol. As an 1889 editorial in *The Hindu* opined, 'Opium may be a great evil, but national bankruptcy is a greater evil.'[8] One of the only major dissenting voices was Dadabhai Naoroji, who refused to touch the opium profits of the firms he had invested in. In his own words, 'This opium trade is a sin on England's head, and a curse on India for her share in being the instrument.'[9]

Most of the other nationalist leaders found no contradiction in arguing for the independence of their own country on humanitarian grounds while continuing to exploit the citizens of another country. Many openly criticized the anti-opium lobby in England. The Indian National Congress passed their first resolution against opium only in 1924. In the same year, they formed a committee headed by a British priest, Charles Freer Andrews, to investigate the first Indian opium epidemic. In the colonial tea plantations in Assam, the government and rich planters found common interest in the mass availability of the drug for their workers.

In the eighth chapter, 'Endings and Legacies', the opium trade finally comes to an end. In 1909, thirteen nations came together to discuss the opium problem at the first international conference in Shanghai. A few years later, these nations met again in The Hague in the Netherlands and signed the International Opium Convention, which bound them to 'control' the opium trade. In 1913, the last shipment of Indian opium reached China where they promptly set it on fire as a symbolic gesture of defiance. A decade after the Shanghai conference, and after the desolation of Europe during the First World War, a global version of this convention would be added to the 1919 Treaty of Versailles.

The ninth chapter, 'Opium, Cotton, Sugar, Slavery', zooms out of the opium triangle that dominated one section of the globe and moves laterally to explore the ways that the opium trade intersected with various other systems across the world. Through Britain's thirst for tea, there was a boom in the demand for sugar. Sugar and cotton plantations drove the horrific Atlantic slave trade. This coexisted for a few years with the coolie trade – where indentured labour from India and China were shipped across the world. Whether the plantations were in Malaysia or Cuba, opium was used by the owners as a form of social control: dependent workers were much more pliable.

The tenth chapter, 'Opium Smoke and Mirrors', explores the drug's literary legacy. Apart from its mark on Romantic poets like Keats, Shelley and Coleridge, opium and the broader trade have found their way into Indian writing in English as well. In *Narcopolis*, Jeet Thayil tells the story of opium pipes and dens in 1970s Bombay. Amitav Ghosh's magisterial Ibis trilogy claims the entire history of the opium trade as its canvas, with the characters moving between the central locations and events that mark this period in history.

Finally, in the eleventh chapter, 'Opium Today', the story continues from the end of the India–China trade to the present day. A global anti-drug regime has emerged through international cooperation but has been dominated by the rhetoric of the USA's War on Drugs. Promoted by a series of right-wing presidents,

America's War on Drugs led to a militarized, disastrous and fundamentally ineffective series of interventions across the world. And even as they pursued these policies, there have been multiple instances of their efforts being undermined through actions of their intelligence organization, the CIA. In its long-running fight against the spectre of communism, the shadowy intelligence agency allegedly collaborated with multiple criminal organizations engaged in illegal drug trafficking.

Today, the opium landscape looks very different. For decades, the source of the world's illegal opium was a small patch of mountainous jungle in the crux of Laos, Thailand and Myanmar. Now, almost 90 per cent of the illegal production of opium comes from Afghanistan. Legal production of opium still occurs in a few countries across the world, including in India. While production is strictly controlled, there are more than 60,000 farmers who are opium license holders. Despite being engaged in a state-sanctioned activity, these farmers constantly live under a cloud of criminality. All of them are suspected of secretly supplying the illegal drug trade in India – which domestic intelligence agencies continuously link to near-mythic Pakistani drug lords and terrorists, ignoring the role of our own political leaders.

Over the course of the last century, pharmaceutical companies have synthesized a number of different drugs that bind to the same receptors in the brain as opium. These drugs, like fentanyl and methadone, are called opioids but they don't have any connection to the poppy plant. Drugs that are produced from the poppy are called opiates and include substances like heroin, morphine and codeine. While all of these were used medicinally, they all contributed to a series of devastating epidemics that ravaged and still ravage several countries across the world, including the USA. In 2018, there were more than 70,000 deaths by drug overdose in the USA, most of them from opioids.

Closer to home, a 2015 study led by the All-India Institute of Medical Sciences estimated that there were more than 200,000 people who suffered from opioid addiction in Punjab.[10]

In the 1950s, Mao Zedong would take ruthless measures to curb the opium epidemic: arresting people with addictions, executing dealers and destroying opium crops. It might sound vicious (because it was) but it was a problem that had been systematically cultivated by a cartel of European countries for centuries. It's hard to calculate how many people were actually addicted to opium in a debilitating way. Different historians have estimated that 1 per cent to almost 10 per cent of the population were smoking the drug daily by the end of the nineteenth century. But despite these large numbers, it's important to note that a lot of the scaremongering imagery about opium – emaciated people with addictions wasting away in dingy opium dens – was invented as propaganda for political purposes and often racially motivated. These nested layers of propaganda and counter-propaganda cloud every issue revolving narcotic drugs. But what is clear is that for more than a century, the British government and the East India Company believed that the drug was dangerous and continued their trade anyway.

The story of the opium trade (though as historian Amar Farooqui argues, 'trade' is too kind a characterization[11]) isn't just about the narcotics that were stored in chests and packed into ships. It's about how this system that existed for more than a hundred years shaped the world we live in today. The legacy of the opium trade in India, whether it's the poverty of Bihar or the wealth of Bombay, is something that we still do not discuss in textbooks or teach in schools and colleges. Like many institutions in India, the story is one of immense pain for many and huge privileges for a few.

Notes

1. Matthew Boulton, industrialist and partner of James Watt, the inventor of the steam engine, quoted in Berg, Maxine. 'Macartney's Things. Were They Useful? Knowledge and the Trade to China in the Eighteenth Century.' From Global Economic History Network (GEHN) Conference, vol. 4, 2002.
2. Berg, Maxine. 'Macartney's Things. Were They Useful? Knowledge and the Trade to China in the Eighteenth Century.' From GEHN Conference, vol. 4, 2002.
3. Chung, Tan. 'The Britain–China–India Trade Triangle (1771–1840).' *The Indian Economic & Social History Review* 11, no. 4 (January 1974): 411–31.
4. Greenberg, Michael. *British Trade and the Opening of China 1800–42.* Cambridge University Press, 2008, p. 110.
5. Bauer, Rolf. *The Peasant Production of Opium in Nineteenth-Century India.* Brill, 2019, p. 79.
6. Lovell, Julia. *The Opium War: Drugs, Dreams, and the Making of Modern China.* eBook, Abrams, 2011.
7. Nye, Eric W. 'Pounds Sterling to Dollars: Historical Conversion of Currency.' https://www.uwyo.edu/numimage/currency.htm. Accessed 19 October 2019.
8. Chandra, Bipan. *The Rise and Growth of Economic Nationalism in India: Economic Policies of Indian National Leadership, 1880–1905.* Har Anand Publications, 2010, p. 508.
9. Chandra, Bipan. *The Rise and Growth of Economic Nationalism in India: Economic Policies of Indian National Leadership, 1880–1905.* Har Anand Publications, 2010, p. 506.
10. Ambekar, A., A. Agrawal, R. Rao, A.K. Mishra, S.K. Khandelwal and R.K. Chadda, on behalf of the group of investigators for the National Survey on Extent and Pattern of Substance Use in India. *Magnitude of Substance Use in India.* Ministry of Social Justice and Empowerment, Government of India, 2019.
11. Farooqui, Amar. *Smuggling as Subversion: Colonialism, Indian Merchants, and the Politics of Opium.* New Age International, 1998, p. 4.

1

The Poppy Pioneers

Early History

In the Iraklion Archaeological Museum, on the island of Crete in the Mediterranean Sea, sits the Poppy Goddess. She's 78 centimetres tall and dressed in arresting attire. A standing collar frames her regal neck. At the back, the dress is open, a triangular section cut away to reveal skin down to her waist.[1] It's high fashion – from more than 3500 years ago. Apart from proving that fashion is cyclical, the Poppy Goddess is the earliest depiction of a person with opium symbolism. In her hair, there are three moveable hairpins in the shape of opium buds. The buds have harvest notches on them – delicate incisions that let the sap leak out. The Greek archaeologist who discovered the terracotta figure in 1937 wanted to call her 'the goddess of ecstasy',[2] as he saw in her face a beatific expression: she seemed to be spectacularly high. The dominant theory is that she's part of a pantheon of deities of the Minoan civilization, named after the mythical King Minos who let the half-bull half-human Minotaur wander around in his labyrinth in what can only be described as an irresponsible manner. The Minoans are one of the earliest civilizations in the European sphere, overlapping for centuries with the Indus Valley civilization thousands of kilometres away.

The Minoan Poppy Goddess has come to be associated with Demeter, the Greek goddess of grain and harvest. She's tied to medicine and fertility. There are other figurines like her, similar in general design but differing in specific details. Some have snakes on their arms or doves in their hair. All of them have their hands raised in gestures of benediction. To the modern viewer, though, they might look like they've been caught in the middle of a crime and are telling the police not to shoot. While that is a joke, there are theories that the Poppy Goddess isn't a goddess at all. The outraised hands might not be a benediction but rather arms lifted in praise or surrender. She might represent the worshippers – a stand-in for their role in whatever ritual is being conducted.[3] But that enigma aside, the crown of poppies in her hair is probably the first hint of opium's complicated role in the ancient world.

There is evidence of opium in Egypt where the Ebers Papyrus recommends it as a cure for crying children, albeit a temporary one. In Hellenic Greece, Hippocrates and Aristotle mention it as a medicine. Homer makes multiple references to it – as a way of numbing the spirit as much as the body. On the island of Kea, off the coast of Greece, senior citizens held what Lucy Inglis calls 'suicide parties'.[4] On reaching the age of sixty, Keans who felt they were turning into a drain on society might throw a funeral celebration with their friends and drink a cocktail of poppy, hemlock and wine. Alexander the Great's armies cut a wide swathe from Macedonia to India, potentially bringing opium with them and trading portions of it with multiple groups along the way.

Another iconic emperor is the prime candidate for the first identifiable person with an opium addiction. Marcus Aurelius is best remembered for *Meditations,* a tortured account of his attempts at self-improvement, now considered a classic in the canon of Stoic philosophy. Ever since his death in 180 CE, Aurelius's commitment to virtuous leadership has made him someone that men in power (well, usually men) like to cite as an influence. Even today, *Meditations* is a firm favourite of the billionaire CEO and the aspiring politician who needs to conjure a reading list to signal depth and insight to the common public. But cynicism aside, Marcus Aurelius the man was an inspiring figure. He became emperor of Rome at the venerable age of forty and was committed to living up to the image of a 'good emperor'.[5] He catalogued his strengths (keen honesty, material simplicity) and weaknesses (a quick temper, a slow wit) with great self-awareness. The sculpted images that we have of him reveal a man of gravitas with large eyes and a noble nose, short curls on his head, and a well-kept beard wreathing his jaw. Contemporaries often decried his soft voice and tolerance as weaknesses, which remain strange criticism of a man who had his sons-in-law killed when they threatened his son's ascendancy to the throne after him.

But the most striking characteristic of Marcus Aurelius is the sadness and suffering that pervades every aspect of his life and work. He was an insomniac and seemed to suffer chronic pains in his stomach and chest. As he aged, he seemed to become more and more physically weak and began spitting blood. Beyond these physical symptoms, his writings are shot through with melancholy, and misandry – completely lacking in humour.

Modern scholars who try to diagnose his condition have several hypotheses including hypochondria, stomach ulcers, depression or a combination of all three. Whatever it was, even the emperor of Rome wasn't in a position to be treated for it. As he grew older, this took a huge toll on Marcus Aurelius. He began to detest his body and its weaknesses, and tried to find refuge in intellectual and philosophical concerns.

Aurelius's doctor was the most famous physician in the Roman empire, Aelius Galenus or Galen. If Western philosophy can be seen as a series of footnotes to Plato, Western medicine for hundreds of years would be footnotes to Galen. Galen prescribed a medicinal concoction called theriac to Marcus Aurelius. Theriac was derived from an even older medicine called mithridate or mithridatium, which was considered the medicine of kings – a painkiller, a cure-all, a universal antidote against the poisons of assassins. It was supposedly invented by a king who was so successful with the medicine that when he lost a battle and tried to commit suicide by poison, he was completely immune. Theriac, from which we get the word 'treacle', was considered one of the most valuable medieval remedies in the European world.[6] Galen wrote an entire book on the medicine which he served as a pill to be drunk with a glass of wine. Marcus Aurelius initially mixed poppy juice with the wine and when he later tried to stop because it made him too drowsy, he found he couldn't sleep at all.[7] Of course, while there are persuasive comparisons of his dream-like prose to the visions of people with addictions, it's not conclusive that Marcus Aurelius was addicted and that will probably be the case forever. According to the historian of science Joseph Needham, missionaries may have introduced a version of Galen's theriac to China around the seventh century. He found theriac listed in *Tsao Kang Mu* and *Thang Pen Tsao*, two ancient Chinese medical treatises.[8]

Stepping forward in time and eastward in geography, opium could also be found in the writings of the eleventh-century polymath Ibn Sina (also known under the latinized moniker Avicenna). As per his own account, Ibn Sina was a child prodigy. He had memorized the Quran by the age of ten and began studying arithmetic, Islamic law, philosophy and medicine in his teenage years. Before he was eighteen, he was summoned by the court physicians to attend to the emir who was sick. He succeeded in aiding the emir, and from then, there was no stopping him. He wrote book after book – and all of them were original, insightful and influential. The picture painted by his peers is of an exceedingly handsome man, turbaned and bearded as was traditional, who lived a life of tremendous exuberance and hedonism. He never married and had few friends or allies, possibly due to his consistent nonconformity, especially in theological matters. He also carried around a massive ego which ensured his unpopularity with most other intellectuals of his day. Once when he was criticized for a lack of expertise in Arabic philology, he avenged himself through an elaborate prank. He studied philology for three years and then authored some 'long-lost' odes which he aged artificially to make them seem ancient. Then, he had the emir present the text to his critic and ask for his opinion. Ibn Sina simply stood back and revelled in his enemy's stumbling public struggle to interpret the anachronistic words and phrases. Eventually, the elaborate joke was revealed and the critic was suitably embarrassed.[9] The incident seems almost too strange to be true – like something a petty supervillain might do in a comic book.

His magnum opus was the five-volume medical encyclopaedia *The Canon of Medicine*, which was used as a textbook at least till the seventeenth century. In the *Canon*, Ibn Sina devotes a whole chapter to opium, discussing its applications for severe cough, diarrhoea, insomnia and pain relief. The positive applications, though, are overshadowed by his elaborate notes on all the negative effects opium can have on the body. 'Used with circumspection,' he wrote in the *Canon*, 'it may achieve by stealth and through the mind what more drastic medications of the body fail to do. It is one of Allah's signal gifts for which He should be thanked every day. But even divine gifts can be mishandled by bumptious men.'[10] This acute awareness didn't help when, in the middle of a severe illness, a servant who had been stealing from him, according to his student and biographer, poisoned him with a huge dose of opium when giving him his requested medication. Ibn Sina barely survived that overdose and his health never recovered. He died soon afterwards.

The fakirs or dervishes of the same time period used opium and hashish as a part of their spiritual practice, using it to attain a state of trance or to experience visions of heaven.

While there are many examples of doctors in the medieval era calling opium a miracle drug especially for curing diarrhoea, it is useful to repeat at this point that most of these scholars were also very aware of the dangers of opium. Al-Biruni, another polymath and contemporary of Ibn Sina, saw people die from opium suppositories. He also observed that people living in tropical climates who took opium as a way of handling the extreme heat were constantly increasing their dosage till they eventually died.[11]

One of the many Islamic scholars who carried Ibn Sina's work forward was the physician Hakim Imad al-Din Mahmud ibn-Mas'ud Shirazi who was born in 1515 CE. Imad's father was a physician as well, and even in his relative youth, he worked for the emir in modern-day Azerbaijan. Due to some unknown faux pas, Imad provoked the emir's ire and was punished by being immersed in a pool of freezing water for an entire night.

To survive, Imad chewed on opium throughout that long night. He made it to the next morning but at a huge price – his body was wracked with pain, some parts paralysed, some parts forever shivering.[12] And it seems that he continued taking opium and addicted himself. This was extremely common in Persian Iran at that time. Iranian high society consumed opium as an intoxicant at social gatherings – it was a party drug like ecstasy. But opium didn't stay limited to the upper classes for long; it spread to all sections of society till opium addiction became a large-scale problem.

Imad would write the first textual study of opium addiction as a medical and social problem, *The Book of Opium*. He explored everything from the botanical nature of the poppy plant to the advantages and disadvantages of prescribing opium as medication. He exhaustively listed the various symptoms of a person with an opium addiction – nausea, anxiety, mood swings, weight loss, reduced appetite and so on – and formulated techniques for the treatment of addicts. He even invented two techniques to aid people with addictions during the season of Ramadan when they would be required to fast. One was an 'extended release opium tablet' made with almond oil, melting wax and sugar. The other was a 'sustained release rectal suppository' that contained 'equal amounts of opium and beaver testicles ... dispersed into a melted base of tragacant or acacia'.[13] Truly, a magical recipe.

Opium in India

In the early sixteenth century, in the northwest frontier of India, the man who would found the Mughal empire was growing restless in Kabul. Babur was only eleven when he ascended the throne of his tiny kingdom of Ferghana in Central Asia. He was a descendant of Genghis Khan on his mother's side and Timur on his father's. Babur would live his whole life in the shadow of Timur, the almost mythical undefeated conqueror and his great-great-great-grandfather. But unlike Timur, Babur would see defeat after defeat. While he tried to conquer Samarkand, he would lose Ferghana. Then, he lost Samarkand and wandered for years, trying to gather allies and launch futile attempts to regain his lost legacy. At twenty-one, he gave up, and with just 300 men turned his back on his homeland and marched across the Hindu Kush mountains to Kabul. He would launch four attacks on India before the final one, each with some degree of success. Finally, in 1526, at the age of forty-three, during his fifth invasion of India, he marched into Delhi, not to sack the city like Timur but to rule it. His dynasty would take the Persian name of his mother's ancestors, the Mongols.

During the decades of wandering, as he sat around campfires in the cold desert nights, Babur would narrate the story of his life. As the masterful historian Richard Eaton describes them, these memoirs were a mix of 'a diary, a gazetteer, a chronicle and a father's advice to his son' and were 'pervaded by themes of defeat, humiliation, displacement and exile'.[14] The *Babur Nama* is also scattered with references to drinking and drugs. He routinely drank wine until he blacked out. While he declared that his body couldn't tolerate opium (because it made him vomit), he was addicted to ma'jun. This was a part-drug, part-sweet – made of ganja leaves (marijuana), milk, sugar, poppy seeds and other ingredients. According to historian Meena Bhargava, Babur was an alcoholic and addicted to ma'jun. His extreme consumption was 'the main cause of his several illnesses and his alarming bed-ridden condition thrice'.[15]

The two emperors after Babur were both described as tiryaqi, meaning opium eaters, in Abul Fazl's *Akbar Nama*. Humayun, Babur's eldest son, allegedly pre-decided how many opium pellets he could have in a week and then gave them to his bodyguards to ration out to him, vowing not to eat more. He usually took these pellets along with a glass of rose water. By the reign of Humayun's son, Akbar, opium was widely grown across Mughal territory. Opium and other drugs were such an integral part of Akbar's court that they were one of the elements (along with gold, silk and other luxuries) of the weighing ceremony, where he donated materials equal to his body weight. Even when he was very sick, he didn't stop drinking or taking opium. The Mughals would also drink kuknar, which comes from the Persian word for opium, but was a beverage made from opium seeds, sometimes mixed with ganja.

Akbar's son, Jahangir, was also apparently addicted. The Englishman William Hawkins wrote that the emperor would drink wine and chew opium till he passed out. Jahangir's hedonism seems to have spilled over into his parenting as well. His son Shah Jahan did not drink till he was twenty-four and was only convinced to try by his father's repeated coaxing. Shah Jahan also used opium for very different purposes. When he had prisoners he couldn't execute for political reasons, he locked them away in the dungeons of Gwalior fortress and slowly poisoned them with poust. This was a concoction made by soaking crushed opium in water for at least one night.[16] The result was a powerful narcotic that would be administered till the victim was addicted, losing all desire for food and withering away. The truly macabre part of this was that the process could be as drawn out or as quick as the emperor felt, allowing him to modulate the suffering of those who languished in those bleak cells. Francois Bernier, a French traveller in Mughal India, writes of a handsome prince who was brought before Aurangzeb and begged 'that if it were intended to give him the poust to drink, he begged he might be immediately put to death'.[17]

Another use of opium for the Mughals was to ensure hunting expeditions went as planned. When an emperor wanted to hunt a lion, his aides would make sure the lion's last meal was an opium-drugged donkey. The opium would get into the lion's system and allow it to be caught in a net and dragged to an appropriate location so that the emperor and his retinue could have the pleasure of the kill.

Among the more working class members of Mughal society, opium was one of the ways of dealing with hunger and holding pain at bay. Messengers known as halcarras carried letters over hundreds of miles, powering themselves on nothing more than rice, water and opium.[18] Even before the Mughals, in the times of the Delhi Sultanate, there is evidence of widespread opium use in the form of the occasional ban or prohibition. In the fourteenth century, Allauddin Khilji banned opium in Delhi.[19]

It isn't clear how far back India's relationship with opium goes. Most of India's famous texts on medicine don't mention opium at all. Sanskrit literature is mostly bereft of any references to the poppy. The earliest mentions of opium in Ayurveda literature seems to be in the fourteenth and sixteenth centuries.[20] But some scholars argue that opium production started on India's western coast as early as the eight century. We do know that by the time the Portuguese arrived in India at the end of the fifteenth century, opium was one of the many goods traded along the Malabar Coast as a part of the bustling Indian Ocean trade network that connected the Middle East and Africa to China and South East Asia. Multiple Portuguese sources, especially in Cochin, mention opium being traded by Muslim and Chinese merchants.[21] Afonso de Albuquerque, the Portuguese general, wrote to his king in 1513 declaring that so high was the demand for opium in India that all the fields in Portugal should be sown with the seeds of poppies.

The Portuguese were the first to sweep eastward, sniffing for spices. Albuquerque and other Portuguese warlords like him sailed the seas with the blessings of their god and saw it as their duty to disrupt the Muslim trade networks that dominated the Indian Ocean. It was a violent and brutal rewriting of relationships that had existed for hundreds of years. The Portuguese effectively militarized Muslim communities on the Malabar Coast and around the Indian Ocean who had till then been primarily traders. For almost a century, till the mid seventeenth century, the Portuguese were the primary European power in South and South East Asia. They were also the first European power to build a permanent base in China. In the mid sixteenth century, they negotiated a lease for the land in what is now known as Macau (or Macao). The Ming dynasty seemed to have viewed the idea of a European settlement at Macau as a way of benefiting from trade but controlling it so that it didn't get out of hand. By 1640, Macau's population was said to be around 40,000 people, with about 2000 of them being Portuguese.[22] Macau became one point along the Goa–Japan trade route that brought much wealth to the Portuguese. At various points, these ships carried silk, pepper and other spices, and silver and other precious metals. While opium was shipped to Macau, it remained a minor commodity for now, though the port would become central to European interests in China for centuries.

The Portuguese also established a base in modern-day Vietnam that they named 'Cochin-China'. The first part is a reference to the existing Malay name for the land, Kuchi. The Portuguese added 'China' to distinguish it from the city of Cochin where they also had a base. Cochin-China was another stop on the route from India to China and then Japan.

Then came the Dutch.

The Dutch East India Company

The Dutch learned much from the Portuguese and they understood the synergy between profits and violence. Jan Pietersz Coen, one of the Dutch empire's most vicious and most successful conquerors, captured the ethos perfectly: 'Trade cannot be maintained without war, nor war without trade.'[23]

The Dutch kicked the Portuguese out of the Malabar Coast in 1663. They had been fighting for years before that – taking ships, hanging merchants. The Dutch were obsessed with pepper and negotiated an export monopoly on the spice with the Malabar rajas. Simultaneously, they fought for and won an almost complete import monopoly on opium. This was the first opium monopoly in history, a century before the British. At the same time, they began to export opium from Bengal to South East Asia.

Suddenly, in the late seventeenth century, the opium trade began to flourish. Not to China but to the Dutch-controlled ports like Batavia (currently Jakarta), Malacca and Manila in the Philippines among others. Alexander Hamilton, a Scottish sailor (no relation to the American founding father who inspired the titular musical), wrote about the beginning of the Dutch opium trade in his book:

[it] was not known to the Dutch before 1685, that one Mr. Lucas, a Factor in the Company's Service at Malacca, was advised by a Malay to send some Surat Baftees dyed blue, and some Berams, dyed red, which are both coarse Cotton Cloth much worn in that Country; and Ophium is as much in Request there, as Tea is with us. In 10 Years that he kept that Trade wholly to himself, tho' in other Mens Names, he got an Estate of 10 or 12 Tuns of Gold, or about 100,000 Pounds

English, and then revealed the Secret to the Company, who took that Trade altogether into their own Hands.[24]

By the end of the century, opium exports from Bengal were forty-three times higher than they were at the beginning. And it would only keep going up. According to historian Hans Derks, 'for the whole of the 18th-century, on average 112,000 pounds of raw opium were exported each year from Bengal and apparently also imported in Batavia, which comes to the unbelievable amount of 11 million pounds in a century'.[25] Through Batavia, a small amount of opium was exported to China but this was just a trickle compared to the flood that was to come.

Derks also claims that the Dutch East India Company (VOC) gave us the first-ever drugs baron. Jacob Mossel was born in 1704 in Enkhuizen, a port town in the northern part of the Netherlands. His family weren't nobles but they weren't destitute either. Mossel was prone to displaying his family's coat of arms, which implied some family glory, however distant. But most importantly for him, Mossel received a decent education. He learned how to read and write and do basic sums. At the age of fifteen, like so many other young boys at the time, he set out on a ship to join in the grand adventure of profiteering and colonization spearheaded by the VOC in Asia. After a year at sea, he landed at Nagapatnam in modern-day Tamil Nadu and began working his way up through the ranks of the VOC.

Within four years, he became a bookkeeper, which earned him at least three times as much as being a sailor would have. Another four years later, at the age of twenty-four, he married the stepdaughter of the local governor. Now, his prospects were blooming. He got promotion after promotion with his father-in-law's help. Eventually, at the age of thirty-eight, as a senior official, already relatively wealthy, he was transferred to Batavia, where real fortunes were waiting for those unscrupulous enough.

Just as Mossel arrived at Batavia, the opium trade of the VOC began to skyrocket, tripling in three years. In 1745, a group of private traders negotiated a ten-year contract with the VOC to take over the distribution of opium. This private group called themselves the Amphioen Sociëteyt or Opium Society. The first director of the Society was Jacob Mossel, and after some clever politicking, he became the single largest shareholder as well, holding twice as many shares as anyone else. The official reasoning for this lucrative distribution contract was to put an end to smuggling. The VOC was inefficient, everyone knew that. The real reason was of course profiteering. The terms of the contract essentially put the entire burden of risk on the VOC while giving the Opium Society a profit on every trade. It was free money. And they didn't really have to do anything about smuggling either as they just directed the Dutch navy to handle the problem. Everyone who could have or would have objected was simply given shares in the Society. Even the Prince of Orange, Wilhelm IV, became a shareholder, reaping the dividends of the opium trade.

Five years after the founding of the Opium Society, Mossel became the governor general of the Dutch East Indies. The VOC was like a gigantic, ungainly ship ridden with leaks. Everyone was stealing from the VOC as much as they possibly could. But to Mossel, the clever bookkeeper, and his friends, stealing seemed unnecessary when you could just sign the appropriate paperwork so the VOC just gave you the money legally. Mossel had the mind of a bookkeeper. Even as he grew more and more absurdly wealthy through his corrupt activities, he was the kind of man who would write a book chastising those who flaunted their wealth and laying out 'more than 120 rules related to the proper design of houses, the use, and shape of walking sticks, buttonholes and shoe-buckles'.[26]

But eventually, corruption and a series of poor economic decisions led to the downfall of the VOC. Riddled with financial problems, the VOC ceased trading in the eighteenth century. As their influence shrank, the English East India Company moved in to take their place.

The British Develop a Taste

But meanwhile, back in England, a new form of opium was becoming all the rage: laudanum. Born on the cusp of the sixteenth century in Switzerland, Theophrastus von Hohenheim would become a notorious figure in history though most people have only heard his nom de plume: Paracelsus. He was one of the great kooks of history, alternating between legitimate medicine and alchemy, theology and mystical gibberish that would inspire some of the many other great kooks of history. But he's only relevant to this story for his gift of a name. He labelled one of his many miracle cures laudanum.

A century later, an English physician, much more modest in his visions, would compound a medical tincture using an extract of opium and invoke Paracelsus's cure, calling it laudanum. The physician's name was Thomas Sydenham. Before Sydenham invented his version of laudanum, opium was commonly available in pill form, concocted by apothecaries who mixed the ingredients themselves. Also, pills were notoriously variable in standard and dosage, based on the eye and hands of the druggist or apothecary. Sydenham combined opium with saffron, cinnamon, cloves and, probably most importantly, sherry (which is a kind of wine that has been fortified with extra spirit for potency). Sydenham then made the recipe freely available, and soon, this new easy way to receive the becalming effects of opium spread throughout England and Europe. It also received a boost after Sydenham used it to ease the pain of one of doctor-turned-philosopher John Locke's patients, the Countess of Northumberland.[27]

One of Sydenham's pupils, a man named Thomas Dover, would invent a powdered form of opium that was called Dover's Powder. The powder was a mix of saltpetre and opium, and was often drunk with wine and milk. It too became a huge hit with people in search of a general cure-all. Laudanum, Dover's Powder and another opium-based drug called paregoric became some of the most popular medicines in England and Europe for the next two centuries. These weren't the only opium-based magic medicines, of course. There were also Ayer's Cherry Pectoral, Mrs Winslow's Soothing Syrup, and Hamlin's Wizard Oil.[28] And back then, these drugs were available in grocery stores – no doctor or prescription needed. When traders with the East India Company came to India, some of them probably had a personal store of one or more of these little miracle cures in their baggage.

To the extent that it affected world history, the East India Company had a humble beginning. English merchants, jealous of the Dutch success in trading with the 'Indies', came up with the plan to look east as well. After decades of underperformance, they realized that the Dutch were too deeply entrenched in the 'Spice Islands' and so they turned their attention to the textile trade of the Indian subcontinent instead. This turned out to be an excellent idea. Through a combination of luck and patronage, the fortunes of the East India Company turned. Their profits from textiles, spices and jewels from the Indian subcontinent soon began to outpace the Dutch. Slowly, they began to set up forts along the Indian coast, with the first being at Madras,[29] Bombay and Calcutta coming later. It's important to remember that none of these early successes came through military power.

When an English soldier was killed by Siddi sailors in Bombay in 1683, the governor – terrified of the repercussions if they started a war – refused to seek revenge. Some of his soldiers were less cautious and took their honour into their own hands, forcing the Siddi ships to leave Bombay. Their departure was temporary. The Siddis came back with an overwhelming force and besieged Bombay till the British ran out of food and were forced to sue for peace.[30] Three years later, the British would send a fleet of nineteen ships to attack the Mughals, smarting under their consistent taxation. The Mughal army smashed the expedition and continued to capture all the existing Company forts. After the Company sued for peace, Aurangzeb, the Mughal emperor at the time, seemed to forgive them out of the kindness of his heart and returned the conquered forts and prisoners.

In the century and a half between the founding of the East India Company and the Battle of Plassey, it was diplomacy and a willingness to work within the rules of the existing powers that served the Company well. They spent a lot of energy and money on currying favour with local powers including sending diplomats to spend years developing relationships with specific leaders. While this has been acknowledged, what may not be as well known is that they also spent a lot of energy and money currying favour in Britain. Even as the royal charters that guaranteed the power of the Company were renewed, there were allegations of and investigations into the large sums of money paid out as 'gifts' to government officers and members of Parliament. Estimates of the total amount spent on this proto corporate lobbying varied from £90,000 to £200,000: Rs 150–300 crores in modern terms.

As is the case with many corporates today, the Company's primary reason for all these bribes was to preserve their monopoly powers. The Company detested private traders and considered them 'worse … then [sic] Pirates & deserve as much to be hanged'.[31] In 1682, one such private trader, Thomas Sandys, took them to court arguing that their government-granted monopoly was illegal. He argued that 'free trade' was the right of every English merchant and the Company had to scramble to find a justification for their need to hold this monopoly on trade with India. This became 'the great case of monopolies' and was the talk of London for a time. As one scholar puts it, 'mercantilism itself was put on trial'.[32] The Company's lawyer fell back on fearmongering – a strategy that has always paid dividends. He argued that free trade was well and good when done with fellow civilized Christians. But Asia was a land of non-Christians, he declared, and thus traders were in danger; so it was for their protection that restrictions had to be placed. Of course, Sandys and other private traders knew this argument was nonsense. They had been doing business with Indian kingdoms safely and happily for years. But this was less of a question of facts than politics. And those who held power in Britain, including the king, were convinced that what was best for them and their purses was if the Company maintained its monopoly.

The East India Company loaned the British government millions of pounds. In exchange for these long-term loans, the Company was allowed to issue short-term debentures or bonds. Through the sale of these 'India bonds' on the burgeoning London Stock Exchange, the Company raised large sums of money,[33] some of which they used to loan more money to the government. These loans weren't idle transactions. They enabled

Britain's military growth and development. And the government responded by actively using that military to aid in the economic enterprise of the Company. Quid pro quo, as the saying goes.

Notes

1. 'Conversation: Minoan Masterpieces.' *Archaeology Magazine*, 2010. https://archive.archaeology.org/1003/etc/conversation.html.
2. Kritikos, Pan G., and S.P. Papadaki. 'The History of the Poppy and of Opium and Their Expansion in Antiquity in the Eastern Mediterranean Area.' *UNODC Bulletin on Narcotics* 19, no. 3 (1967): 17–38.
3. Gaignerot-Driessen, Florence. 'Goddesses Refusing to Appear? Reconsidering the Late Minoan III Figures with Upraised Arms.' *American Journal of Archaeology* 118, no. 3 (2014): 489–520. https://doi.org/10.3764/aja.118.3.0489.
4. Inglis, Lucy. *Milk of Paradise: A History of Opium.* eBook, Pegasus Books, 2019.
5. The biographic details of the life of Marcus Aurelius are based on: McLynn, Frank. *Marcus Aurelius: A Life.* Da Capo Press, 2009.
6. Fabbri, Christiane Nockels. 'Treating Medieval Plague: The Wonderful Virtues of Theriac.' *Early Science and Medicine* 12, no. 3 (2007): 247–83. https://doi.org/10.1163/157338207X205115.
7. Africa, Thomas W. 'The Opium Addiction of Marcus Aurelius.' *Journal of the History of Ideas* 22, no. 1 (January 1961): 97. https://doi.org/10.2307/2707876.
8. Trocki, Carl. *Opium, Empire and the Global Political Economy: A Study of the Asian Opium Trade, 1750–1950.* Routledge, 2012, p. 20.
9. McGinnis, Jon. *Avicenna.* Oxford University Press, 2010, p. 25.

10. Dormandy, Thomas. *Opium: Reality's Dark Dream*. Yale University Press, 2012, p. 32.

11. Hamarneh, Sami. 'Pharmacy in Medieval Islam and the History of Drug Addiction.' *Medical History* 16, no. 3 (July 1972): 226–37. https://doi.org/10.1017/S0025727300017725.

12. Golshani, Seyyed Alireza, Behnam Dalfardi, Ezzat Motahari, Mehdi Hesampour, Mahsa Ansari and Hassan Yarmohammadi. 'Hakim Imad Al-Din Mahmud Ibn-Mas'ud Shirazi (1515–1592), a Physician and Social Pathologist of Safavid Era.' *Galen Medical Journal* 2 (1 December 2013): 169–73.

13. Soleymani, Samaneh and Arman Zargaran. 'A Historical Report on Preparing Sustained Release Dosage Forms for Addicts in Medieval Persia, 16th Century AD.' *Substance Use & Misuse* 53, no. 10 (24 August 2018): 3. https://doi.org/10.1080/1082 6084.2018.1432648.

14. Eaton, Richard M. *India in the Persianate Age: 1000–1765*. eBook, Allen Lane, 2019.

15. Bhargava, Meena. 'Narcotics and Drugs: Pleasure, Intoxication or Simply Therapeutic – North India, Sixteenth–Seventeenth Centuries.' *Medieval History Journal* 15, no. 1 (April 2012): 114. https://doi.org/10.1177/097194581001500104.

16. Arnold, David. 'The Social Life of Poisons.' In *Toxic Histories: Poison and Pollution in Modern India*. Cambridge University Press, 2016, pp. 17–40. https://doi.org/10.1017/CBO9781316411414.002.

17. Derks, Hans. *History of the Opium Problem*. Brill, 2012, p. 180.

18. Trocki, Carl. *Opium, Empire and the Global Political Economy: A Study of the Asian Opium Trade, 1750–1950*. Routledge, 2012, p. 20.

19. Khan, Waseem, Jahanzeb Khalil and Manzoor Ahmad. 'History of Opium Cultivation in Pakistan: Socio-Economic Significance and Politics of Opium Eradication.' *Science International* 28, no. 2 (2016): 6.

20. Chopra, R.N. and I.C. Chopra. *Indigenous Drugs of India.* Academic Publishers, 1994, p. 205.

21. Bhargava, Meena. 'Narcotics and Drugs: Pleasure, Intoxication or Simply Therapeutic – North India, Sixteenth–Seventeenth Centuries.' *The Medieval History Journal* 15, no. 1 (April 2012): 103–35. https://doi.org/10.1177/097194581001500104.

22. Subrahmanyam, Sanjay. *The Portuguese Empire in Asia, 1500– 1700: A Political and Economic History.* John Wiley & Sons, 2012, p. 217.

23. Derks, Hans. *History of the Opium Problem.* Brill, 2012, p. 208.

24. Trocki, Carl. *Opium, Empire and the Global Political Economy: A Study of the Asian Opium Trade, 1750–1950.* Routledge, 2012, p. 37.

25. Derks, Hans. *History of the Opium Problem.* Brill, 2012, p. 179.

26. Derks, Hans. *History of the Opium Problem.* Brill, 2012, p. 243.

27. Inglis, Lucy. *Milk of Paradise: A History of Opium.* eBook, Pegasus Books, 2019.

28. Haq, M. *Drugs in South Asia: From the Opium Trade to the Present Day.* Springer, 2000, p. 39.

29. William Dalrymple suggests that the location of this fort – Fort St George – was decided based on the home of a Tamil woman who was a British officer's object of affection. Dalrymple, William. *The Anarchy: The East India Company, Corporate Violence, and the Pillage of an Empire.* Bloomsbury Publishing, 2019.

30. Wilson, Jon. *India Conquered: Britain's Raj and the Chaos of Empire.* eBook, Simon & Schuster, 2016.

31. Stern, Philip J. '"A Politie of Civill & Military Power": Political Thought and the Late Seventeenth-Century Foundations of the East India Company-State.' *Journal of British Studies* 47, no. 2 (April 2008): 253–83. https://doi.org/10.1086/526759, p. 268.

32. Stern, Philip J. '"A Politie of Civill & Military Power": Political Thought and the Late Seventeenth-Century Foundations of the

East India Company-State.' *Journal of British Studies* 47, no. 2 (April 2008): 253–83. https://doi.org/10.1086/526759, p. 269.

33. Erikson, Emily. *Between Monopoly and Free Trade: The English East India Company, 1600–1757.* Princeton University Press, 2016, p. 42.

2

From Calcutta to Canton

Calcutta's Birthday

In 2003, the Calcutta High Court pronounced their verdict on an unusual question: when should the city's birthday be celebrated? It had traditionally been thought to be 24 August 1690, the date when the English trader Job Charnock (or Job Charnayak, as the case delightfully listed his name) bought some land and built a factory. To answer the question, the court formed a committee of academic historians to probe the history of Calcutta's founding. After the committee deliberated and tabled their nuanced response, the high court declared that 'Calcutta does not have a birthday'. Admirably, there was no nationalist pandering to the idea of a 'true founder' of Calcutta (despite the plaintiff clearly aiming for that angle). The committee wrote: 'Determination of truth in history is a question of different interpretations ... Historians do not act as Judges.'[1]

The history of the East India Company's relationship with Calcutta becomes concrete (pun intended) with the building of Fort William. The fort was named after William III, prince of Orange (modern-day Netherlands) and king of England after what is called the Glorious Revolution in the late seventeenth century. The fort, an unremarkable building, would become the fulcrum of events that would lead to the birth of the British empire in India.

In 1755, the directors of the East India Company received disturbing news: the French were preparing for war.[2] The French and the English were perennial rivals, and now, with imperialism, this rivalry played out across the globe. The East India Company guessed the French were planning an attack in India, probably on Calcutta or Madras. The two nations had already drawn blood in the subcontinent. The French had even captured Fort St George in Madras a few years earlier. The directors quickly passed on this vital piece of intelligence to Calcutta where, despite being explicitly banned from doing so by the Mughals, they began to rebuild the walls to prepare for this impending French attack.

A part of the British confidence in this brazen flouting of the nawab of Bengal's orders came from their belief that they were dealing with the elderly, peaceful Aliverdi Khan. When he heard about the British activities at Fort William, Aliverdi Khan did try to diplomatically convince them to halt their illegal fortification. But while these negotiations were taking their course – through message and messenger – Aliverdi Khan died. He left no obvious successor. The man best placed to succeed him – through political favour and vicious temperament – was his nephew, Siraj ud-Daula. Siraj was, simply put, a psychopath. He was violent, sadistic and arrogant. And now, as he consolidated his position as the new nawab of Bengal, he was the man the East India Company had to deal with.

When Siraj heard about the British refusing to obey orders, he marched a gigantic army to Calcutta and smashed the city's puny defences. He humiliated any Company leaders he could find and then marched away, leaving behind a force that looted and pillaged the city. When news of the fall of Calcutta hit Madras, it reached the ears of another psychopath (this one on the British side), Robert Clive. This was Clive's second stint under the Company. He had started his first stint as a simple accountant but then, through a talent for cunning and violence, had won promotion and amassed enough illicit wealth to go back to England. There he spent his fortune trying to buy himself a political office but it didn't work out. He found himself back with the Company. But this time, he was in command of the troops the British had sent to stop the foreseen French attack. His army was a mix of Company men, hired Indian soldiers, and the official squadron of ships and cannons that the British government had sent. But that vital piece of intelligence of French plans would turn out to be wrong. No attack was forthcoming. So Clive had an army on his hands and no enemy to fight. Also, he had lost his investments in the Calcutta trade. He persuaded the other officials around him that this engine of war could be directed at this new enemy.

After a few months of careful planning, Clive's fleet – the largest army the British had ever amassed in India – sailed to Calcutta. It was still less than 2000 men but Calcutta was a husk of a city and weakly defended. They reconquered the city but, decimated as it was, there were no rewards to reap. The real test came when Siraj returned to Calcutta to retake the retaken city. Despite his overwhelming numbers again, this battle would follow a different script. A surprise attack in the middle of the night pierced Siraj's defences and threw his camp into chaos, spooking their commander who immediately retreated. Siraj's priorities must've been elsewhere – potentially with the Bengal economy which had suffered without the bustling English trade – and he sued for peace. Robert Clive had somehow done it again. As Siraj's army turned around and marched home, it would've seemed that with this new peace treaty signed, the story was over.

But it was only the beginning. Siraj ud-Daula's arrogance had won him few allies amongst the power brokers of Bengal. And it had made an enemy of the most powerful of them all: the Jagat Seth. Frustratingly, little is known about the family of the Jagat Seths. They were merchants, originally from Marwar but had moved to Patna and then Murshidabad (then the capital of Bengal). In Bengal, they flourished as moneylenders and bankers, often funding the schemes and stratagems of the nawab of Bengal. In 1717, the then patriarch of the family, Fateh Chand, was given control of the Murshidabad mint by the nawab. With this, their place in the power politics of Bengal became entrenched. Five years later, the Mughal emperor Muhammad Shah bestowed the title of 'Jagat Seth' on Fateh Chand.[3]

From then, the wealth and political acumen of Jagat Seths always lurked behind whoever was enthroned as the nawab of Bengal. And unlike his uncle, Siraj did not show them the proper deference. According to a contemporary historian, Siraj once slapped Mahtab Rai, who held the title of Jagat Seth at the time, and repeatedly threatened him with circumcision. The Jagat Seths decided it was time for a new nawab.

They found the perfect fit in Mir Jafar, one of Siraj's commanders. Mir Jafar and the Jagat Seth sent out tentative feelers to Robert Clive and the Company, whose army had just bested Siraj. The Company was well aware of the Jagat Seths, who had been lending credit to the various foreign powers in Bengal for years by then. Even as they approached the English

East India Company for military aid at this point, they continued lending lakhs of rupees to the Dutch and French East India Companies.

When Clive and the Company heard the offer, they must've been ecstatic at the opportunity that had fallen into their laps. Not only would this allow them to rewrite the equations of power in Bengal, but they were also being offered a colossal amount of money. And the Company haggled for more. As per the final deal struck, they were set to receive more than £4 million – more than Rs 5000 crores today.[4] Once terms were agreed, Mir Jafar and the British signed a physical contract in secret that outlined their terms – one for each party.

With that deal in place, the Company concocted a story of how Siraj had broken their peace treaty and declared war. It is obvious that their motivator was wealth but it's still interesting to note that Clive and the Company stress in their deliberations that Siraj was an untrustworthy business partner (probably true) and a violent monster (almost definitely true). Of course, both those criticisms are equally true of the Company. The story of the Battle of Plassey is well known so it won't be recounted here. Mir Jafar's betrayal stunned Siraj's army and the rest, as they say, is history. Clive received a personal share of the money promised by Mir Jafar and the Jagat Seth and overnight became one of the richest men in England. And the East India Company, using the might of the official British Army, had suddenly gone from traders to conquerors. Mir Jafar would prove to be a weak leader, firmly under the thumb of the Company, who used him as a puppet as they systematically plundered the wealth of Bengal over the next decade. He would also become addicted to opium.

According to historian Thomas Timberg, the Jagat Seths miscalculated in their scheme with the British. The East India Company quickly usurped their role in the economy of Bengal.

With declining wealth came declining prestige and soon the Jagat Seths were kingmakers no more. In the nineteenth century, they were reduced to requesting pensions from the British for their past services.[5]

A New Government Department Is Born

Opium had been a state monopoly even under the Mughals. By 1688, Bihar produced more than 4000 chests of opium every year.[6] After the Battle of Plassey, when the Company claimed monopoly rights in 1773, they justified it as a mere extension of the Mughal state's old policies. And this was true for a few decades. Even though the British would eventually operate on an insofar unimagined scale of operations, they started by restricting opium production to 4000 chests a year in their Bengal territories. This artificial restriction raised opium prices in China as demand slowly began to grow – which was what the British wanted. In a roughly twenty-year period from the beginning of the nineteenth century, Bengal opium prices increased by more than 400 per cent.[7]

In 1830, all attempts at restricting trade – in Malwa or Bengal – were unceremoniously ended. Between 1830 and 1839, the area under cultivation doubled in size.[8] Opium exports tripled. Then, there was a period of decline as the British waged the First Opium War. By 1860, the area of opium cultivation had almost doubled again. Then, in three years, by 1863, it had doubled *again*! So over the century, the lands devoted to opium cultivation went up by almost 800 per cent. There were eventually one million peasant households cultivating opium on approximately half a million acres of land. Despite being called 'Bengal opium', these crops were grown across a rectangular area around 250 kilometres wide that began around Agra in the west and stretched all the way across the Gangetic plains to Bihar and Bengal.

To oversee such a vast operation, the British had to construct the bureaucratic behemoth of the Opium Department. Born in 1797 as a part of Lord Cornwallis's 'permanent settlement' reforms,[9] the Opium Department was managed directly by the Board of Revenue. It had two distinct halves: the Benaras Opium Agency, which oversaw modern-day Uttar Pradesh and beyond, and the Bihar Opium Agency, which oversaw the lands in Bihar and Bengal. The Benaras Opium Agency operated out of a large factory in Ghazipur near Varanasi, and the Bihar Opium Agency from a factory in Bankipore near Patna.

The lives of these peasants were miserable. They were trapped under the twin heels of the zamindar and the Opium Department. While they accepted lifelong indebtedness for the ability to subsist, their work generated obscene profits for those above them. Peasant farmers rented their lands from zamindars. Zamindars paid a land tax to the government that was due four times a year. The dates of payment of the land tax coincided with the time of harvests. But the zamindar collected rents from the farmers a few weeks before the land tax was due. This meant that the farmers had to pay their rents before the harvests could be sold. Where would they get the money from? The simple answer is that they would borrow it. Sometimes from a sahukar or moneylender. Or they might decide to plant opium for which they could get a cash advance. The farmers probably knew the cash advance would end up being less than the eventual price of the harvest but had limited choices. They could accept the advance from the Opium Department or they could take a loan from the rapacious village sahukar. As one commentator described the situation, 'the Plowman, flying from the Tax Gatherer is obliged to take refuge under the wings of the Monopolist'.[10]

What was worse was that zamindars charged higher rents
from farmers who decided to cultivate opium. This was
completely illegal according to existing tenancy laws but was
widely practised. The British turned a blind eye to it because
it was a part of the system of exploitation that had emerged.
The British paid money to the farmers and the zamindars took
that money away from them. The only role the peasants had in
the process was to do the work and hold the money briefly as it
passed between these two powers. While some historians have
argued that the higher rent was a way for zamindars to discourage
poppy cultivation, it seems more likely that the zamindars didn't
care what was grown. They saw an opportunity to extract more
money and grabbed it.[11]

As the due date to pay rent to the zamindar neared, a
lambardar (in the Benaras Opium Agency) or khatadar (in the
Bihar Opium Agency) would travel through the village. They
were the middlemen in the opium cultivation process. The
khatadar would prepare a list of farmers that he would represent.
His big advantage was that he could read or write, unlike the
farmers. A khatadar probably had thirty or so farmers that he
oversaw. At one point, the Bihar Opium Agency could count
25,000 khatadars who represented 700,000 farmers.[12] The
contracts for the growing of opium was signed by the khatadar,
on behalf of the farmers. These contracts stipulated the terms
and conditions for the advance and the punishments for failing
to deliver the agreed amount of opium at the time of harvest.
But the fact that these contracts were legally binding on farmers
who had never seen them was just one of the stark illegalities of
this system.

Any farmer who cultivated opium without such a contract was
quickly punished. The official amount that they could be fined
could go up to Rs 500 which would've taken the average farmer

decades to pay. The law explicitly included special rewards for those who reported illegal cultivation. According to a statement by a contemporary police officer, this law was abused to harass innocent people. Similar to how illegal drugs are placed by police officers on innocent people to frame them, anybody with a grudge could place some opium in the house of their enemy and then work with the police to ruin their lives.

The khatadar received the advance from the department and then distributed to the farmers – after taking a cut for themselves. The khatadar did not receive a salary of any kind. They received a commission from the department based on how much opium they delivered and they supplemented this income by taking cuts from the money meant for the farmers. This kind of 'contractor' system is still common today. And if the khatadars were at all similar to their modern counterparts, they exploited and abused those who depended on them, cheating them out of as much as they could. The farmers had no system to hold the khatadar to account. They had little direct contact with the Opium Department. The department was aware of this. In 1832, a deputy opium agent wrote, 'It appears to me that two principal circumstances form the chief obstacles to an extensive poppy cultivation in this district, viz., the inadequate price the cultivators receive for their opium and the oppression to which they are subjected from the gomastahs.'[13] An earlier report, dated 1820, found that the farmers were getting swindled of most of their profits by the various intermediaries in the process.[14]

The khatadar would submit his list of farmers to a zilladar who was an official employee of the department. The zilladar was a field officer who went from village to village, managing the khatadars. The zilladar would survey the lands under cultivation and inspect the farmers' crops to make sure they met whatever standards had been dictated by the department. There would be around ten to twenty-five zilladars in a kothi, which was the basic administrative unit of the Opium Department. Every kothi probably contained around 10,000 to 15,000 farmers. The kothi was managed by a gomastah who was solely responsible for the smooth collection of harvested opium and the distribution of the cash advances. The gomastah reported to a sub-deputy opium agent or his assistant who were the lowest rung of British officers in the department.

Poppy was a rabi crop which meant it was sown in 'winter' – October to December – and harvested in 'spring' – February to April. The crop needed to be watered around once a week. At the same time, too much water would damage the plants. The department would provide a special kind of loan to any farmers who needed to dig wells to irrigate opium fields. Growing poppy is labour intensive. According to one estimate, one kilogram of opium would take around 387 man-hours of work.[15]

Around harvest time, the zilladars would meet the khatadars and give them a list of dates when each of their farmers should come to the kothi's opium office to hand over their produce. This office was usually less than twenty kilometres from the farmer's lands. To harvest the ripe opium pods, the farmer's entire family (and the agricultural labourers they had hired, if necessary) would pierce each opium pod with three small blades and then slowly scrape the extract into a brass vessel or clay pot. The act of harvesting the opium buds involved repeatedly licking the blade to keep it wet, which often unwittingly addicted the harvesters to the drug. The farmer would carry their harvest, which was usually just one large pot containing a few kilos of opium. When they arrived at the opium office, the farmers would watch as their produce was weighed and tested for adulteration. A person, called a purkhea, was specially appointed to test for adulteration. They would dip their hands in the gooey white liquid and feel the consistency and texture with their fingers. If the opium was suspected to be adulterated, it would be set aside and tested more thoroughly at the opium factory where they had developed techniques for checking if sand, flour or vegetable extracts had been added to increase the weight. The khatadar had the right to scrape whatever opium was stuck to the inside of the clay pots after the department was done transferring it to their own vessels.

From the kothis, the opium harvests would be sent under armed guard to the nearest opium factory – either Ghazipur or Bankipore, depending on which agency was in charge. In Ghazipur, the factory overshadowed the town. In 1888, Rudyard Kipling, an Indian favourite despite his effervescent love for the colonial empire, visited the factory. The agent at the time, Harry Rivett-Carnac, was an old friend of the family. Kipling, who had tasted the black smoke of opium when he was only eighteen, wrote, 'On the banks of the Ganges, forty miles below Benares as the crow flies, stands the Ghazipur Factory, an opium mint as it were, whence issue the precious cakes that are to replenish the coffers of the Indian Government.'[16] The role of opium as a pillar of the economy of the country must have been common knowledge at this point.

The factory at Ghazipur was a large, imposing warehouse that sometimes employed one out of every ten people who lived in the town. Whole families were employed there – including the children. There are reports of young mothers leaving swaddled infants in a corner as they worked their shift. The air in the factory was thick with the smell of opium, which would've assaulted the nostrils of any visitors. One British resident of Patna who visited the factory described it as an 'odour of indescribable nastiness'.[17] Despite this stench, these opium factories appeared in travel guides and were often tourist destinations for British visitors.

When the pots of opium arrived there, hundreds at a time, neatly packed in large baskets, they would first be meticulously examined and weighed by agents. Their paperwork would be scrutinized and new paperwork would be drawn up. The sheer volume of paper that travelled with the opium moved Kipling to write that there 'never was such a place for forms as the Ghazipur Factory'.[18] Once approved, the next step was to coax the different batches of opium, from different fields and different farmers, into some kind of uniform consistency. In jars, the opium was mixed and stirred, slowly turning from milky white to a darker hue. Then it was poured into wooden drawers where labourers kneaded the semi-solid substance with their bare hands. From these drawers, the opium was poured into long, shallow vats. Labourers would get into the vat, and standing knee-deep, mix and knead the opium using their legs.

Then, once the opium was the right consistency, it would be taken over to the cake makers. These labourers would squat on low wooden palette-like platforms with a small table in front of them. They would each have a small brass cup, which they would layer with leaves that had also been purchased from the opium farmers. These leaves were soft and pliable as they had been steamed carefully for hours, usually by the farmer's wife. Children would pour standardized dollops of opium into the cups. They would then fold the leaves around the opium, moulding it into large balls that were almost the size of a human head, weighing more than a kilogram. Like this, each labourer would make around seventy cakes per day[19] – one every four minutes, as per the boast of a British supervisor.[20] These balls were then left to rest for two or three days before being transferred to shelves where they sat for the next few months under the watchful gaze of tenders on the lookout for signs of breakage or mildew. These shelves towered above the ground, stacked on top of each other till they reached the high ceiling of the factory building. Children were employed here as well. They would make their way through the shelves, climbing up scaffolding and ladders, to check on the balls – insects had a habit of laying eggs there – and turn them over slightly. A factory employed around sixty-five boys for every 10,000 balls.[21]

When the adult labourers and children left the factory at the end of the day, they were carefully searched. It was easy to pinch a little opium after a full day of working directly with it – and a pinch was worth a lot. The factory staff went to the extent of washing down the workers as they left. After all, the opium that stuck to their bodies had a value. As one visitor to a factory wrote, 'the washing of a little boy well rolled in opium is worth four annas (or sixpence) in the bazaar, if he can escape to it'.[22] It's no wonder that Kipling would describe the Ghazipur factory as a place where 'no one trusts anyone'.[23] Though it's important to note that when Kipling says 'no one', he only has space in his head for the British and their employees.

The opium that was potentially adulterated went through a series of tests so that the adulterant could be identified and then eliminated if possible. Sometimes this involved washing the opium with cold water or the addition of iodine or ammonia. But the otherwise complex process of distillation and filtration needed to be done with equipment that most readers would've last seen in their school chemistry labs. Indian labourers performed these tasks as well – an image that clashes with the usual picture of masses of poor, untrained, unskilled factory labour.

The Patna factory had an attached mill where around fifty labourers worked to produce the mango wood chests used for packing. Each chest would eventually hold forty balls of opium, arranged in two layers like sweet boxes. By the end, the chest would weigh around 60 kilograms and would bear the brand

'Patna Opium' on the side. For 150 years, Patna Opium was a recognizable product all over the British trading world. From the Suez Canal to Hong Kong, newspapers carried quotations for the price of Patna Opium. These wood chests were loaded on to fast ships that took them down the river to Calcutta where they were auctioned to the highest bidder. A relatively small portion was directed towards sales from government-controlled retail outlets. The rest then began their journey to China in the cargo holds of private ships.

There would've been only two auctions per year in Calcutta till the 1820s. After that, with the arrival of opium clippers that, with the power of steam, zipped from Patna to Calcutta with ease, these opium auctions were held once every month. The department kept an eye on the market price and demand, modulating the amount of opium that was available for action to ensure the maximum return. These auctions were held at an earmarked location called the Opium Sale Room. Here, wealthy traders or their agents would take their seat, reserved for them by name, and then bid on the stock of opium for sale. The range of acceptable prices was more or less agreed upon beforehand, and while competing for the limited opium stock, these big merchant firms probably had a collegial relationship with each other. Till the late 1830s, American traders were banned from participating in the Calcutta auctions and so they traded in Turkish opium instead, which was significantly less lucrative.

The City at the End of the Rainbow

Canton is an inland port. To get there, a ship would have to navigate Zhujiang known as the Pearl River. The ship would probably sail to Macao and report to the authorities there about their intention to sail onwards to Canton. They then had to hire a local pilot, a skilled seaman who had obtained an official license to guide ships up the Pearl River. These pilots would employ teams of twenty to fifty local sailors based on the size of the ship they were guiding. Every ship would also be assigned two customs officers or tidewaiters who would accompany the ship till it reached Canton and then return with it to Macao when it was ready to depart again. Other than the pilots, the sailors and the tidewaiters, no other Chinese men or women were allowed to travel on foreign ships. This entire route became reserved for merchant vessels. Locals who wanted to travel between Canton and Macao had to take another route.

As the merchant ships sailed up the river, they would stop at several toll booths where every member of the crew would have to be accounted for – to ensure that nobody disembarked or boarded midway. As historian Van Dyke puts it,

> If fifteen foreigners, thirteen Chinese, six slaves and one milk cow left Macao, then fifteen foreigners, thirteen Chinese, six slaves and one milk cow had to arrive in Canton a couple of days later. If a person or animal died en route (which happened), the corpse had to complete the journey so there was an accurate account on arrival.[24]

Once they sold their cargo at Canton, traders had to bank their silver immediately with the Company 'bank'. In return, they received a document that could be encashed in London. This method of moving money across the world before the banking system really existed became the most efficient way to transfer fortunes back to London from India. Soon, privateers who made fortunes in India would invest in opium and use these documents as a way of transferring wealth back home to England – regardless of how they made their fortune in the first place.

At Macao, the ships would be measured as port fees were calculated based on length and width. There was also a charge called the 'emperor's present' which was a fixed fee every ship had to pay that went straight to the imperial treasury. Then there were duties which were based on the units of cargo. For example, opium was measured in piculs, which was a standardized weight of around 60 kilograms. It's important to note that none of these taxes were based on the value of the cargo, and so, as inflation mounted and the value of these goods rose, these charges became cheaper for foreign traders. This was an elaborate system with a fee for every type of activity and every rung of government. In 1836, according to one comprehensive tally, traders had to pay sixty-seven separate fees between Macao and Canton.[25]

At Canton, the ships would anchor on Whampoa Island. The sailors would then use smaller boats to cross towards the factories where they stayed. The use of the term 'factories' is a bit misleading. It does not mean that manufacturing happened there. It usually refers to a warehouse or trading station. There were seventeen such buildings the Canton authorities had built and then leased out to foreign traders. Each factory and ship had to hire a maiban or comprador, a generic term used for the local facilitators of foreign traders. Factory compradors, like the dubash in India, were in charge of supplying and maintaining these factories. They ensured all provisions were available and managed the myriad Chinese workers who did all the cooking and cleaning in these buildings. Compradors, like pilots, were officially licensed. They wore their licenses as wooden signs around their waist to identify themselves.

Apart from compradors, tidewaiters and pilots, the other official role attached to every factory or ship was the linguist or translator. Mostly these men spoke Portuguese which they had probably learned in Macao. Though, with time, as the British began to dominate trade, the language we refer to as 'pidgin English' arose and became the default trading tongue. All of these various officials formed the backbone of the formal Canton trading system but they were also the mainstay of the illegal opium trade. Over the seventeenth and eighteenth centuries, the system of smuggling too became reliable and straightforward. The rates that they charged – their 'smuggling fees' – became standardized as various districts competed amongst each other and the Portuguese for the illegal trade. Eventually, smugglers could accurately predict their costs and profits as easily as their legitimate counterparts. These fees were much lower than all the brokerage costs the legitimate merchants had to pay.

It wasn't just the English who traded in Canton. Far away from the conflicts that raged in Europe, Canton was a place where enemies and allies rubbed shoulders constantly. There were ships from France, Sweden, Spain, Greece, Denmark and America, among dozens of others. And because Europeans weren't in control of the port, it was welcoming to any ship as long as they were interested solely in trade. There were Muslims, Arabs, Parsis, Jews, Africans and South East Asians. Only the Russians and the Japanese weren't allowed in Canton as they had separate designated ports as per treaties they had negotiated with China. Canton did not discriminate based on colour or religion – only gender. No non-Chinese women were allowed in Canton.

Chinese women were very visible around the ships, many of them on their own small boats, receiving and delivering clothes they would wash on the shore of Whampoa.[26] But no women were allowed in the factories themselves, though the authorities seemed to turn a blind eye to the sex workers who plied their trade there. Brothels, or flower boats, could be found stationed along the Pearl River. Another common sight was the small army of barbers that milled around, sometimes paddling on the river on loose boards. China had strict regulations on how hair must be worn so barbers were a vital part of social life. And, much like today, they were hubs of gossip. New arrivals to Canton might head straight to a barber for a haircut and to quiz them on job opportunities and local news. Like taxi drivers outside airports, they could also point them towards lodgings.

Another standard part of the milieu around the factories were the sights and sounds of Hog Lane, the market street that ran between the buildings. Hog Lane was crowded with carts and stalls selling everything the foreign sailor might want to purchase. From keepsakes and trinkets to household odds and ends to food and drink, Hog Lane had it all. Apart from porcelain and silk dealers, there were:

> picture painters, glass blowers, sculptors, calligraphers, sign board and lantern makers, limners, weavers, embroiderers, silk fabric painters, herb and tea specialists, hatters, furniture makers, furriers, tailors, shoemakers, fishmongers, moneychangers, copper smiths and silver smiths. Shops selling dried fruits and meats, fans, lacquer ware, rattan mats, baskets, pewter and tin ware, fragrant woods, incense, bamboo blinds, jewellery, carvings (ivory, wood, bone, etc.) and numerous others could be found.[27]

When a prospective customer first visited one of these stores, they would receive a gift of some kind, usually a silk handkerchief. But if a customer didn't then buy anything, the other stores would be informed of their miserliness and there would be no more gifts from any other stores they visited.

It's hard to estimate the number of foreign sailors in Canton. In 1837, there were at least 158 white British sailors in Canton.[28]

Large ships like those run by the East India Company sometimes took four or five months to fully unload and restock. And while this was happening, the sailors often had nothing to do but get drunk and fight in the crannies of Hog Lane. While there were Chinese guards stationed to keep the peace, they mostly ignored these conflagrations if they could.

The Story of Pan Zhencheng

As mentioned before, the only merchants that foreign traders could do business with were the Hong. One such Hong merchant was Pan Zhencheng, also known as Pan Qiguan or Pan Wenyan. The foreign sailors, whose records are often the only ones we have, usually referred to him as Poankeequa. When he died, they referred to his children by the same name. Born in 1714, even before the Yongzheng emperor first banned opium, Pan Zhencheng lived to witness almost the entire arc of eighteenth-century life in Canton. Pan's father was a trader from Fujian who worked in Manila of modern-day Philippines. Because Pan spent his teenage years in the Spanish-speaking docks of Manila, he became fluent in the language – learning how to speak, read and write. His father died when he was twenty-three and he was forced to work for other merchants, using his knowledge of the Manila markets and the Spanish language to make himself vital to their operations. By the time he was in his thirties, he had settled in Canton and was working for himself, quickly becoming one of the largest merchants in the city.

Pan's greatest strengths were his fluency with the Spanish language and his ability to lobby the local administration to get what he wanted. Silver, either raw or in the form of Spanish dollars, was the primary currency for the foreign trade in Canton. And Pan developed a near monopoly on the import of silver from the Spanish with the help of Catholic members of his family in Manila. He also had a close relationship with the Swedes. Despite the volumes of these trade never reaching the dizzying levels of the English East India Company, they were steady and reliable. These relationships allowed him to survive when those who had pegged their fortunes to the English were at the mercy of their whims. It's hard to overstate how complex and interwoven the economic life of Canton was. It was common for three or four parties of different nationalities to be involved in any given transaction. The Swedes might borrow money from an Armenian to underwrite a voyage by a Chinese merchant who wanted to trade in Vietnam or Indonesia.

Pan primarily traded in silk which came from lands near his homeland of Fujian. Like most commodities that were sold in Canton, silk arrived via a human caravan that traversed hill and river, stretching thousands of miles and consisting of thousands of people. These people would carry the silk or tea on their backs on routes across mountain passes. Then their loads would be placed on barges or boats and sailed down a river. The route to Canton involved multiple stages of this process. Goods were carried across mountains, floated down rivers, transferred to bigger boats, carried across land again, loaded on other boats, and so on. From start to finish, this journey could take four to eight weeks. There were as many as 30,000 porters employed in this trade. These men and women were paid pitiful wages for their backbreaking labour. In 1773, there are records of these porters going on strike for an increase of 0.002 taels per catty (which is a unit of load weighing around half a kilogram). Their masters refused to pay them this raise and the porters brought the entire tea trade to a screeching halt.[29]

The officially licensed Hong merchants like Pan occupied a strange position in the economic system of China at the time.

They were tools of the empire's foreign and internal trade policy. Balancing revenue generation and cultural beliefs, the empire instituted the Canton system, which was a unified system to handle diplomacy, foreign affairs, exports and imports. While it worked reasonably well from a macro perspective, the Hong merchants themselves were more or less disposable. They were constantly going into debt or becoming insolvent but there was always someone else waiting to take their place and so the system continued. In 1817, five Hong merchants became insolvent, cumulatively owing more than a million dollars to their creditors. Even Pan was, at one point, 200,000 taels in debt. The Hong merchants were collectively responsible for the debts of any individual merchant. The merchants maintained a fund for this, collected through a small 3 per cent charge on all trade. This system came to be known as the 'Canton Guaranty System' and became the inspiration for the first American bank deposit insurance statute, the Safety Fund Act of 1829.

At the time, in the state of New York in the USA, a banking crisis was looming. This was very much the Wild West of finance (arguably, Wall Street today is no better). Banks were essentially printing money by giving out loans. But their recklessness in this regard made it clear that many of them might go bust at any moment. A former judge, Joshua Foreman, proposed the Safety Fund Act based on his view of the longstanding stability of the Canton system. His proposals were quickly accepted and became law. Every bank had to contribute 3 per cent of their capital to a fund. If a bank failed, the fund would liquidate its assets and take on the responsibility of paying back the depositors. The prevailing wisdom is that, in the modern era at least, knowledge flows from the West to the East. This is one small example, of many, to the contrary.

Technically, at the time, it was illegal for Chinese merchants to take loans from foreigners. But credit was so essential for the smooth working of the Canton system that these loans were ubiquitous. Hong merchants would take loans from foreigners to fund the purchase of commodities like tea or silk from inland China and to bring it to Canton for sale. Even though these debts were illegal, the Qing government protected foreign merchants from losses by standing in guarantee of their debts to the Hong. A government guaranteeing an illegal loan is a hard thing to fathom but that was the case. Also, point to be noted, no such guarantee was provided to Chinese merchants. This asymmetry, revealing where governments' priorities lie, can still be seen in third world nations that are dependent on exports today.

Chinese merchants were also banned from speaking directly to foreign administrators to improve trade regulations. The Qing government saw these communications as threats to their control and the punishment could be as serious as being put to death. For the empire, the health of their trade and its resulting revenue was the primary concern. Any attempt at personal profit that threatened the trade as a whole was dangerous and quickly shut down. In the mid eighteenth century, three of the largest Hong merchants formed a kind of 'triple alliance'. The Qing administration didn't immediately shut it down because this 'cartel' wasn't hurting trade. The person it did hurt was Pan who found himself outside of this group.

But Pan didn't take this lying down. He lobbied the government and formed a council known as the Co-hong. The Co-hong was a collective entity of Hong merchants to self-govern themselves to some extent. Pan became one of the leaders of the Co-hong and this neutralized the cost of being outside of his rivals' alliance. The Co-hong was meant to standardize and systematize rates and processes when it came to the Canton trade but merchants constantly found ways around its rules. After all, the ability to give favourable rates to your favourite customers was an essential part of maintaining your business. Even Pan himself was guilty of this. All merchants had to pay 3 taels on every picul to the Co-hong to defray their costs. In 1762, he secretly sold 15,000 piculs of tea to the Swedes. He didn't report the transaction or pay the Co-hong charge, essentially saving 45,000 taels. This grift isn't the whole story. The interesting part is that he was caught a few years later and brought before a court where he apologized and was forgiven. He claimed the grift was the idea of one of the Swedish merchants. This excuse seems to have been accepted because he only had to pay half the amount to the Co-hong, not the entire sum.[30]

Eventually, in 1771, the Co-hong ended amidst allegations of another bribe. Historians believe the East India Company paid Pan the sum of 100,000 taels to lobby for the Co-hong to be shut down. The devious Pan seems to have accepted the bribe, knowing the Co-hong was going to be terminated anyway. As a tool for controlling trade, it had stopped being useful to the Qing administration. With the end of the Co-hong, Pan tried to retire from the trade but that was easier said than done. He succeeded for a little while, letting his son take over. But within the decade, the governor approached Pan and requested – in a way that made clear that acceptance was the only option – he return to officially being a Hong merchant again. Pan probably had to use the 100,000 taels bribe from the English East India Company to 'buy' his retirement in the first place. Now, the governor gave him a huge sum of money to 'buy' him back. This shows how, according to one Chinese historian, the merchants were just 'instruments of government trade' and were used to ensure that 'most trading profits came to the government's revenue and mandarin pockets'.[31]

Pan seems to have only half-heartedly participated in the parallel smuggling economy. Opium smugglers bypassed the Canton system entirely. Some of the personnel on the Chinese side were the same. Tidewaiters, translators and pilots had to take out loans to buy their official licenses. The illegal opium trade was one of the best ways to earn enough to repay those loans. For smugglers, the route to China was the same. Their first stop was Macao as usual but from there, they journeyed to Lintin Island (now known as Nei Lingding Island), which was a tiny island in the Pearl River. Lintin Island became the hub of the illegal opium trade from around 1815 onwards. Around the island, old ships were permanently anchored as floating warehouses. Chinese buyers would row to these anchored warehouses on smaller boats referred to as centipedes, fast crabs and scrambling dragons. These boats were manned by twenty to seventy armed sailors to protect their precious cargo.[32] These buyers had already paid silver and purchased little chits at Canton. They would exchange these chits and a further 'gift' per chest to receive their opium.[33]

If they wanted to make greater profits, the smugglers would bypass the Canton area entirely and try to reach less accessible locations where demand was high. If they chose well, local merchants would flock to the ship, eager to make a quick profit. Lines would form as merchants waited for their turn. Without translators, they would communicate purely through sign language and the calculation of the abacus. These smugglers were making a lot of money. The system was working well till rumours began that opium from elsewhere in India was coming into Macao. And not just in one or two ships. There seemed to be a complete parallel system of opium cultivation outside the Bengal monopoly.

Notes

1. 'Sabarna Roychowdhury Paribar ... vs The State of West Bengal and Ors. on 16 May, 2003.' https://indiankanoon. org/doc/782056/.
2. Dalrymple, William. *The Anarchy: The East India Company, Corporate Violence, and the Pillage of an Empire*. Bloomsbury Publishing, 2019. The description of events that led to the Battle of Plassey draws heavily from Dalrymple's detailed recreation.
3. Timberg, Thomas A. *The Marwaris: From Jagat Seth to the Birlas*. Penguin UK, 2015, p. 22.
4. Conversion based on Nye, Eric W. 'Pounds Sterling to Dollars: Historical Conversion of Currency.' https://www.uwyo.edu/ numimage/currency.htm. Accessed 26 October 2020.
5. Timberg, Thomas A. *The Marwaris: From Jagat Seth to the Birlas*. Penguin UK, 2015, p. 23.
6. Bauer, Rolf. *The Peasant Production of Opium in Nineteenth-Century India*. Brill, 2019, p. 11.
7. Cederlöf, Gunnel. 'Poor Man's Crop: Evading Opium Monopoly.' *Modern Asian Studies* 53, no. 2 (March 2019): 633–59. https://doi.org/10.1017/S0026749X17001093.
8. Land areas are measured in bighas, which is often a variable measure of land. It's hard to convert bighas accurately into modern measures like hectares or acres.
9. The 'permanent settlement' regulations were land and tax reforms introduced by Lord Cornwallis in the 1790s, first in Bengal and Bihar.
10. Trocki, Carl. *Opium, Empire and the Global Political Economy: A Study of the Asian Opium Trade, 1750–1950*. Routledge, 2012, p. 47.
11. There was definitely some diffidence amongst the zamindars about encouraging opium cultivation as is evidenced from the amount the Opium Department spent on 'gifts' for them.

12. Bauer, Rolf. *The Peasant Production of Opium in Nineteenth-Century India*. Brill, 2019, p. 78.

13. Kranton, Rachel and Anand V. Swamy. 'Contracts, Hold-Up, and Exports: Textiles and Opium in Colonial India.' *American Economic Review* 98, no. 3 (May 2008), p. 29. https://doi.org/10.1257/aer.98.3.967.

14. Kranton, Rachel and Anand V. Swamy. 'Contracts, Hold-Up, and Exports: Textiles and Opium in Colonial India.' *American Economic Review* 98, no. 3 (May 2008): 967–89. https://doi.org/10.1257/aer.98.3.967.

15. Trocki, Carl. *Opium, Empire and the Global Political Economy: A Study of the Asian Opium Trade, 1750–1950*. Routledge, 2012, p. 68.

16. Kipling, Rudyard. 'In an Opium Factory.' In *From Sea to Sea and Other Sketches: Letters of Travel (Volume 2)*. Macmillan and Co., 1899, p. 301.

17. Childers, Hope Marie. 'Spectacles of Labor: Artists and Workers in the Patna Opium Factory in the 1850s.' *Nineteenth-Century Contexts* 39, no. 3 (27 May 2017), p. 178. https://doi.org/10.1080/08905495.2017.1311987.

18. Kipling, Rudyard. 'In an Opium Factory.' In *From Sea to Sea and Other Sketches: Letters of Travel (Volume 2)*. Macmillan and Co., 1899.

19. Bauer, Rolf. *The Peasant Production of Opium in Nineteenth-Century India*. Brill, 2019, p. 77.

20. Kipling, Rudyard. 'In an Opium Factory.' In *From Sea to Sea and Other Sketches: Letters of Travel (Volume 2)*. Macmillan and Co, 1899.

21. Trocki, Carl. *Opium, Empire and the Global Political Economy: A Study of the Asian Opium Trade, 1750–1950*. Routledge, 2012, p. 70.

22. Childers, Hope Marie. 'Spectacles of Labor: Artists and Workers in the Patna Opium Factory in the 1850s.' *Nineteenth-Century Contexts* 39, no. 3 (27 May 2017), p. 179. https://doi.org/10.1080/08905495.2017.1311987.

23. Kipling, Rudyard. 'In an Opium Factory.' In *From Sea to Sea and Other Sketches: Letters of Travel (Volume 2)*. Macmillan and Co, 1899, p. 303.

24. Van Dyke, Paul Arthur. *The Canton Trade: Life and Enterprise on the China Coast, 1700–1845*. Paperback ed. Hong Kong University Press, 2007, p. 53.

25. Van Dyke, Paul Arthur. *The Canton Trade: Life and Enterprise on the China Coast, 1700–1845*. Paperback ed. Hong Kong University Press, 2007, p. 85.

26. Van Dyke, Paul A. and Maria Kar-wing Mok. *Images of the Canton Factories, 1760–1822: Reading History in Art*. Hong Kong University Press, 2015, p. 17.

27. Van Dyke, Paul A. and Maria Kar-wing Mok. *Images of the Canton Factories, 1760–1822: Reading History in Art*. Hong Kong University Press, 2015, p. 19.

28. Chen, Song-Chuan. *Merchants of War and Peace: British Knowledge of China in the Making of the Opium War*. Hong Kong University Press, 2017, p. 8.

29. Van Dyke, Paul Arthur. *Merchants of Canton and Macao: Politics and Strategies in Eighteenth-Century Chinese Trade*. Hong Kong University Press; Kyoto University Press, 2011, p. 51.

30. Van Dyke, Paul Arthur. *Merchants of Canton and Macao: Success and Failure in Eighteenth-Century Chinese Trade*. Hong Kong University Press, 2016, p. 66.

31. Zhuang, Guotu. *Tea, Silver, Opium and War: The International Tea Trade and Western Commercial Expansion into China in 1740–1840*. Xiamen University Press, 1993, p. 18.

32. Lovell, Julia. *The Opium War: Drugs, Dreams, and the Making of Modern China*. eBook, Abrams, 2011.

33. Downs, Jacques M. 'American Merchants and the China Opium Trade, 1800–1840.' *Business History Review* 42, no. 4 (1968): 418–42. https://doi.org/10.2307/3112527.

3

Smugglers from Malwa

Competitors in Crime

At the beginning of the nineteenth century, the bigwigs of the East India Company in Fort William in Calcutta received some disconcerting reports. Indian opium was being sold in Macau and Canton – opium that wasn't coming from Calcutta. This didn't completely catch them on the wrong foot. They knew that the Marathas were producing opium in the Malwa region but didn't know at what scale. After some basic investigation, they were horrified to discover that opium was becoming a major crop in the region and a sophisticated trade network to China had already developed. Lord Wellesley, India's governor general, foresaw that if unchecked, this alternate source of opium would hobble Calcutta's profits. Especially because this 'Malwa opium' seemed to be easier to smoke and more potent than Bengal opium and Chinese 'customers' were already starting to prefer it. This obviously could not be tolerated.

Malwa is an uneven triangular plateau of around 40,000 square kilometres. The historical region overlaps with a large section of modern-day Madhya Pradesh and a small part of Rajasthan and Gujarat. The farmers of Malwa had been growing opium since at least the sixteenth century when the Mughal empire controlled the entire region. European travellers described it as growing in abundance. With the beginning of the China trade, Malwa opium had become a distinct brand. Unlike in Bihar, Malwa farmers stored the opium sap in pots with linseed oil to preserve the moisture. The opium mellowed in these pots sometimes for months. This transformed the flavour and consistency of Malwa opium and became part of the region's 'brand' in China. The preservative effect of the oil also meant that the opium lasted a year longer than Bengal opium. Farmers prized certain wells for irrigation over others as the source of water affected the flavour of the opium.

In Malwa, there was no central authority like the Opium Department. The entire supply chain was completely in the hands of sundry zamindars and sahukars – landlords and moneylenders. The sahukars advanced money (or sometimes grain instead of money) to the farmers before the harvest. They charged interest measured in opium juice. The same was the case for taxes on the sale of opium in villages. Instead of specifying a rate in money, it was directly expressed in opium. Despite there being no centralized agency, there was still a fixed procurement price. Just before the harvest, the sahukars would all get together out of the heat of the Malwa sun. There, in the shade, after their greetings and small talk, they would politely discuss and decide the price for the coming season. The farmers weren't invited. Based on the price agreed together, the moneylenders would decide how much of the advance paid to the farmers was recovered and make a note in their account books. It might be tempting to imagine that the farmers of Malwa were more free or prosperous than the farmers in Bengal. But sadly, that is not the case. They were as trapped in a cycle of exploitation in the supposed 'free market' of Malwa as they were in the government monopoly in Bengal.

After the harvest, the farmers would hand over the opium to middlemen at local markets. The middlemen would weigh and measure everything, recording the values in the appropriate ledgers. Over the next few weeks, these middlemen would form the opium into balls. Similar to the process in the Patna and Ghazipur factories, these balls would be wrapped in poppy leaves and watched for months to stave off insects. Once they dried, the middlemen would sell them to a wholesaler who was often an agent of an affluent merchant from Bombay or Ahmedabad. They packaged the opium balls in bags made of the same cloth as dhotis, then placed them in baskets or chests. The wholesalers sent these chests to Portuguese-controlled Daman or other ports in Rajasthan or Gujarat from where they were loaded on ships to China. If it was Daman, it was sent on the backs of mules or bullocks. If it was headed to Jaisalmer or maybe Karachi, it would be loaded on camels to cross the Thar Desert.

The wholesale price of opium couldn't be communally decided. It varied based on factors like the price in China. This meant that speculation by sahukars was common. They would execute contracts to buy stocks at fixed prices at some future date. These contracts were bought and sold, like bills of exchange. In all these cases, money rarely exchanged hands. Everything was just entries in ledgers.

In 1805, the British outlawed opium cultivation in Malwa. But since they had no direct control over this region at the time, enforcing a monopoly in this region was easier said than done. Instead of slowing down and then stopping, production began to increase. Malwa opium became more and more popular in China. A network of Indian merchants were 'smuggling' the drug to China through every possible port on the west coast. One by one, the British tried to close these smuggling routes. They signed treaties with the Gujarati kingdoms on the coast to buy their promise that opium would not be exported from their harbours. But however much they tried, the smugglers seemed to simply find another way, slipping through their fingers like water. As ports in Gujarat became closed to them, the smugglers started ferrying opium through Sindh to Karachi. According to one Chinese historian, the Company conquered the kingdom because Sindh consistently refused to cooperate with their requests to block all opium transport through its territories.[1]

The Maratha Confederacy

After the death of Aurangzeb and Shivaji, the Peshwas came to control political power in central India. The Peshwas were a dynasty of prime ministers rather than emperors. By the mid eighteenth century, five noble houses divvied up the entire region and formed the Maratha Confederacy. The Peshwas positioned themselves at the head of this alliance. The other four houses were Bhonsle, Gaekwad, Holkar and Scindia. Of these, Holkar and Scindia controlled most of Malwa between them. Many other smaller kingdoms and chieftains in the region rose and fell around these houses over the years.

In the late eighteenth and the early nineteenth centuries, the British barged into the politics of central India. They fought a series of extended conflicts that we now refer to as the three Anglo-Maratha wars. The members of the Maratha

Confederacy were never able to form a united front. Divided, they found themselves floundering against the British. By the end of the Third Anglo-Maratha War in 1818, the British were the preeminent force in the region – and the whole country. But rather than knocking their thrones to the ground and setting an office chair in their place, the Company decided on a different course. The leaders of the erstwhile Confederacy still governed their kingdoms but the British pulled all the strings.

This system of indirect rule was a contentious issue. One of its key proponents was Sir John Malcolm, a passionate ideologue of the British empire and self-appointed expert on the politics and culture of central India. Malcolm, unlike some others, was very clear that trade and profit couldn't be the sole aim of the Company in India. In his eyes, they were meant to rule this land. He was the son of a sheep farmer in Scotland, one of seventeen children. His mother's family connections helped his family by getting the older male children jobs with the East India Company. Malcolm was twelve years old when he was signed up as a cadet with the Company and shipped to Madras. By the end of the Second Anglo-Maratha War in 1805, he was thirty-seven. He had been a Company man longer than he had been a child. In over two decades in British India, he had fought in military campaigns and negotiated diplomatic treaties. The only interludes were campaigns in Persia and a brief stint as a commander in the Napoleonic wars in Europe.

A pompous man with a receding hairline, Malcolm almost retired early in 1819 because the Company snubbed him for the governorship of Bombay. The post went instead to Monstuart Elphinstone, whose name can still be found on various landmarks in the city. Elphinstone was Malcolm's personal friend and was a man he had recommended as a potential successor. The fact that he had beaten Malcolm to the position was unbearable. In what Malcolm must've seen as the second twist of fate's cruel knife, another old friend, Thomas Munro, became the governor of Madras in the same year. But Hastings, governor general of India at the time, convinced him to delay retirement and remain in Company service. Malcolm comforted himself by scheming to become lieutenant governor of central India, a post that didn't exist. He dreamed of a 'mountain throne' for himself from where he would govern the rocky landscape of Malwa. He was a man susceptible to flattery, which the locals seem to have indulged – at least according to him. In his letters home, he described people shouting 'Jai Malcolm Jai' as he passed them on the road. His name became a powerful mantra that people chanted to ward off evil. Apparently, women tied a string on the right arm of their children 'whilst the priest pronounced the name of Malcolm three times' as 'a sovereign cure for a fever'.[2]

He was appointed the commissioner of the Malwa region and immediately began working on a report. This report would become, in his eyes, both the bedrock of colonial knowledge about this region and a testament to his value as a Company official. He was so committed to this magnum opus that he didn't even want to take a break to travel to Calcutta to receive his Grand Cross, the award of knighthood. Hastings sent it to Bombay instead so he could be spared the trip. The finished report came to be called *Memoirs of Central India* but it wasn't an autobiography. It talked about everything from politics to geology – as well as contained notes on the opium trade. His friend Munro described this work as a 'Malwa Encyclopaedia'.[3] The careful statistics in the book were compiled by Captain Frederick Dangerfield, a dynamic Company man who started his career in the Bombay Infantry, and who worked under Malcolm. Dangerfield's landmark survey of the opium cultivation in the region was the result of months in the field. He traipsed across

Malwa, interviewing legions of farmers and traders who tried to ignore him as much as they could. Their intransigence annoyed Dangerfield but the resistance of the farmers should come as no surprise. Dangerfield's careful data collection was never going to be of any help to them.

Apart from the data and lengthy descriptions, the footnotes of Malcolm's report are full of anecdotal insights into how caste, class and gender intersected with opium. In one banal section about the duties charged on opium, Malcolm decries how in one district of Malwa, brahmins and banias were charged zero or lower rates of tax on their goods.[4] In another footnote, he recounts a second-hand tale from someone clearly trying to win his favour. In this dark story, a thakur, hearing that his wife has given birth to a daughter, instantly starts to prepare a pill of opium to kill the baby. Luckily, the storyteller intervenes to stop the infanticide. Whether or not it happened, Malcolm seems to have been impressed.

The Company Changes Tactics

For about fifteen years, the Company's stance on Malwa opium was completely adversarial. Their official policy aimed to shut down production by any means necessary. But slowly it became clear this wasn't going to happen. Simultaneously, the demand for opium was far outpacing the supply in Calcutta. The Company began to see Malwa in a new light. Once again, they would turn a problem into a solution.

Two officials, George Udny and J.P. Larkins, convinced the Company to control the Malwa trade rather than eliminate it – to domesticate the wolf rather than shoot it. So, they sent an agent, James Taylor, to Malwa to buy opium to sell in Bombay. It's a bit of a mystery why Taylor, in particular, was chosen to be their first agent in Malwa. He was a junior employee, only holding minor postings before this. Suddenly, he was thrown into a bustling, sophisticated market with a large amount of money and no experience. It was like sending a child with a brand new deck of cards into a professional poker game. Predictably, the Indian traders who controlled the opium markets tried to rob him blind. And they succeeded at least once, in a particularly devilish fashion.

In 1822, a firm in Bombay run by one Premji Purshottam reached out to the Company, offering to supply them Malwa opium at Rs 75 per panseri, a unit of measurement of opium. This was much, much lower than the current price of around Rs 90 per panseri. The firm was told to get in touch with the Company's agent in Malwa, Taylor. When Taylor heard of this lucrative offer from officials in Bombay, he stopped buying from the open market and waited for Premji Purshottam to get in touch. The wait dragged on for a long time because while Taylor was politely waiting, Purshottam's agents started buying up all the opium available. When Taylor finally gave up waiting, he found that the market price had risen to around Rs 105 and was still rising. It was a trick that could only work once but demonstrates how the Company had completely underestimated the cut-throat competition.[5]

During his tenure as the agent, Taylor was constantly under criticism from senior officials – either for the prices he was paying or his inability to halt the smuggling. Reports from Macau and Canton claimed that Portuguese opium sales had only increased since Taylor began his work. In fairness to Taylor, there wasn't much he could do. The prices he paid might have been relatively high, but much of the criticism aimed at him was likely driven by ulterior interests. A representative of Bombay Presidency, he was not part of the old boy's club in Calcutta, and they wanted one of their own in charge – no doubt with one eye on the large budget that came with the post. The officials in Calcutta also chafed at Bombay's supervision of the trade and griped and complained till they had their way. In 1823, a Calcutta resident, Samuel Swinton, took over from Taylor, and with that, the Company's methods began to change. The job of the opium agent began to transform from financial to political, and the Company abandoned the open market for backroom deals albeit with the veneer of an official trade agreement. Captain Dangerfield, whose report was still the best source of on-the-ground data at the time, was appointed as his deputy.

Swinton began negotiating treaties with the various kingdoms of Malwa and Gujarat, aiming to fix rates, quotas and tariffs.[6] The Company sent agents to each kingdom, and despite the negotiations happening simultaneously, they took three years to finish. Most of the kingdoms that were producing opium did sign agreements – except one, the Scindias (or Shindes) of Gwalior. Early on, the Company decided to centre their operations in Indore, allying with the Holkars and thus further straining their relationship with the Scindias.

The Company's primary representative in Indore was Gerald Wellesley, son of Richard Wellesley, one-time governor general of India who 'conquered more of India than Napoleon did of Europe'.[7] As official resident of Indore, Wellesley tried to convince the opium traders in the Scindia-controlled markets to deliver to Indore (which was controlled by the Holkars) and was frustrated and baffled when they wouldn't. He seemed to be curiously ignorant of the Holkar–Scindia rivalry, which defined the geopolitics of that region in more ways than one. He eventually wrote many angry letters to his superiors (and to the traders who became quite upset) complaining that 'reasoning and ordinary appeals to duty' were lost on these agents. This intransigence of the merchants from Gwalior further convinced the Company that Indore had to be their base of operations, and they redoubled their efforts to make it the headquarters of their opium trade.

Eventually, Wellesley would go on to become the opium agent after Swinton. While not related to opium, there's an interesting piece of historic gossip attached to Wellesley: throughout this period, he harboured a secret. He had three children with an Indian woman whom we only know as 'Culoo'. Wellesley never acknowledged these children or gave them his surname, but he sent them to England and looked after them. When they were baptized, their father was listed as a 'Charles Fitzgerald'. Records suggest that they lived perfectly normal lives in England. Wellesley, on the other hand, died in 1833, only a few years after returning home.[8]

Swinton's tenure as opium agent and his treaties with the Malwa kingdoms were a colossal debacle. Because they happened simultaneously, there was no way to learn from experience or to homogenize terms across treaties. One example is the negotiations with the kingdom of Kota, which was a producer of opium as well as a point of intersection of many different smuggling routes. Captain Caulfield, the Company official in charge of the negotiations, pushed hard for a treaty and eventually won fairly agreeable terms – but only for six months. The issue with a six-month treaty is that by the time you sign it, it's time to start working on the next one. To Caulfield's dismay, most of the merchants in Kota were completely against renewing the treaty.

After much back and forth, it was eventually renewed but, this time, with major concessions to Kota, including a bonus for not allowing any opium to pass through the kingdom. The treaty also had a much larger contract value, meaning that the

Company had agreed to buy a sum of opium from Kota that exceeded, as far as they knew, what they could produce.

When the officials in Fort William in Calcutta heard about this, they were shocked: the bonus for not allowing any opium to transit through the kingdom was calculated on every unit of opium sold to the Company. This was tantamount to an incentive to boost cultivation! The Company's official policy was still to decrease smuggling while vacuuming up what was available in the market. Caulfield had also guaranteed that the Company would match the price paid to any other kingdom, which was something that could be easily manipulated if the kingdoms colluded.

But even as Calcutta was figuring this out, Wellesley and Swinton were putting the finishing touches on a deal with Holkar to buy more than double his current production capacity. Even worse, they guaranteed payment even if production didn't hit targets. This meant that Swinton had essentially promised Rs 7 lakhs per year even if Holkar didn't produce anything at all. If Caulfield's treaty had the potential for collusion, this one was a disaster from the beginning as far as Calcutta was concerned. But Swinton vigorously defended himself, arguing he had no choice but to agree if he wanted the treaty to go ahead.

But Calcutta could not and would not accept this. They wanted to set aside the treaties despite Swinton's pained admonishments that this would ruin the Company's relationship with these states. This was to no avail. The Company wanted fixed rates for purchase: anything else was too dangerous. So Swinton and his team reopened negotiations, and in 1826, they drew up a whole new set of treaties. But over the course of these negotiations, something interesting happened. The Company had, without explicitly deciding to do so, switched strategies in Malwa. Instead of limiting production in the region, they were now incentivizing production while trying to monopolize distribution. The treaties with Kota and Indore had subtly reversed the Company's entire opium policy. By the time the Company realized this, it would be too late. They couldn't go back. And there was only one way forward. In 1830, after two years of bandying the idea around, the Company finally decided that anyone could export opium through Bombay as long as they paid a transit duty. The department set up scales in Indore, Ajmer and Ahmedabad where opium meant for Bombay could be weighed and assessed. Once the duty was paid, it would be stamped and sent to Bombay. They hoped that a low enough transit duty here would render most other smuggling routes economically unviable – and they were right. Opium began to pour into Bombay.

And this money was essentially 'free' compared to their revenue from the opium in Bengal. The transit duty was about half the price of a chest in Calcutta. For which, in the words of Rolf Bauer, 'they paid over a million peasant households, and ran an Opium Department and two factories with thousands of employees'.[9] Suddenly, they now realized the benefits of leaving the trade in the hands of local traders, bankers and merchants.

Opium's Local Powers

In the Holkar court, the locus of power was a Brahmin merchant called Tatya Jog.[10] Named Vithal Mahadev at birth, he began as an apprentice to a Malwa moneylender named Hari Pant Jog. Jog was patronized by Ahilya Bai, who ruled the Holkar kingdom after her husband died. With Ahilya Bai's death, Mahadev managed to leverage a friendship with a European commander of Holkar's army to take over a section of his employer's business. He also absorbed his name in the process and became 'Tatya Jog'. He was the power behind the Holkar throne in many ways. When John Malcolm wanted to understand Malwa, it was Tatya Jog who provided him with reams of documents. Malcolm lavishes praise on Ahilya Bai in his book, recounting anecdote after anecdote of her qualities as a governor. Most of these glowing anecdotes seem to have come from Jog. He wasn't the kingmaker the Jagat Seths were in Bengal but he was still indispensable. Jog represented the Holkars in treaty negotiations with other native kingdoms as well as with the British. It was Jog who negotiated Holkar's opium treaty with Wellesley, driving the hard bargain that got Caulfield in so much trouble. But while he might haggle over prices, once a deal was finalized, he directed his entire network of opium agents and wholesalers to work with the British. Swinton wrote that Tatya Jog, through his various firms, 'had a share in all opium smuggled to Daman'[11] in 1822. He traded in goods all across India, from Pune to Calcutta to Hyderabad.

In Gwalior, Gokhul Parakh, one of Scindia's chief ministers and a powerful merchant, used his influence to oppose collaboration with the British. Parakh was one of the financiers of the Scindia government, loaning large sums of money to the treasury in their times of need. He was given titles and lands in return. According to John Malcolm, his influence was vast. Most of the mercantile community of Ujjain took their cue from Parakh. When he had come into prominence out of nowhere, the old powers of Scindia's court had tried to run him out of town. But when their courtly intrigue backfired, his power was only consolidated. It helped that he was closely allied with Baiza Bai, the Scindia queen, who was a banker herself.

But despite the seeming neat split between a friendly faction and a not-so-friendly one, Malcolm warned Taylor against Indore as a base of operations. For all the help of Tatya Jog,

Malcolm knew a spider web when he saw one. In his own words, the British would be 'surrounded by an influence and an intrigue that would not be favourable'.[12] Yaswantrao Holkar's 'licentious passions ... brooked no control'. His affairs with his minister's wives were the focus of much scheming by Tatya Jog and others.[13] Malcolm had no stomach for this sort of courtly drama. One can only assume because he was bad at it.

Another of Scindia's chief merchants was Appa Gangadhar. His family had controlled the Mandsaur district of Malwa in Scindia territory for three generations. He exercised almost total control over the farmers in the district, both through political authority and by being the capital behind most moneylenders in the region. As a zamindar and a tax collector, Gangadhar easily exploited the peasants under him, charging them double the standard rent for the land on which they cultivated opium. For every rupee they paid to the state, they also paid a rupee into his personal treasury. Like Tatya Jog for Holkar, Gangadhar was one of Scindia's chief mercantile negotiators of the opium treaties with Swinton. Even in these negotiations, he seemed to have had an eye primarily on his own wealth, offering to clinch the deal if a major portion of the opium purchased came from Mandsaur.

Unlike the other bankers, Appa Gangadhar exercised direct control over the farmers of one of the highest opium-producing regions in Malwa. He wasn't just in the business of lending or speculating. He financed his own caravans, protected at all times by armed guards. Other traders who wanted to send their goods to Daman or some other port could consign their goods to his protection for a fee. If they were lost or captured, Gangadhar would bear the cost.

These merchants were the driving force of the Malwa opium trade. The reins stretched back to the large firms in cities like

Bombay where a cordial relationship had developed between the British and their Indian subjects. Unlike in Calcutta, the two groups seemed to work and thrive together in this new city on the western coast.

Notes

1. Markovits, Claude. 'The Political Economy of Opium Smuggling in Early Nineteenth Century India: Leakage or Resistance?' *Modern Asian Studies* 43, no. 1 (2009): 89–111.

2. Kaye, Sir John William. *The Life and Correspondence of Major-General Sir John Malcolm, G.C.B.: Late Envoy to Persia, and Governor of Bombay*. Vol. 2. 2 vols. Smith, Elder and Company, 1856, p. 318.

3. Harrington, Jack. *Sir John Malcolm and the Creation of British India*. Palgrave Macmillan US, 2010, p. 106.

4. Malcolm, John. *A Memoir of Central India, Including Malwa and Adjoining Provinces: With the History, and Copius Illustrations, of the Past and Present Condition of That Country*. Vol. 2. 2 vols. Kingsbury, Parbury, & Allen, 1823, p. 81.

5. Farooqui, Amar. *Smuggling as Subversion: Colonialism, Indian Merchants, and the Politics of Opium*. New Age International, 1998, pp. 115–16.

6. The details of Swinton's negotiations are based on the extensive work done by Amar Farooqui in *Smuggling as Subversion: Colonialism, Indian Merchants, and the Politics of Opium*. New Age International, 1998.

7. Dalrymple, William. *The Anarchy: The East India Company, Corporate Violence, and the Pillage of an Empire*. Bloomsbury Publishing, 2019, p. xiv.

8. Makepeace, Margaret. 'Gerald Wellesley's Secret Family.' British Library's Untold Lives Blog, 20 April 2017. https://blogs.bl.uk/untoldlives/2017/04/gerald-wellesleys-secret-family.html.

9. Bauer, Rolf. *The Peasant Production of Opium in Nineteenth-Century India*. Brill, 2019, p. 33.

10. The details about the ministers and power brokers in this section come from Amar Farooqui's *Smuggling as Subversion: Colonialism, Indian Merchants, and the Politics of Opium*. New Age International, 1998.

11. Farooqui, Amar. *Smuggling as Subversion: Colonialism, Indian Merchants, and the Politics of Opium*. New Age International, 1998, p. 112.

12. Malcolm, John. *A Memoir of Central India, Including Malwa and Adjoining Provinces: With the History, and Copius Illustrations, of the Past and Present Condition of That Country*. Vol. 2. 2 vols. Kingsbury, Parbury, & Allen, 1823, p. 98.

13. Malcolm, John. *A Memoir of Central India, Including Malwa and Adjoining Provinces: With the History, and Copius Illustrations, of the Past and Present Condition of That Country*. Vol. 1. 2 vols. Kingsbury, Parbury, & Allen, 1823, p. 289.

4

The Bombay Boom

Unwanted Islands

In 1662, the Portuguese gave Bombay to the British as a wedding present. Catherine of Braganza, the infanta, was a cherubic twenty-three-year-old when her mother arranged her marriage to the ruler of England. Having lost her father when she was a teen, and raised in a convent under the watchful gaze of her mother, Queen Luisa de Guzman, she had mostly lived a quiet, cloistered life. Like most royal weddings of that time, this one was both a business agreement and a political alliance. Portugal was a potent imperial power but had recently lost the French as an ally and needed another country's aid in its war against Spain. In England, after the death of Oliver Cromwell and the collapse of his republican regime, monarchy returned and the exiled prince Charles II was crowned king. As the wedding preparations began with the typical royal razzle-dazzle, behind the scenes, the two countries hashed out the real deal. The English would get trading privileges and benefits, 2 million Portuguese crowns and the territories of Tangiers in Africa and Bombay in India. In return, the English would provide naval support to the Portuguese in their war against Spain.

While the political alliance was smooth sailing, the marriage was racked with storms. Charles II was a serial adulterer and had fathered children with several other women. Catherine miscarried three times, almost dying in the process. There was also the question of her faith. Catherine was devoutly Catholic, which was a never-ending source of resentment in Protestant England.

During her marriage negotiations, the British had promised her the freedom to pursue her faith, but the Protestant ministers of England never stopped their plotting. They tried to pressure Charles II into divorcing her multiple times but he staunchly refused. They even accused her of trying to poison the king – anything to get rid of her – but Charles II shut down all attempts to put her on trial. Despite this cultural dissonance, Catherine potentially altered the course of history by popularizing a bitter drink among the English high society: tea.

In Portugal, tea was already a mainstay of the aristocracy, but in England, it was rarely drunk. Over the course of her life, Catherine's enthusiasm for the drink transformed it into a marker of taste and discernment. As one poet would write, 'The best of Queens, the best of herbs, we owe.'[1] She contributed to the birth of a national obsession – an obsession whose fervent flames would be felt on the opposite end of the world.

Despite accepting it as a gift, Charles II soon decided he had no need for Bombay and leased it to the East India Company for the nominal sum of £10 in 1668. Charles II's apathy ran so deep that the British didn't take control of the islands of Bombay for three years after the wedding. When they initially arrived to claim the islands, the Portuguese garrison refused to hand over possession, claiming they had not been informed of any such deal. Only in 1665 were the British finally allowed to land and take control of the settlement, but by then, most of the original force had died from disease and exposure as they waited for political powers to sort the matter out.[2]

At first, the East India Company's primary port on India's west coast was Surat. It was there that they set up their first factory in 1612, and after a few years, inveigled themselves into positions of power and governance. Surat was a bustling coastal town where the opulence of princes rubbed shoulders with the squalor of brothels and arrack bars. And as a common point of embarkation for the devout souls going on their Hajj, it was one of the pearls in the crown of the Mughal empire. But as the Mughals declined so did Surat, till it seemed to fall off a precipice, never to regain its lost dominance. Emerging to take its place was a low-lying mess of islands that made up the city of Bombay.

Today Bombay revels in its position as the commercial capital of India but this commitment to mercantilism is surprisingly telegraphed in the intentions of its earliest English settlers. When he was not spending his time overseeing the reclamation of land from the sea, Gerald Aungier, the second governor of Bombay, was actively recruiting traders and merchants to the city. Of course, in India, this took on a very obvious caste colour where banias and other mercantile communities were specifically invited to come and make a home in Bombay and aid in the city becoming a port of commerce. There is the famous case of Nima Parakh, a bania from Diu, who negotiated with Aungier for the money to build a house, immunity from being arrested without notice, and a contract promising that banias (and banias alone) wouldn't be forced to convert to Christianity.[3]

The banias were a highly organized community in that way. They had an organization called the Bania Mahajan that had on multiple occasions negotiated with the Company on behalf of the community as a whole, including after the riots in Surat in 1795. Describing the situation in Surat, historian Lakshmi Subramaniam says the city was governed by an 'Anglo-Bania social order'.[4] The same could be said of Bombay where many of the city's early political projects were bankrolled by banias who, in turn, enjoyed regular interest payments and other privileges. Other mercantile communities that moved in large numbers were Parsis, Marwaris, Gujaratis and Konkani Muslims.

Bombay's topography lent itself to shipbuilding which, alongside rising cotton exports to Britain and China, fuelled the city's growth. But even a century later, in 1788, Lord Cornwallis was complaining that large sums were being diverted from Calcutta to pay for Bombay's upkeep. The port's expenses far exceeded its revenue. Unlike in Calcutta, British control on this side of the country was still minimal. They were surrounded on all sides by the kingdoms of the Maratha Confederacy. If it wasn't for their naval power, they would've been a peripheral entity on the western coast. This would change in 1818, after the Third Anglo-Maratha War, but till then the Company's (and Britain's) ambitions for India's western coast far exceeded their actual power.

So when they heard of the large-scale production of opium in the Malwa plateau, they cycled through multiple strategies in their attempts to wrest control of the trade before eventually giving up. Eventually, they allowed any merchant who paid them a transit duty to export opium to China from Bombay.

This duty was calculated to make the long smuggling routes to Karachi and Sindh obsolete. The economic logic of this was sound, and soon, opium was flooding into Bombay. The British collected their fee, the Indian merchants maintained their profits, everyone was happy. Everyone, except the British government. Malwa opium was substantially cheaper than Bengal opium. The Bombay transit fee system was inordinately cheaper than the Calcutta system with its advances to thousands upon thousands of farmers and supplementary bureaucracy. With the transit fee system, almost the entire money collected went straight to government coffers as revenue. And as no restrictions were placed on how much opium could be exported out of Bombay, officials in Calcutta were sure this would harm their profits from the monopoly trade in eastern India. According to historian Amar Farooqui, the Calcutta officials were right.[5] Within a year, opium prices in China fell by 10–30 per cent. As Calcutta's profit margins began to shrink, it became clear that they needed a way to increase consumption of opium in China even further. As the logic of corporations has dictated forever, when organic demand fails to suffice, inorganic demand would have to be created. Within a decade, the First Opium War would break out.

But for now, under this new system, the city of Bombay flourished. Between 1836 and 1862, less than three decades, Bombay's population tripled, almost reaching one million people.[6] During roughly the same period, exports from Bombay, 90 per cent of which was opium and cotton, multiplied six times.[7]

An Opium Baronet

In 1805, at the age of twenty-two, Jamsetjee Jejeebhoy was already on his fourth voyage to China. Since the death of his parents when he was sixteen, Jejeebhoy had been working in some capacity or another for members of his extended family in Bombay. While none of his previous voyages had been without incident, this journey was going to change his life forever. On 11 July 1805, four days before his of twenty-second birthday, Jejeebhoy was aboard the ship *Brunswick* when he heard the news that a French ship had been spotted on the horizon.

It was the middle of the Napoleonic wars, and the French were prowling the Indian Ocean, harrying British vessels. When the *Brunswick* had stopped in Bombay, it had been in dire need of repair and French prisoners of war were press-ganged into service. These prisoners were later loaded on a boat and sent home to be exchanged for British prisoners. On their way to France, the ship carrying the prisoners was intercepted by the French admiral Charles-Alexandre Léon Durand, the Comte de Linois, on his magnificent flagship, the *Marengo*. Linois learned from the prisoners when the *Brunswick* was going to ship out and where it was heading. He quickly formulated a plan.

Off the coast of Pointe de Galle (now known as just Galle) in southwestern Sri Lanka, Linois ambushed the *Brunswick*. The Captain of the *Brunswick*, James Grant, had little choice. The *Marengo* was a seventy-four-gun ship but the *Brunswick* was primarily a trader. Grant fired once, but his heart wasn't in it. Soon enough, he lowered the British flag that was flying from the mast of his ship and surrendered. Linois boarded the ship and took most of the officers as prisoners aboard the *Marengo*. Then, he outfitted the *Brunswick* with a new French crew and the two ships set course for the Cape of Good Hope. Jejeebhoy and the other passengers and crew must have been terrified as the *Brunswick* altered its course from China to South Africa, on the opposite side of the globe.

Before this tragedy struck, Jejeebhoy had been keeping the company of another young man on the ship, William Jardine, the Scottish surgeon's assistant. Jardine was twenty-one years old and had been aboard the ship for the last two years. Now, being taken hostage forced these two acquaintances closer together. By the time they arrived in South Africa in September, they had the beginnings of a friendship that would last a lifetime and would change the face of the world.

William Jardine would, in 1832, alongside future partner James Matheson, found what was arguably the most important British trading house of the nineteenth century. Matheson was another Scotsman who had come to India to apprentice with a merchant house. The two of them met in Canton and formed what would eventually become the trading firm Jardine and Matheson. For almost three decades, they would dominate the opium trade as the foremost smuggler among smugglers. By 1834, they would be involved in almost one-third of the entire opium trade.[8] And this share kept rising, peaking in the 1860s. Through their profits, they began to become a driving force behind British expansion in China. To Matheson, the Chinese were 'a people characterized by a marvellous degree of imbecility, avarice, conceit and obstinacy'.[9] They funded newspapers that lionized smuggling as 'free trade' and bellowed for Britain to go to war against China. Jardine would actively counsel the foreign minister Lord Palmerston on a plan of attack during the First Opium War, leveraging their experience with the Qing government. After the war, they celebrated the fact that opium hadn't been officially legalized because it meant more power for them. It kept out, in Jardine's words, 'men of small capital'.[10]

Jardine and Matheson also pioneered the opium clipper. Traditionally, the China trade was at the mercy of the seasons. The northeast monsoon prevented ships from making the trip across the Strait of Malacca as the wind and rain fought them every inch of the way. The traditional East Indiaman ship built at Surat, Bombay or Calcutta for the China trade was huge and rounded, built for carrying tonnes of cargo. They travelled with the monsoon and took around two years to complete a round trip. Opium clippers were 'a new style of vessel with a relatively small cargo space, a slim, streamlined hull and as much canvas as it could possibly carry without capsizing'.[11] Designed for the opium trade, these clippers could carry their small but high-value cargo to Canton against the monsoon. The first such clipper was named *Red Rover* and was built in Howrah, part-owned by Jardine and Matheson. It broke the speed record that existed at the time, outracing every other ship from Calcutta to Lintin.

They would both be wealthy beyond imagination. The novelist and politician Benjamin Disraeli would obliquely refer to Jardine in a book as 'richer than Croesus, one Mr Druggy, fresh from Canton, with a million in opium in each pocket'.[12] James Matheson would become so rich that he would buy his own island – the Isle of Lewis – off the coast of England. At one point, he was the second-largest landowner in Britain and spent £500,000 building a literal castle on his island as a summer home.[13] Today, Jardine Matheson Holdings Limited, the descendent of that original trading firm, has revenues of almost Rs 290,000 crores and is one of the most valuable publicly traded companies in the world.

Jejeebhoy too would become ridiculously rich. He would retire from business with an estimated wealth of around Rs 40 crores and then devote his life to becoming the first baronet of Bombay. This kind of wealth doesn't just happen. It requires an engine to power it and a system that enables it. The engine was opium and the system was a global drug-smuggling operation that propped up an empire.

The Parsi community was involved in the opium trade from its beginnings in India. Hirji Jivanji Readymoney was trading with China as early as 1756. (The name Readymoney seems to have originally been a cheeky nickname that was later officially adopted by the members of the family.[14]) They were an important part of the mercantile community of Surat but many of them moved to Bombay – even before it became the capital of the Presidency. At the time of the 1881 census, more than 5 per cent of Bombay's population was Parsi, which is a huge percentage compared to today. More than half of the entire Parsi population lived in Bombay at the time.[15] When Jejeebhoy first met Jardine on that fateful voyage in 1805, the Bombay opium boom had not yet begun. But when it took off a few years later, he was aptly placed to ride the wave, reinventing himself as needed.

From his earliest days, Jejeebhoy was conscious of his public persona and took steps to change certain details of his life to better fit his desired narrative. For example, he claimed to have been born in Bombay, but some historians believe he was actually born in Navsari in Gujarat. He also referred to himself with the Gujarati-sounding Jamsetjee rather than Persian-sounding Jamshed, which was his actual birth name.[16] Undoubtedly the capital and networks of the broader Parsi community were essential to his success, but in this sense at least, he was a self-made man.

His parents, whom he lost when he was only sixteen, were from a Parsi priestly community. His father worked as a weaver in Navsari in Gujarat. But after they died, Jejeebhoy moved to Bombay and began working for his maternal uncle, buying and selling empty liquor bottles. He earned the nickname 'Batliwalla' or 'bottle seller' and seemed to revel in it, often signing letters with the moniker as if it were his real last name. At the age of twenty, he married his maternal uncle's daughter, Avabai, who was around ten years old at the time. As an employee of firms owned by various relatives, he began to participate in international trade and made his first few trips to China. None of these trips directly made him rich, but they did help him develop vital connections across South and East Asia, including the aforementioned fortuitous meeting with William Jardine. Jejeebhoy would do his best to turn the Malwa opium trade into a monopoly for Jardine and Matheson but never quite pulled it off.

He began his trading firm, Jamsetjee Jejeebhoy & Co., with three other partners, each from a different community and each of whom brought specific expertise to the enterprise. There was Motichund Amichund who was Jain and had close ties with the opium producers in Malwa. There was Mohammed Ali Rogay, a Konkani Muslim, who was sometimes referred to as nakhuda, meaning shipowner or captain. Like Jejeebhoy, Mohammed Ali Rogay was a community leader and a member of the highest of Bombay high society. His family had been sea traders for generations and Rogay became one of the most sought-after agents for Bombay traders who wanted to ship to Canton. He was a veteran of the trade even when Jejeebhoy was still learning the ropes. In 1825, when drought gripped Bombay, he built a large public water tank in what is now called Azad Maidan, spending the equivalent of Rs 2 crores in modern currency.[17]

And last but not least, there was the Goan Catholic Rogeria di Faria who had connections with the Portuguese authorities who controlled the port at Daman. His father had been a merchant in Calcutta but Faria moved back to Bombay and integrated himself into Portuguese trade networks. He owned multiple ships that travelled from ports like Mozambique to Macao. In 1807, the Portuguese royal family fled to Brazil after an invasion by Napoleon's forces. In 1822, Brazil became independent and Faria became the honorary consul for Brazil at Bombay. In 1838, when he was sixty-eight, Faria went bankrupt after throwing his capital behind a disastrous military expedition. He had to retire from the world of business completely. Jejeebhoy stepped in and provided Faria with a pension to survive on for the rest of his life. His gravestone can still be found at the Gloria Church in Byculla in Bombay.[18]

The second act of Jejeebhoy's life can be seen both as a continuation of his earlier life and a sharp break from it. When his son Cursetjee was old enough, Jejeebhoy began to step back from the business to focus on civic life. While opium was seen as just another item of trade within these mercantile circles, it seems that Jejeebhoy wanted to distance himself publicly from the drug trade. Opium prices were freely published in newspapers, and few merchants felt any sympathy for the Chinese when the First Opium War broke out. Jejeebhoy and the others seemed to be primarily interested in claiming compensation for destroyed stocks and impatiently waiting for when regular trade would resume. But in his burgeoning career as a public figure, he might have been worried about its potential damage to his reputation.

Various historians have noted that between European merchants and their Indian counterparts, there was a sense of shared community and mutual respect in Bombay. But that was not the case among the citizenry and the government. The Parsis had repeatedly displayed their support for the British through financial contributions and were rapidly becoming the most Anglophile of all Indian communities.[19] For them and the other elite of Bombay, charity and public work were a way of building a common moral and ethical ground with the British – a way of proving their shared humanity. Simultaneously, the British were looking to ensure that the local elites saw a common benefit in continued British rule.

At the forefront of this push to use philanthropy to forge bonds with Bombay's rulers was Jejeebhoy. His donations were prolific. By 1855, his commercial empire was mostly finished and he devoted himself entirely to philanthropy and public life. In his biography, the historian J.R.P. Mody calculates that Jejeebhoy donated £245,000 over the course of his life. In current terms, that would be around £10 million or Rs 100 crore.[20]

This astronomical level of charity has left its mark on Bombay and Pune. He paid two-thirds of the entire cost of the Pune water works with the balance coming from the government. His wife Avabai single-handedly paid for the entire construction of the Mahim causeway that connects the island of Mahim to Bandra, ensuring the government wouldn't charge a toll from citizens. He created the JJ School of Arts where Lockwood Kipling, father of Rudyard, would be dean in the 1860s. The same school would be the cradle of the Progressive Arts Group, the troupe of modernist painters like M.F. Husain who changed the landscape of art in independent India. Because of a hefty tax on cattle grazing at public grounds instituted by the British, Jejeebhoy bought one such field and then let cattle graze there for free. This act remains preserved for history in the name Charni Road (charni means grazing), a common stop on Bombay's western train line.[21] Probably most notable of all his contributions to the public of Bombay was the founding of JJ Hospital, to which he eventually donated both land and a large sum of money. The hospital had been entirely Jejeebhoy's idea, and when he wrote to the British government, they received the idea enthusiastically. But the process became extremely drawn out when sharp differences emerged in how they believed the hospital should function. Jejeebhoy wanted it designed around class and caste lines, but the government refused. Finally, when the hospital was built, there were some concessions made, such as a separate kitchen for Brahmins.

Because of his philanthropic work, Jejeebhoy's reputation among the British grew. In 1834, along with his business partner, Mohammed Ali Rogay, he became one of the first Indians to be appointed Justice of the Peace. This was one of the very few official positions in local government that Indians could participate in. A Justice of the Peace held a seat in the Court of Petty Sessions, the de facto municipal authority. In 1842, he became the first Indian to be knighted by the queen, officially receiving a Sir prepended to his name. But Jejeebhoy wasn't done. In secret, he began a campaign to receive a hereditary title. Thomas Williamson Ramsay, the former revenue commissioner of Bombay, wrote a glowing account of his numerous good deeds, and with the help of many well-wishers, this account was widely distributed among the Lords of England, even reaching the hands of Prince Albert himself. In 1856, a profile of Jejeebhoy was published in *Illustrated London News*. Apparently, Lord Palmerston, the man whose shadow looms over the opium wars, was the one who first broached the subject with the queen on Jejeebhoy's behalf. The campaign was eventually successful though it was by no means simple.

In 1857, Queen Victoria named him the first baronet of Bombay. But it took four years for him to finally obtain the title because the British government was unsure of Parsi inheritance law and whether it would complicate the process of handing down the title. To secure the baronetcy, Jejeebhoy had to place a property in trust (officially referred to as Mazagaon Castle) along with a sum of Rs 25 lakh. And now that Jejeebhoy had set a precedent, the British eventually opened up the honours system to colonial subjects. They used the gesture to portray a united and homogenous global empire. Between 1890 and 1911, seven baronetcies were granted to citizens of Bombay Presidency, and sixty-three Parsis were knighted by 1946.[22] Despite being such a small community, various Parsis would endow more than 400 educational and medical institutions over the nineteenth and early twentieth centuries.

The Jewish Connection

In the mid 1850s, it looked like Bombay would overtake Calcutta as the major economic powerhouse of the British empire in India, but for various reasons, this never happened. Around that time, as India moved from Company Raj to British Raj, the first cotton mills started in Bombay. Many of these mills were started by notable Parsi families that had amassed their wealth in the opium trade. In fact, many Parsis were slowly getting out of the opium business as the years went on. They were embracing the turn towards industry. When the American Civil War broke out in 1861, the cotton trade from India hit a flashpoint. The Confederates or the American South, one of the largest producers of cotton in the world, were embargoed for their use of African slaves on their cotton plantations. Bombay became the global centre for trade of another vital commodity. The city was growing increasingly larger now as people flocked to it from all over the country – and even from all over the world.

One such group that would come to replace the Parsis in the opium trade and make their mark on Bombay was the Sassoon family. The Sassoons were one of the most eminent Jewish families in Baghdad. Their patriarch, David Sassoon, who first came to Bombay around 1832, had been treasurer to the governor of Baghdad like his father before him. But under the new pasha, Jews were being persecuted and many had fled the city. Sassoon would not have been even forty years old when he arrived in Bombay with his children and his second wife. His first wife had died a few years earlier. He quickly made a name for himself with the British as a savvy merchant with a fine trade network across the Arabian Sea. This was despite not speaking a word of English himself.

Though he initially focused on cotton, Sassoon also exported opium and sent his son to Canton to be his agent there. After the Treaty of Nanjing, he set up branches in both Hong Kong and Shanghai, and hence was able to capitalize on the huge boom that happened after the war was over. One of Sassoon's key advantages came from integrating himself into the existing Malwa system. He began advancing money to the high-level Malwa traders and they, in turn, passed that money downstream till, essentially, Sassoon was advancing money to the farmers themselves. This was unique to him. Nobody else wanted to risk money by investing directly in the cultivation. By gaining such direct control of the Malwa supply chain, Sassoon eliminated all competitors. According to historian Carl Trocki, 'This put Sassoon in a position somewhat analogous to that of the Indian government in Bihar and Benares. The firm acted as the "banker" to finance the Malwa opium crop, making advances to an already established group of dealers and, in effect, purchasing the crop before it was even planted.'[23]

Using this control of the Malwa trade, he expanded into the Calcutta side of the trade, manipulating the prices by stockpiling and artificially limiting supply. According to one Chinese scholar, it was the speculative power of Sassoon's firms over the opium trade that reduced the profits of Jardine and Matheson and eventually forced them to diversify their interests outside opium.[24] By 1871, Sassoon had a powerful hold over the opium trade from both Calcutta and Bombay. After almost three decades of dominance, Jardine and Matheson, along with their Indian partners like Jamsetjee Jejeebhoy, no longer controlled the trade.

Sassoon made multiple contributions to the urban landscape of Bombay, including the Sassoon Reading Room and Library which remains a recognizable landmark near Kala Ghoda, a neighbourhood in Bombay known for art and culture. But they were overshadowed by the legacies of his children. His oldest son, Abdullah, financed the first wet dock in Bombay, still called Sassoon Docks. Abdullah and younger brother Elias would, through their respective trading firms, also come to own the largest number of cotton mills in the city. At their peak, during the 1880s, these mills would employ over 15,000 people. Jacob Sassoon, Elias' son, would become the single largest employer of factory labour.

Abdullah, who took the name Albert, moved to England in the 1870s and ran the business from there. He would eventually become a baronet. His son would marry a woman from the Rothschild family, an amusing fact given that the Sassoons would soon earn the nickname 'Rothschilds of the East'. Elias was one of the first waves of traders to see the potential in Shanghai and established a base there as early as 1850. When his father died, Elias would start his own firm and focus on Shanghai. Because of this presence, Shanghai soon attracted more Baghdadi Jews. As in Bombay, the homes of the members of the Sassoon family became centres of the Jewish community, places for people to come together and talk. Arthur Sassoon, another of David's sons, would become one of the founding committee members of the Hong Kong and Shanghai Bank, which would grow into what we know today as HSBC. Arthur was originally named Abraham but changed his name without telling his father when he was in Hong Kong, partially to avoid anti-Semitism and partially because it was a better fit for his anglicized lifestyle.

David Sassoon's grandson-in-law, Sassoon Jacob Hai David, is another prominent figure from that time. He was a wealthy businessman and held multiple public offices, including Sheriff of Bombay. He was also made a baronet in 1911. When the Bank of India was formed in 1906, he was one of the lead promoters and acted as chairman for a little while.[25] When the Gateway of India was built to commemorate the arrival of the British monarch George V in India in 1911, he was one of those who financed the construction of that iconic monument. Famously, the Gateway wasn't built in time for the king's actual arrival and George V saw a crude mock-up, possibly made of cardboard, waiting for him on the Bombay shore.

One notable mercantile community missing from the narrative so far are the Marwaris. While many of them were no doubt involved in the trade, none of them attained the stratospheric level of wealth of people like Jejeebhoy or Sassoon. Sassoon worked with a Marwari trader named Gulraj Singhania who acted as his primary, if not sole, broker. This would imply that Singhania would've been trading in huge volumes. According to one source, in the mid nineteenth century, Singhania was paying Rs 27,50,000 annually as customs duty towards his opium business.[26] But the direct involvement of Marwari firms in the export of opium in their own names seems to have occurred relatively later, towards the beginning of the twentieth century. This was when the opium trade was already on the decline, as international pressure to end the trade began to grow.

In the history of the colonization of India, the nineteenth century is a long one. As the tentacles of the British empire crept over the subcontinent, they accelerated a subtle shift in power. Bankers and merchants were slowly becoming the real power brokers. The Mughal empire had provided centuries of stability that had allowed these communities to grow and flourish but the British made them essential to the governance of their imperial project. But as we've seen, this imperial project was at its base a narco-state. The mercantile community's ability to negotiate and profit in their dealings with this narco-state was built on an ability to ignore the morality of their actions.

But the blood on the hands of the opium trade was only going to grow. The British were going to force two wars on China, beginning what some refer to as the Century of Humiliation. China was pried open, and like sailors feeding the furnace of a steamship with coals, the British empire began to shovel more and more opium into what they saw as an engine for making money. But money has a gravity of its own. It begins to warp everything around itself, rearranging people and objects in subtle and terrible ways. For one thing, opium money became a vital source of income for the government in India. This meant that the nationalist movement, as it gained purpose and momentum, remained curiously silent on opium. In their pragmatism, they didn't want to risk winning the independence of an impoverished nation. In Britain, an anti-opium lobby was running a vociferous campaign to stop the trade. But it would take almost a century for this lobby to win even the smallest victory.

Notes

1. The poem is 'On Tea' by Edmund Waller.
2. Dalrymple, William. *The Anarchy: The East India Company, Corporate Violence, and the Pillage of an Empire.* Bloomsbury Publishing, 2019.
3. Fernandes, Naresh. *City Adrift: A Short Biography of Bombay.* eBook, Aleph Book Company, 2013.
4. Subramanian, Lakshmi. 'Capital and Crowd in a Declining Asian Port City: The Anglo-Bania Order and the Surat Riots of 1795.' *Modern Asian Studies* 19, no. 2 (1985): 205–37.
5. Farooqui, Amar. *Smuggling as Subversion: Colonialism, Indian Merchants, and the Politics of Opium.* New Age International, 1998, p. 156.

6. Fernandes, Naresh. *City Adrift: A Short Biography of Bombay*. eBook, Aleph Book Company, 2013.

7. Markovits, Claude. *Merchants, Traders, Entrepreneurs: Indian Business in the Colonial Era*. Palgrave Macmillan, 2008, p. 144.

8. Chen, Song-Chuan. *Merchants of War and Peace: British Knowledge of China in the Making of the Opium War*. Hong Kong University Press, 2017, p. 14.

9. Lovell, Julia. *The Opium War: Drugs, Dreams, and the Making of Modern China*. eBook, Abrams, 2011.

10. Trocki, Carl. *Opium, Empire and the Global Political Economy: A Study of the Asian Opium Trade, 1750–1950*. Routledge, 2012, p. 107.

11. Trocki, Carl. *Opium, Empire and the Global Political Economy: A Study of the Asian Opium Trade, 1750–1950*. Routledge, 2012, p. 105.

12. Lovell, Julia. *The Opium War: Drugs, Dreams, and the Making of Modern China*. eBook, Abrams, 2011.

13. Courtwright, David T. *Forces of Habit: Drugs and the Making of the Modern World*. Harvard University Press, 2001, p. 34.

14. Palsetia, Jesse S. *Jamsetjee Jejeebhoy of Bombay: Partnership and Public Culture in Empire*. Oxford University Press, 2015, p. 26.

15. Figures from: Guha, Amalendu. 'The Comprador Role of Parsi Seths, 1750–1850.' *Economic and Political Weekly*, vol. 5, no. 48, 1970, pp. 1933–36.

16. Palsetia, Jesse S. *Jamsetjee Jejeebhoy of Bombay: Partnership and Public Culture in Empire*. Oxford University Press, 2015, pp. 12–15.

17. Kidambi, Prashant, Manjiri Kamat and Rachel Dwyer. *Bombay before Mumbai: Essays in Honour of Jim Masselos*. Oxford University Press, 2019, p. 27. Converted to pounds at the rate 1/15 which is provided at https://www.cs.mcgill.ca/~rwest/wikispeedia/wpcd/wp/r/Rupee.htm and then converted to

modern rates using the converter at https://www.uwyo.edu/numimage/currency.htm.

18. Souza, Teotonio R. de. 'For Goa and Opium.' In *Reflected in Water: Writings on Goa*, edited by Jerry Pinto, p. 316. Penguin Books India, 2006.

19. Palsetia, Jesse S. *Jamsetjee Jejeebhoy of Bombay: Partnership and Public Culture in Empire*. Oxford University Press, 2015, p. 66. According to Palsetia, the Parsis contributed to various patriotic and military funds as well as for the construction of various statues to British political figures like William Pitt and Lord Cornwallis.

20. Palsetia, Jesse S. *Jamsetjee Jejeebhoy of Bombay: Partnership and Public Culture in Empire*. Oxford University Press, 2015, p. 97.

21. Fernandes, Naresh. *City Adrift: A Short Biography of Bombay*. eBook, Aleph Book Company, 2013.

22. Palsetia, Jesse S. *Jamsetjee Jejeebhoy of Bombay: Partnership and Public Culture in Empire*. Oxford University Press, 2015, pp. 144–52.

23. Trocki, Carl. *Opium, Empire and the Global Political Economy: A Study of the Asian Opium Trade, 1750–1950*. Routledge, 2012, p. 113.

24. Goldstein, Jonathan. *The Jews of China: Historical and Comparative Perspectives*. Vol. 1. eBook, EM Sharpe, 1999.

25. 'Sir Sassoon Jacob David, Merchant-Philanthropist, Dies in Bombay, Aged 77.' Jewish Telegraphic Agency, 29 September 1926. https://www.jta.org/1926/09/29/archive/sir-sassoon-jacob-david-merchant-philanthropist-dies-in-bombay-aged-77.

26. Calangutcar, Archana. 'Marwaris in Opium Trade: A Journey to Bombay in the 19th Century.' *Proceedings of the Indian History Congress* 67 (2006): 745–53.

5

The Opium Wars

The Onslaught of Commissioner Lin

In late 1838, the Daoguang emperor finally made a decision. His son was discovered smoking opium in one of the Forbidden City's temples. At the same time, 3700 kilograms of opium (about the weight of the adult male Indian elephant) had been seized from smugglers less than 150 kilometres away from the capital. He sent off one of his famous missives and summoned an administrator with a burgeoning reputation for honesty and reliability: the now legendary Lin Zexu.

For a famous government official, Lin Zexu's roots were humble. His family were minor landholders who had failed to qualify through the government exams for four generations. With each generation that failed to earn an official posting, the family's wealth and reputation had dwindled. To remedy this, Lin Zexu's father began coaching him when he was three years old, hoping his son would succeed where he, his father and his grandfather had failed. This dedication to (or obsession with) prestigious exams should sound familiar to the Indian reader. Lin would later write how he and his father would sit and work together 'through freezing days and endless nights, in a broken-down three-roomed apartment, with the north wind howling angrily, one lamp on the wall ... till the night was out'.[1]

The relentless preparation paid off. At the age of twenty-six, on his third attempt, he passed the metropolitan exam and won an official posting. Over the next twenty-seven years, he lived the life of the effective civil servant – being transferred from town to town and promoted from appointment to appointment. But whether he was river superintendent or judicial commissioner, Lin Zexu was seen as incorruptible, earning him the nickname 'Lin Clear-as-the-Heavens' (Lin Qintian). He clearly had very robust ideas of right and wrong. You can't be incorruptible without an ironclad moral vision of one kind or another. So as the empire lost silver and gained an opium crisis, Lin was one of the few men of repute to openly identify as 'anti-opium'. As the emperor looked around for someone to handle the crisis, Lin Zexu was at the top of a very short list. The emperor summoned him to the royal court. And if the wavering emperor was looking for someone with clarity of purpose and a reassuring faith in their own ability, he found it in Lin Zexu. This was a man who was confident he knew what to do and how to do it. Lin had no sympathy for opium smokers: his judgement was ruthless. To him it was clear that people with addictions had to give up their 'evil' habit or be put to death.

The emperor appointed Lin Zexu as the commissioner of Canton and charged him with terminating opium smuggling once and for all. Lin moved to Canton and began to implement his stratagems with haste. Not because his heart burned with zeal for the cause, though. Oh no, for Lin Zexu, this was an opportunity to impress the emperor and thus earn what he truly desired: the power to reform the empire's grain transport and irrigation systems. Lin Zexu had extensive opinions on opium but they were nothing compared to his extensive opinions on boosting agricultural productivity and food safety. To Lin Zexu, Canton and opium constituted an interlude in his career – one that he hoped to complete as soon as possible. So when he arrived at the port with the European factories perched outside, he wasted no time. Lin's strategy weaponized public surveillance. He organized the residents of Canton into 'security groups' of five, each of whom had to keep watch on the others, ensuring that they stayed clean from the taint of opium. It seems to have worked well. As historian Julia Lovell writes in her fascinating book on the opium wars, 'Within two months of his arrival, Lin had arrested 1,600 people for opium offences, and confiscated nearly fourteen tons of opium and almost 43,000 opium pipes; within another two months, he had imprisoned five times more opium-felons than the provincial governor had in three years.'[2]

While he focused on his countrymen, Lin sent an ultimatum to the Europeans: give up your opium stocks or get out. The Europeans – used to working with the corrupt Hong for so long – simply ignored this cranky new bureaucrat. But as Lin raced through the town, gathering up Chinese opium smugglers like teenagers hoovering up evidence of a party before their parents get home, he also began calling for the arrest of British smugglers. Which, of course, suddenly made this whole thing 'political', and so an urgent alert was sent to the British supervising officer.

Charles Elliot was in Macao when he heard the news that a Chinese bureaucrat was arresting a British citizen and immediately rushed to Canton. Elliot was a thickset man with a large, bushy beard and a large forehead. He, much like Lin Zexu, was an earnest civil servant who took his job seriously. This wasn't as common as you might imagine. It was definitely in stark contrast to his predecessor, Lord Napier, a bombastic aristocrat who, much like the earlier Macartney embassy, managed to insult the Chinese in a number of ways during his time there; he was eventually chased out of Canton and died of fever in Macao. When he took the job, Napier had planned a glorious tenure where he proved British superiority over the Chinese but all he got was ignominious death. Elliot was also from a noble family, but in the enactment of his duties, he was the polar opposite of his predecessor.

Before Lin Zexu arrived at Canton, Elliot as the chief superintendent of the Chinese trade clearly had no love for opium. He disliked the smugglers and drug trade and publicly aired that dislike. From his writing, the picture that emerges is of someone much more empathetic to the Chinese than his average countryman. But he was also a colonial administrator. His job was to look after British interests and citizens, and he never wavered from it. He believed the convenient British logic of the goodness of 'free trade'. To Elliot, the Chinese trading restrictions were misguided and unjust. In fact, he blamed the Chinese for the drug trade. If they legalized opium or opened up their markets to free trade, the drug would become less and less profitable. And the opium trade would wither away. This is probably not true at all – but it was a common logic among the colonial aristocrats who scoffed at the drug trade while owing their careers to it.

But with Lin Zexu's arrival, whatever Elliot's opinions might have been before, he turned into the most pragmatic of colonial servants. Irritated by Elliot's protection of smugglers, Lin Zexu ordered the European factories blockaded and stopped all

Chinese workers from working there. In some accounts, this blockade is called 'a siege' but it was actually far from a violent process. The Europeans were comfortable in their compound. They had enough food stores and the richest were even able to still have food delivered to them from the city. Their primary problem was boredom, which they alleviated by drinking all the time and playing schoolyard games. But as weeks passed, there was no sign of Lin retreating from his demands. The British couldn't leave as Chinese ships blockaded the port, stopping all ships coming in or going out. It wasn't a real war, but it could easily turn into one. Elliot, the man who was technically responsible, sweated over a solution. The British smugglers were vehemently opposed to giving up their stock: their entire livelihoods were wrapped up in these goods. The lines of credit backing these chests of opium reached all the way back to India and London. There were the fortunes of a lot of different people packed alongside the opium.

Elliot's solution to the problem can be seen as either benign or devious. After three days of silence, he sent word to Lin that the British would hand over their entire store of opium – more than 20,000 chests. To convince the horrified smugglers (or merchants, if you prefer), he promised them that the British government would indemnify their losses amounting to almost £2 million. Remember these were supposed to be criminals: the British government had no official involvement in this trade whatsoever. But now they did. Some historians argue that Elliot did this on purpose – correctly guessing this £2 million bill would essentially force Britain to go to war against China. How else were they going to be able to afford it? Others are more sympathetic to Elliot, painting him as man in a tough spot who made a tough choice.

Lin Zexu took the 20,000 chests of opium, and with salt and lime, burned it all. The smoke billowed into the sky. The ash washed into the sea. It took three days.

The Daoguang emperor was delighted on hearing the news and the grapevine was abuzz with how Lin Zexu's star was rising. But the commissioner of Canton wasn't done. He sent Charles Elliot a contract that required the British to pledge they would ship no more opium to China and any smuggler caught in the act could be put to death. When he received the contract, Elliot tore it to pieces. He declared he'd rather die than sign this bond. The entire premise of the contract was ludicrous to Elliot. As far as he was concerned, he could never sign a document that allowed for British citizens to be put to death by another country. Smuggling didn't merit the penalty according to British law, and while Elliot might have agreed that technically Chinese law should apply in China, he couldn't allow this 'technicality' to supersede his duties to protect fellow citizens. 'If ... these bonds be absolutely required, there will remain no alternative but for the English men and vessels to depart,' he declared to Lin.[3] This was perfectly fine with Lin who was happy for the British to go and never come back. It was the British after all who needed China's tea, not the other way around. Regardless, once the stock was handed over and negotiations over the contract stalled, the blockade was lifted. The British left the port of Canton and sailed away to the relative safety of the island of Hong Kong.

In Hong Kong, the British sat and waited for word from London. Elliot fired off letters to Lord Palmerston, each one more impassioned than the last, about how a military attack was required to enforce British rights. He did not receive a reply for Lord Palmerston was a busy man. Henry John Temple, who bore the title Lord Palmerston, was a British politician who was, according to his biographer, 'the very personification of nineteenth-century England. His brimming self-confidence in Britain's greatness and his unhesitating willingness to advertise his nation's virtues to the rest of the world and to identify himself with the British people made him their natural spokesman.'[4] But the historical record of his actions paints a picture of man with various contradictory impulses who had a huge effect on the nineteenth-century world. From an aristocratic background, Palmerston was ushered into politics on the strength of his lineage. But he slowly veered away from the conservative Tory Party and joined the more progressive Whigs in 1830 before leading the formation of the Liberal Party in 1859. While considered a moderate reformer, his domestic record is littered with anti-democratic policies, including stalling attempts at universalizing electoral franchise.

But he is most remembered (and widely criticized) for his role in world affairs: he routinely pushed foreign nations to the brink of war for the sake of British interests. In the dramatic international incident known as the Don Pacifico affair, Palmerston attacked the Greek government for not defending a questionably British subject whose house had been attacked by an anti-Semitic mob. This was partially done to force Greece into paying back overdue loans but at the risk of poking Russia and France who were both co-guarantors of Greece's independence. Palmerston was dragged before Parliament to be censured and it looked like his career was over. But he turned the tables on his critics, giving a speech still remembered as his *civis romanus sum* moment. He praised Britain as a model nation that guaranteed its citizens protection and liberties wherever in the world they might be. The country was a model of freedom and governance

– much like the enlightened world of ancient Rome. At the end of the day, he was more popular than he had ever been.

The question of the rights of British citizens abroad became very relevant in the story of the opium war when legal jurisdiction became the crux of a new international incident. A handful of British and American sailors slipped away to the Chinese coast for some supplies. Discovering a stash of local liquor, they got drunk, vandalized a nearby temple, and in the ensuing fight, killed a Chinese man. Elliot tried to pay some compensation to the dead man's family and hush up the matter but Lin soon found out and demanded that the guilty soldiers be handed over to be executed. Elliot of course had no intention of doing so. He held a trial on the ship, finding five of his men guilty of riot and assault. He claimed there wasn't enough evidence for murder which Lin found preposterous, declaring that 'a wooden dummy would have done better'.[5] The guilty sailors were then packed off to London to serve their sentence, but on reaching their homeland, they were released as the British authorities declared that Elliot had no judicial authority to hold a trial. It's unclear if Elliot knew this would happen or this was genuinely his best attempt at justice. Understandably insulted by this refusal to submit to Chinese law, Lin banned all trade with the British – even essential supplies and drinking water. Chinese war junks parked themselves off the Chinese mainland, blocking the British ships in Hong Kong from restocking at the mainland.

After a few weeks, their drinking water store dwindling, Elliot demanded they be allowed to travel to the villages on the coast of the mainland to buy supplies. The Chinese ignored him. With three ships, he sailed to the Chinese war junks and threatened to fire. When they refused to let them pass, he fired. His British canons tore through the Chinese ships and he grimly sailed past the wreckage. Surprisingly, Lin wasn't angered by this. In fact, he relented, allowing the British to restock and reopening negotiations. He wanted the murderous sailors handed over to him but Elliot repeated that the murderers' identities could not be ascertained. He also refused to sign Lin's proposed contract, instead offering that British goods be searched and opium confiscated. Elliot, in many ways, was just playing for time. He needed word from London. His opinion was clear: a short, violent reprisal by British forces would quickly make the Chinese change their stance.

But back in London, Lord Palmerston, on whose desk Elliot's letters landed, was taking his time. This was despite the fact that Elliot wasn't the only one trying to get the foreign secretary to take action. William Jardine had fled Canton to return home just before the trouble with Lin Zexu started. When he finally arrived in London, he immediately began the process of lobbying Lord Palmerston to declare war against the Chinese. But Palmerston, alongside the rest of the ruling Whig government, had important things to focus on. The 'Chinese question' was important, of course, but far more important was the 'Turkish question'. In their attempt at saddling the whole world, the British government had a whole platter of 'questions' to deal with. As the foreign secretary at this time, Lord Palmerston was a busy man – and quite aware of his own importance. He was nicknamed Lord Pumice Stone by those annoyed by his abrasive personality.

When Lord Palmerston finally met William Jardine, he extracted as much information as he could and gave no promises in return. But Jardine convinced him that the prior intelligence collected by the British was correct. A relatively small force armed with artillery could smash through most of the Chinese coastal fortifications. If they blockaded the eastern seaboard, they could choke the vital food supply route from Nanjing. Then, chokehold in place, they could push towards Peking and press the emperor to agree to their terms. Palmerston's fellow Cabinet members were more worried about who was going to pick up the bill, especially since Elliot had declared that the government would indemnify those pesky merchants. When Palmerston volunteered that the Chinese could pay the bill, recently inducted Cabinet member and every Indian's favourite colonizer Thomas Macaulay apparently applauded in response. With that masterstroke, it was decided. Word was sent to Lord Auckland in British India to ready ships and soldiers. As Lin and Elliot glared at each other across Chinese waters, preparation for war began.

When the British Parliament heard about this, they were aghast. The country had essentially gone to war without Parliament approval. Of course, much of the outrage was manufactured to bring down the ruling government. In April 1840, the Tories, Britain's Conservative Party, brought a no-confidence motion to Parliament but the ruling Whig government survived with a majority of nine. Maybe history would've been different if those nine men had voted differently. But probably not.

Time for War

Readers today, accustomed to planes that jet across the world in hours, might find it hard to fully realize how slow war was in the mid nineteenth century. In September 1839, Lord Palmerston and the Cabinet agreed to go to war. It took till November for word to reach Lord Auckland in India and for his preparations to start. Lord Auckland's armed force – a fleet of twenty-two warships and more transports containing around 3600 soldiers, many of whom were Indian – reached China only in July 1840.

Which makes this almost a year after Lin Zexu had blockaded the British and Charles Elliot had written requesting that a violent response be sanctioned. During this relatively quiet year, the world did not stop spinning. The Qing government continued to wrestle with numerous problems of managing a sprawling empire. Lin Zexu received his commendations from the emperor for his success. He continued to diligently govern Canton and root out people with opium addictions. Even though the opium trade had almost completely ceased, the British community in Hong Kong continued to live out their lives in peace. They continued to depend on local Chinese communities for the resources to survive even as news filtered through that the hammer was set to fall.

When the British fleet arrived at the island of Zhoushan to begin their military expedition, the Chinese thought they were opium smugglers trying to avoid the new rules at Canton. They expected to charge a hefty bribe and then let the English through. For the corrupt administrators of Zhoushan, Canton's loss would be their gain. But instead, the admiral of the British fleet declared they were here to conquer the island and demanded surrender. There were ships from the Chinese navy in Zhoushan but their admiral knew they didn't have a chance. They simply were not prepared. He also knew he could not turn and flee without fighting. Punishments for that sort of thing were severe. So the defenders of Zhoushan tried to make a fight of it. They dusted off their ancient cannons on their fort's battlements. They lined up their ships and sailed to meet the British.

The fighting lasted nine minutes. There was a tremendous crashing of cannon fire ripping through wood, smashing and splintering and breaking everything in its way. And then it was over. The residents of the town fled. Any soldiers left alive fled. The governor committed suicide. Calmly, the British took control of the island. And the First Opium War had officially begun.

But the Daoguang emperor had no idea he was supposed to be at war with the British for months. Even when the situation became clear, the term 'war' hardly seemed fitting. In the Qing court, it probably seemed like the dozens of other clashes they continuously dealt with across the empire, including border clashes with bandits and pirates. The Chinese only understood why the British were attacking in August 1840. When the British sailed into Tianjin, the port closest to Peking, they sent a letter from Lord Palmerston to the emperor that outlined their grievances. The letter also had a list of demands: a large sum of money to compensate for the destroyed opium, the island of Hong Kong to act as a British base, and so on. The emperor ignored all of those demands and instead focused on their complaints against Lin Zexu. In his response, he promised to have Lin punished if the British would turn around and go back to just trading in Canton.

The Daoguang emperor's chosen representative was a governor named Qishan, who has been demonized as a traitor in nationalist Chinese history for his role in the opium war. Qishan was one of the wealthiest men in China and his primary method of communicating with the British was to give them generous gifts of food and compliments. He seemed to have made such an impression on Elliot that the British officer was completely won over. The exceedingly polite Qishan seemed far removed from the brusque Lin Zexu. By a very thorough massaging of the truth, Qishan convinced the British to turn around at Tianjin and return to Canton where further negotiations would happen. By telling the British the emperor could be convinced to accept their demands (though he was in no position to assume that), Qishan won the Chinese vital time. But in his report to the emperor, he made it seem like the war was over. So the Chinese did not spend the few months of peace that he won them preparing their defences. Rather, the emperor returned to worrying about other things, after appointing Qishan to Lin Zexu's position at Canton to finish the negotiations and return matters to the previous status quo.

But, of course, the war was not over. It would go on for another two years – only officially ending in 1842 with the Treaty of Nanjing. For the next year, the Chinese and the British would clash sporadically but violently in the moments between 'official' negotiations among the emperor's representatives and the British commanders. Over the course of this 'war', the British appear to have never tasted defeat. Which might've suggested a quicker end to the violence but in their reports back to the Chinese emperor, his military generals and representatives felt obligated to reverse the truth. If they lost, they would usually simply lie, claiming great victories. So for most of this period, the Daoguang emperor believed they were always on the verge of ending the war. This, as you might imagine, was a disastrous situation. The emperor probably only had himself to blame: he initially punished anyone who admitted the British were the stronger military power. Eventually, he realized the reports he received were false and began to collect them from multiple sources, threatening punishments if discrepancies were found. But the outcome of the war had been more or less decided by then.

When the Qing empire was founded, their army had been a fearsome, disciplined fighting force. But those days were long gone. The Qing dynasty had been ruling for two centuries and both the empire and the army were in a very different state. At the time of the opium war, the salaries of most soldiers were pitiful. Soldiers – who were more 'law enforcement' than 'professional army' by this time – typically supplemented their income with bribes or crime. Which isn't very different from law enforcement today. According to Lin Zexu, most aspiring soldiers wanted to join the navy because opium smugglers were a great source of bribes.

In fact, the most complicated part of the opium war was the existing relationship between the Chinese people and the state. Even as the British conquered coastal forts and pushed towards the capital, the average Chinese peasant continued to provide them food and aid in return for coin. Every military general the emperor sent to stop the British complained about the 'collusion' between Chinese peasants and the British forces. But while the voices of the British and Chinese ruling class make up the historical record, the voice of the Chinese people is much harder to access. China, like most large states at the time, was a highly unequal society. There was deep-seated antagonism between the nobles and the commoners, the haves and the have-nots. The rebellions, like the Taiping Rebellion, that would soon wrack the country harnessed the people's desire for change. But for the time being, the Qing dynasty continued to hold on to power.

In December 1840, after months of negotiating, Elliot finally grew impatient. Over the course of these negotiations, he had lowered his demands more or less continuously. Elliot was a bad negotiator – from the British point of view at least. He actually wanted his counterpart, Qishan, and thus China, to come out of these negotiations on a satisfactory footing. To do that, he had to ignore or compromise on much of what was on Lord Palmerston's original list of demands. In his mind, pressing for all of Lord Palmerston's demands would've damaged any positive long-term future relationship with China. Elliot clearly did not realize that Britain did not want a positive long-term relationship. They didn't want any relationship that did not have them firmly in the driving seat. They simply weren't interested in being equals. But after months of earnest conversation that ended up going nowhere, he gave the Chinese a deadline, and when it wasn't met, he ordered his men back to war.

In early 1841, a monster of iron and gunpowder drifted out of Indian waters towards China. It was named *Nemesis*. Built for the opium war, it was an all-iron steam ship – a juggernaut that fed on 11 tons of coal per day. It shrugged off Chinese artillery, easily manoeuvred around their coastal forts, and smashed any ships that got in range. The *Nemesis's* captain, remembering the ship in action, wrote how one of the enemy junks

> blew up with a terrific explosion, launching into eternity every soul on board, and pouring forth its blaze like a mighty rush of fire from a volcano ... The smoke, and flame, and thunder of the explosion, with ... portions of dissevered bodies scattering as they fell, were enough to strike with awe ... the stoutest heart that looked upon it.[6]

His poetry stands in stark contrast to the gut-wrenching carnage of what he was describing.

The British found the initial resistance weak and desperate. The forts were crowded with soldiers, but this only meant that when they were shelled, the death toll was immense. When the British captured towns, many residents committed suicide. The inability of the conquering forces and the terrified defenders to communicate with each other didn't help. Sometimes soldiers killed their families rather than let them be taken prisoner for fear of what the British would do. In most instances, the British casualties were minor. Malaria and other diseases were often a greater threat than being killed in battle.

In March, the British sailed into Canton, moved back into their old factories, and declared that trade must reopen. Qishan's replacement, a wrinkled career soldier named Yang Fang, acceded, and in the middle of the war, trade resumed. Tea began to flow once again in huge quantities to England. How did this square with the emperor? Well, he simply wasn't told. Yang Fang continued in the vein of Qishan and Lin Zexu before him. In his reports, he simply lied to the emperor, fabricating increasing progress against the British threat. Yang Fang's immediate superior was the military general Yishan. With Yishan, the emperor had finally decided to pull out all the stops. He ordered thousands of men to Canton and demarcated a huge sum of money to fund what he hoped would be a decisive blow. When he found out that trade had reopened, he was furious. Not just because he wasn't informed. The news confused his picture of the war front even more. Which is understandable. The British reopening trade in the middle of a military expedition is inexplicable if you're not aware how much the closing of the tea trade hurt British tax revenues.

In the end, Yishan's massive attack went ahead. But coordinating a large army was hard to do with any secrecy and the British had plenty of local informants. Even though the British had been given ample time to prepare, the battle outside Canton was one of the fiercest fights the British would see throughout the first war. But once again, the lack of professional soldiers on China's side led to another rout. The British chased the retreating army back to Canton and began to bombard the city. It was only a matter of time before a truce was announced and the governor of Canton agreed to pay $6 million if the British would take their guns and leave.

The British gracefully accepted the truce and retreated, but as they did so, they looted and pillaged the countryside. Their rapacious soldiers had been cheated out of pillaging Canton so they took out their energies elsewhere. Unarmed peasants ended up receiving the brunt of their violence. Abandoned by their leaders, the peasants rebelled, forming their own militias to attack the British. This peasant army did successfully push the British back but it held as much anger for its own government as it did for the British. Reports of their spontaneous resistance probably wasn't received with joy in Peking. This was inspired by self-defence rather than some burst of abstract nationalism.

What did please the emperor was Yishan's report of the battle at Canton. As was standard practice, he again spun a narrative of his own, rewriting events to turn the truce into victory. He disguised the impending $6 million payment to the British as the existing debts of the Hong merchants. The emperor, convinced that the British were now retreating with their debts paid, disbanded the military preparations he had been making and assumed that the matter was now over. Of course, the British were only retreating from Canton; they had no intention of ending the war. In fact, they were in the middle of getting rid of one of the big factors they felt was holding them back – Charles Elliot.

Everyone – more or less – seems to have been flabbergasted by the progress of Elliot's negotiations with the Chinese. In early 1840, Elliot received a letter from Lord Palmerston angrily complaining about him ignoring the written orders of Her Majesty's government. While Elliot had by no means avoided bloodshed, he had been ready to compromise with the Chinese. This meant he had to be replaced. Elliot's replacement was a man named Henry Pottinger, who had been sent from the British Army in India. Pottinger was seen as a man of decisive action. In this case, that meant he was ready to blow up anything that stopped the British getting the terms they wanted. By the time

Elliot returned to England, his reputation was in tatters. The newspapers portrayed him as either cowardly or incompetent. In the long defence of his actions that he composed, he described himself as the 'worst treated public officer of my day'.[7] It's unclear how much of this criticism affected him or his future prospects but it clearly wasn't too bad. At a costume ball thrown by the queen, he attended dressed as Lin Zexu. It must have helped that Elliot was closely related to the Earl of Minto, whose descendant would be responsible for the influential Minto–Morley reforms in India.

A Treaty Is Signed

Under Pottinger, the opium war takes on an even more brutal tinge. He oversaw a series of lulls punctuated by violent attacks by the British and counterattacks by the Chinese. He conquered Zhoushan again, essentially putting the British almost back to where they were before the negotiations began. Then, they continued onward, brutally destroying Chinese defences and armies in their path. No matter the number of men China amassed, it was never enough. They lacked discipline and experience. They couldn't match British firepower. Eventually, even the emperor's advisors began to publicly declare that they needed to sue for peace and give in to the British demands. Giving up, the emperor appointed negotiators to sue for peace. From British reports, the emperor's representatives were perfectly happy to agree to all of their terms. Their primary goal was to simply get the British to leave as quickly as possible and end the war. These negotiators, though, had a tricky job. They had to lie both to the emperor about what the British were saying and to the British about what the emperor was saying.

On the British side, Pottinger refused to speak to any of the Chinese officials who were of lesser rank than he was. A missionary priest of Prussian descent, Karl Gutzlaff, was the primary negotiator for the British. Gutzlaff, a short man with large dark eyes and comparatively excellent Chinese, worked for various colonial powers as a full-time translator to fund his religious mission. This was quite common for missionaries in the nineteenth century. In fact, the history of missionary activity in China is inextricable from the commercial activities of the colonial powers. The Qing administration expressly prohibited Christian missionaries from entering their lands. But, of course, just as the opium ban didn't stop merchants, this didn't stop the missionaries. They simply joined trading companies as employees and entered the empire under that guise. Gutzlaff, specifically, was highly in demand. Merchants were willing to pay thousands of dollars for a few days of his time. But over the course of the 1830s, he primarily worked for Jardine and Matheson, acting as a guide for their opium-smuggling ships. His justification for participating in a patently illegal activity is a familiar one: it was for the greater good. Jardine promised him a sizeable donation – a percentage of the profits – that he could then use for furthering his religious goals.

For many missionaries, the opening of trade was integral to the spread of religion. But for Gutzlaff, it went one step further. For him, Chinese restrictions on trade went against the will of God who wanted all countries of the world to share their wealth with each other. This acted as a neat justification for him to use the full extent of his powers to aid the colonial project. Throughout the First Opium War, Gutzlaff played multiple semi-official roles and that of priest was the least of them. His primary position in the British apparatus was that of a spymaster. His network of informants was the main channel for intelligence about China's strategies for the British expedition. After the war, Gutzlaff acted as a magistrate of Ningpo, one of the cities the British conquered and retained. An anonymous officer who worked under him at Ningpo described him as the perfect example of how 'knowledge is power'.[8] Of course, he didn't completely forget his Christian mission. During the treaty discussions, he apparently shared copies of the Bible with all the Qing negotiators.

The negotiations over the Treaty of Nanjing were also interesting in what they did not discuss: opium. The entire matter of the drug trade was never even mentioned in the treaty – on the insistence of the emperor's representatives. When they asked Pottinger why the British continued growing the drug in their Indian territories, he just trotted out the standard British evasion: if they didn't allow it in India, it would just be grown elsewhere. As far as Pottinger was concerned, like Elliot before him, it was China's trading policy that was flawed. If they legalized the drug, they would be able to charge duties on its import and it would actually contribute to the treasury. But in this practical response, Pottinger dodged the moral implications of the question posed to him. Despite controlling every aspect of the opium trade, the British, in their discussions, treated it as though it was a mysterious and inevitable force of nature – like the monsoon.

The final terms of the treaty signed at Nanjing directed China to pay the British an indemnity of $21 million. China also had to open up five ports to the English for residence and trade, essentially ending the Canton system and Hong monopoly. The ports were Canton, Amoy, Foochow, Ningpo and Shanghai. The British also gained Hong Kong forever. Also, the British and Chinese were to interact in the future as equals. Once the treaty was signed, the British didn't leave Nanjing till they received the initial payment of $6 million, which covered the losses of the 20,000 chests Lin Zexu had burned in 1839. And thus ended the First Opium War.

Back in England, the success of the war seemed to retroactively prove its necessity. The term 'opium war' was initially coined by critics of the government as a way of pointing out what the war was really about. But after the war, the din of those voices subsided partially because many of those critics cared only about the war in as much as it could be used to hurt the Whig government. But no government has ever been brought down by winning a war, so they dropped it. Only the genuine humanitarians continued but their attempts to shame this act of jingoism and exploitation were drowned out in the deafening cacophony of British power politics. Even in America, John Quincy Adams, the sixth President of the United States, praised Britain for going to war on the principle of universal natural rights. By trying to limit the trade between nations, China had committed 'an enormous outrage upon the rights of human nature and upon the first principles of the Rights of Nations'. For Adams, just as Britain had led the world in the abolition of the slave trade (after profiting from it for decades), they were being a moral paragon here as well.[9] Scholars like Glenn Melancon have argued – persuasively – that it was the idea of 'national honour' that primarily motivated the British Parliament to enter into war. Melancon's analysis relies on parliamentarians' private papers, from which he concludes that their words were not a smokescreen for greed or baser values.[10] But this isn't an argument that exonerates Britain. The idea of national honour is very much wrapped up in ideas of racial supremacy and imperialist fervour.

Of course, the period between the First and Second Opium Wars was essentially an interlude. For the world, it was business as usual. The events of the first war were quickly being turned into history or trivia. In 1845, a statue of Lin Zexu was added to the collection at Madame Tussauds. Merchants like William Jardine were glad that the opium trade wasn't legalized as it kept out the small fry – the 'men of small capital', in his own words.[11] Opium smugglers avoided the five treaty ports and instead developed their own systems and routes. Jardine and Matheson used Hong Kong as their base; they had a 700-ton ship permanently anchored in the harbour as a warehouse. This was also the era where steamships became a part of the nautical landscape. The opium clippers were small and fast. The steamships were large and fast. These ships could make the journey between China and India in fifteen to twenty days. In 1852, a steamship called the *Ganges* carried the largest ever cargo of opium: 2500 chests.

In China, things were only getting worse. In the late 1840s and early 1850s, one of the largest rebellions in history was gathering steam. The Taiping Rebellion began around the strange figure of Hong Xiquan, who pronounced himself the brother of Jesus Christ and the leader of a theocratic movement against the Qing dynasty. For more than a decade, China would be mired in a bloody civil war of epic proportions. At the same time, there were other minor rebellions or outbreaks of civil unrest all across the empire. And like vultures over a kill, the European powers were circling. From the mid 1850s, the British had begun to tentatively discuss potential joint military operations in China with the French, their historic enemies. There were even discussions with the USA. The cause of these secret meetings was probably again economic. In 1854, despite the terms of the Treaty of Nanjing, the trade imbalance between Britain and China was again ballooning. Britain was £8 million in the red. The British tried to broach the subject of revising the treaty to allow trade even with interior China. By this time, the Daoguang emperor had died, and in 1850, the Xianfeng emperor had ascended the throne at the age of nineteen. The Xianfeng emperor refused the British terms outright. The next year Lord Palmerston became Prime Minister of Britain.

A Second War

A lot of ink has been spilled trying to pin down exactly why or how the Second Opium War started. The official British excuse was clear. In 1856, the *Arrow*, a Chinese ship with a British captain allegedly under British protection, was boarded by Canton port authorities and the crew arrested on the charge of piracy. Immediately, the ambitious British consul in Canton, Harry Parkes, rushed to the scene. Parkes was a young man, just twenty-eight years old, but he was already a veteran of British–Chinese politics. He had been an apprentice translator during the negotiations around the Treaty of Nanjing at the age of fourteen. As the acting consul of Canton, Parkes had the authority to act but he also had an axe to grind. Even though the Treaty of Nanjing had given the British permission to access and dwell within Canton, the city's residents had absolutely no desire to have the people who bombarded them become their neighbours. Parkes absolutely detested this continued resistance, repeatedly complaining about the Chinese xenophobia and disrespect for the British. The irony of accusing the Chinese of xenophobia while plotting to invade them was clearly lost on nineteenth-century Englishmen. Whether Parkes was acting on his own or whether he had secret orders to instigate a war isn't clear. But with the precedence of the First Opium War, it isn't too much of a leap to assume that someone like him would know Britain would probably support a war if he could provide the right excuse. The arrest of the crew of the *Arrow* provided him that excuse.

Today, we know the entire *Arrow* incident was manufactured. The *Arrow* was a Chinese ship through and through. The British captain was a purely nominal figure and the man did nothing on the ship. Parkes claimed that the *Arrow* was under British protection but its contract had actually expired. Even after discovering this, he hid the knowledge from his superiors.[12] He also allegedly fabricated an incident where the arrest authorities tore down the British flag that was on the ship. It seems there was never a British flag on the ship. But Parkes exploited this incident, conspiring with his superior officers to besiege Canton. The British cannons bombarded the city's walls and soon a large gaping hole was visible. British soldiers rushed into the gap and took the city – along with a curious ally. Apparently, the US consul at Hong Kong also rushed in with a small detachment and raised the American flag over Canton. Though when the American commander heard this, it was quickly dismissed as completely unauthorized.[13] The Americans had decided to stay 'neutral'.

When the British Parliament heard that Parkes had instigated a full-scale attack on China, they erupted into furious discussion. They debated over the legal technicalities of the *Arrow*'s status, whether it was right to make war, and the commercial importance of the China trade. Of course, in 1856, the British were facing problems in India with the minor matter of the brewing Indian Sepoy Mutiny, or the First War of Independence as we sometimes refer to it today. But the civilian casualties of Canton seemed to generate enough outrage in Parliament that a vote of no-confidence was called for. Unlike what transpired during the First Opium War, this time the ruling government lost the vote and the entire Parliament was dissolved. A new election was called. But as the election was being organized, Lord Palmerston and his colleagues conducted a public relations tour de force and somehow managed to win power back. Of course, Palmerston's campaign was fuelled in no small part by the success of his vitriolic anti-Chinese messaging. But even before the question of war with China had been introduced in Parliament, Palmerston's government had already sent word to begin preparing for war. But this wasn't the only way these discussions were shown to be a sham. In 1858, Palmerston's government survived another no-confidence motion. This time, it was after revelations of an attempt to assassinate Napoleon III, the ruler of France and the nephew of Napoleon Bonaparte. But what is pertinent to the opium trade is how after Palmerston's critics came to power and formed the new government, they immediately forgot their old aversion to war with China and proceeded to vigorously support the ongoing conflict.

As the British Parliament yo-yoed between Whig and Conservative coalitions, the war in China continued unabated. The French joined in and together with the English, they savaged the stretched Chinese defences and besieged Canton again. Lord Elgin, the commanding British officer who oversaw the attack on Canton, would write, 'Whose work are we engaged in, when we burst thus with hideous violence and brutal energy into these darkest and most mysterious recesses of the traditions of the past? I wish I could answer that question in a manner satisfactory to myself.'[14] After capturing the walled city, the European powers forced China to sign another treaty – that of Tianjin in 1858. This opened up even more ports to foreign trade, allowed Christian missionary activity, and also effectively legalized opium. But even then, the war was not over. There were another two years of brutal fighting ahead, culminating in the invasion of the Forbidden City: Peking (now Beijing). And this time, the brutality was captured for posterity as the Second Opium War now had an official photographer.

In these modern times, we're used to war correspondents being sent out to the frontlines of conflict zones and sending back dispatches for the vicarious consumption of the crowds at home. But in the mid nineteenth century, the camera wasn't the portable device it is now. And yet, as Susan Sontag wrote, 'Ever since cameras were invented in 1839, photography has kept company with death.'[15] The Second Opium War was one of the first wars to be photographed as it happened. The man who had this honour was an Italian photographer named Felice Beato – referred to by the British soldiers whom he accompanied as 'Signore Beato'.

When the Second Opium War broke out, Felice Beato had been in Crimea in eastern Europe, capturing images of the aftermath of the Crimean War. This was the war that inspired Lord Tennyson's 'Charge of the Light Brigade', one of the staples of Indian middle school English textbooks. Having made a name for himself, Beato then travelled to India, arriving in Calcutta in 1858. Along with his brother, he set up a practice in India. In India, apart from commercial work, his primary body of work consists of photos of dead mutineers after the revolt of 1857. For one photo, taken in Lucknow, Beato apparently disinterred – or rather, he ordered some poor Indian labourer to dig up – the bones of dead Indian soldiers so that he could arrange the scene as he desired. Looking at the photo, this gruesome detail colours the entire image. The bones look bleached white, very carefully scattered around a courtyard of a derelict palace. In the background, Beato included some living Indians. They sit casually – as if being surrounded by broken ribcages and skulls is the most ordinary thing in the world.

In 1860, he was sent by the British to China and he managed to capture the last stages of the Second Opium War. As the British wrecked fort after fort, Beato took stunning photographs

– including elaborate panoramas – that glorified their onslaught. He often captured before and after photographs so that his audience could better visualize the conflict. One of his most disturbing photos was taken in August 1860 after the capture of Taku, a fort less than 200 kilometres from the Forbidden City. It's another gut-wrenching still. There are half a dozen dead Chinese soldiers, their bodies strewn on the floor of the inner battlements of the fort. One man's head lolls off the edge without support, another has his shirt torn open, revealing his chest. Around the men, the fort looks ruined with gaping holes in the wooden walls.

The Second Opium War ended when the British invaded Peking. The emperor fled, leaving his brother in charge. The emperor's brother was forced by the British and their French allies to sign an even more permissive treaty. The Americans and the Russians claimed a seat at the table too. They all wanted a piece of the pie. Which is why many Chinese historians consider the event an unacknowledged world war. At the signing ceremony, Beato shoved the camera into the chest of the emperor's brother who turned deathly pale, mistaking the camera for a gun. While he was relieved when he discovered he was just having his picture taken, the cheerful Beato probably never noticed his obvious discomfort. He was too busy trying to capture the perfect image. After the treaty was signed, the British looted and ransacked the palace before they retreated. Beato took a share of the spoils as well.

The pillaging of Yuanmingyuan, the emperor's palace, is one of many acts of outright theft that marks European relationships with China. A French interpreter who was there in 1860 said that to describe it, he would need to 'dissolve all known precious stones in liquid gold and paint a picture with a diamond feather whose bristles contain all the fantasies of a poet of the East'.[16]

The European soldiers tore through it, grabbing ceramics, artwork, jewellery, silks – anything they could take back with them. It was chaotic and manic; some senior officers tried to shout them to their senses but the soldiers couldn't be stopped. One British officer wrote that when they first entered the gardens of the palace, it was like 'magic grounds described in fairy tales' but when they left, there was only 'a dreary waste of ruined nothings'. One of the priests who travelled with the soldier wrote, 'Not a vestige remains of the palace of palaces.'[17]

For the opium traders, the next few years were booming. Jardine and Matheson saw their biggest profits in the 1860s. In 1865, they shipped opium worth £300,000 – around Rs 250 crores today.[18] But with the legalization of opium, the systems and networks that funnelled the opium trade into the hands of a few men began falling part. Non-Europeans like David Sassoon and family were able to take over more and more of the trade. The emergence of shipping companies like the Peninsular and Oriental Steamship Company meant that anyone could buy a cargo of opium in India and ship it to China – including Chinese merchants themselves. At the same time, the Chinese began to produce increasing amounts of opium domestically. They weren't reliant only on the import of the drug now that it could be legally cultivated. As the nineteenth century drew to a close, Jardine and Matheson moved out of opium completely, focusing on trading in tea and silk. But they continued to profit off the trade through financial services like insurance and banking and by investing in real estate all across the docks of Hong Kong and Shanghai.

From the very beginning of the opium trade, there were voices condemning it as a grievous crime. But the deafening rain of coins from the sky easily pushed them aside.

Notes

1. This quote is from Yang Guozhen's *Lin Zexu Zhuan* (Biography of Lin Zexu), Renmin Chubanshe, 1981, as found in: Lovell, Julia. *The Opium War: Drugs, Dreams, and the Making of Modern China*. eBook, Abrams, 2011. This chapter owes a huge debt to Lovell's book. For readers interested in a book-length treatment of the opium wars that deals with both Chinese and English sources, Lovell's book is highly recommended.

2. Lovell, Julia. *The Opium War: Drugs, Dreams, and the Making of Modern China*. eBook, Abrams, 2011.

3. This quote is from Chang, Hsin-Pao. *Commissioner Lin and the Opium War*. Harvard University Press, 1964; it has been taken from Lovell, Julia. *The Opium War: Drugs, Dreams, and the Making of Modern China*. eBook, Abrams, 2011.

4. Ziegler, Paul R. Palmerston. *British History in Perspective*. Palgrave Macmillan, 2003, p. 1.

5. This quote is from Waley, Arthur. *The Opium War through Chinese Eyes*. Stanford University Press, 1958; it has been taken from Lovell, Julia. *The Opium War: Drugs, Dreams, and the Making of Modern China*. eBook, Abrams, 2011.

6. This quote appears in W.H. Hall and W.D. Bernard. *Narrative of the Voyages and Services of the Nemesis*. 2nd ed. Henry Colburn, 1845; it has been taken from Lovell, Julia. *The Opium War: Drugs, Dreams, and the Making of Modern China*. eBook, Abrams, 2011.

7. Lovell, Julia. *The Opium War: Drugs, Dreams, and the Making of Modern China*. eBook, Abrams, 2011.

8. Kwan, Uganda Sze Pui. '"A Requisite of Such Vital Importance": The Want of Interpreters in the First Anglo-Chinese War (1839–1842).' *Towards a History of Translating*, edited by Wang-chi Wong, Research Centre for Translation, Chinese University of Hong Kong, 2013.

9. Young, E. 'Chinese Coolies, Universal Rights and the Limits of Liberalism in an Age of Empire.' *Past & Present* 227, no. 1 (1 May 2015): 121–49. https://doi.org/10.1093/pastj/gtv018.

10. Hevia, James Louis. 'Opium, Empire, and Modern History.' *China Review International* 10, no. 2 (2003): 307–26. https://doi.org/10.1353/cri.2004.0076.

11. Trocki, Carl. *Opium, Empire and the Global Political Economy: A Study of the Asian Opium Trade, 1750–1950.* Routledge, 2012, p. 107.

12. For a critical view of the Second Opium War from a Chinese historian, see Wong, John Yue-wo. *Deadly Dreams: Opium and the Arrow War (1856–1860) in China.* Cambridge University Press, 2002.

13. Wong, John Yue-wo. *Deadly Dreams: Opium and the Arrow War (1856–1860) in China.* Cambridge University Press, 2002, p. 7.

14. Ringmar, E. *Liberal Barbarism: The European Destruction of the Palace of the Emperor of China.* Cultural Sociology. Palgrave Macmillan US, 2013, p. 6.

15. Sontag, Susan. *Regarding the Pain of Others.* Picador, 2004.

16. Ringmar, E. *Liberal Barbarism: The European Destruction of the Palace of the Emperor of China.* Cultural Sociology. Palgrave Macmillan US, 2013, p. 3.

17. Ringmar, E. *Liberal Barbarism: The European Destruction of the Palace of the Emperor of China.* Cultural Sociology. Palgrave Macmillan US, 2013, p. 4.

18. The original amount comes from Bauer, Rolf. *The Peasant Production of Opium in Nineteenth-Century India.* Brill, 2019, p. 49. Converted using Nye, Eric W. 'Pounds Sterling to Dollars: Historical Conversion of Currency.' https://www.uwyo.edu/numimage/currency.htm. Accessed 26 October 2020.

6

Anti-Opium Crusades

Opium and Christianity

Christian missionaries were some of the first Europeans to see inland China. The first group of them to come by sea travelled on Portuguese ships in the sixteenth century. They were usually Portuguese or Italian – strange, serious men whose religious fervour had driven them halfway across the world. They were mildly successful and were mostly tolerated by the authorities. But in the early eighteenth century, the Qing emperor declared Christianity illegal and deported as many missionaries as he could. A few dozen managed to avoid capture and spent their lives shuffling between communities of converts.

In the beginning of the nineteenth century, a new wave of Protestant missionaries from Britain and America washed into China. Often, they sailed on the same Company ships that smuggled opium into China. Both were illegal, after all. Some even worked for the smugglers. Men like the missionary Karl Gutzlaff who worked as a translator for Jardine and Matheson were fundamentally compromised when it came to the opium trade. However much they found the drug distasteful, they ignored it. Or worse, they saw it as a part of a divine plan to bring their religion to the country.

But other missionaries did their best to avoid the taint of opium completely. Walter Medhurst was one of the first British missionaries in China. He was trained as a printer and was sent by the London Missionary Society to oversee the printing of the first Chinese Bible and other religious tracts. David Livingstone, who so famously got lost in Africa, was a missionary with the same organization. Even to get to China, Medhurst had to seek the aid of an American philanthropist because he didn't want to travel on an opium ship. On his arrival there, he saw first-hand the damage of the opium trade.

> They may be seen, hanging their heads by the doors of the opium shops, which the hard hearted keepers, having fleeced them of their all, will not permit them to enter; and shut out from their own dwellings, either by angry relatives or ruthless creditors, they die in the streets unpitied and despised. It would be well, if the rich opium merchant, were sometimes present to witness such scenes as these, that he might be aware how his wretched customers terminate their course, and see where his speculations, in thousands of instances, end.[1]

More importantly, unlike missionaries like Gutzlaff who blamed the Qing government, Medhurst understood that the guilt lay primarily with the British.

In his passionate polemics that made their way back home, he tried to exhort the British public to pressure the government to stop the trade. But his motivations were pragmatic. This wasn't about the welfare of the Chinese. Opium, as far as he was concerned, was 'the greatest barrier to the introduction of Christianity which can be conceived of'. He deplored the fact that when he approached potential converts, they responded with:

> Why do Christians bring us opium, and bring it, directly, in defiance of our own laws? That vile drug has poisoned my son – has ruined my brother – and, well nigh led me to beggar my wife and children. Surely, those who import such a deleterious substance, and injure me, for the sake of gain, cannot wish me well, or be in possession of a religion that is better than my own. Go, first, and persuade your own countrymen to relinquish this nefarious traffic; and give me a prescription to correct this vile habit, and then I will listen to your exhortations on the subject of Christianity.[2]

A fair question. After all, as another writer put it, 'the Chinese could not be expected to distinguish between the white missionary and the white opium peddler'.[3] It was clear that religion could not become the opium of the masses as long as actual opium existed.

This realization · wasn't unique to Medhurst. Another missionary ruefully described how when preaching to the Chinese against the evils of opium, it was common for someone to shout: 'Who sells opium?' To which, the red-faced missionary would usually retort: 'Who smokes the opium?' While the response usually silenced the rebellious heckler, it didn't eliminate the shame of the missionary.[4] By the end of the nineteenth century, an even more embarrassing term was born: 'Jesus opium'. The Chinese used the term to refer to the potpourri of pills and substances that missionaries fed to people with addictions as cures.

While these missionaries were writing anti-opium tracts in China, getting these ideas to Britain was easier said than done. Medhurst went to China when he was just twenty-one and his book came out twenty years later, in 1838, just before the start of the First Opium War. While that book and other anti-opium writings were read widely back home, they had little effect on the broader foreign policy of Britain. As discussed in the previous chapter, while there was much public criticism of the First Opium War, the majority of it was aimed at destabilizing the ruling government. Any and all issues were used. Genuine political will to do anything about the opium trade was almost nonexistent at the time.

How the British Treated Opium at Home

The first time the opium question was seriously investigated by the British Parliament was in 1831. The House of Commons appointed a committee to investigate the trade but most of the testimony collected brushed aside any question of wrongdoing. Henry Pottinger, who would take over charge of the First Opium War from Charles Elliot, would say in 1831 that he was 'unable to discover a single case' of misery caused by opium in China.[5] With that, the committee was happy to shelve the question.

Right after the war, in 1843, Lord Ashley (later titled Lord Shaftesbury) dragged the question of the opium trade to the House of Commons again. A middle-aged man with a heightened sense of his own gravitas and impressive mutton chops, Lord Ashley had a reputation as a reformer in his time. His petition on the floor of the House had glaring errors but the zeal caught the government off-guard. However, on the request of the Prime Minister, who worried it would derail the tariff negotiations with China, Lord Ashley withdrew the petition. He might have been a reformer, but first and foremost, he was a gentleman. He dare not be impolite.

From the 1830s, Britain's imports of opium began to rise. More and more, the working class of Britain was turning to opium for medicinal and general pain relief. It was taken for cholera, whooping cough and malaria. It was even mixed with sweet syrup and sold to children as lozenges. It became a part of daily life. For the legion of lower-class agricultural labourers, opium became something they used to survive. As one contemporary doctor put it, the consumers were 'persons who would never think of narcotising themselves; anymore than they would be getting drunk; but who simply desire a relief the pains of fatigue endured by an ill-fed, ill-housed body, and harassed mind'.[6] But it was another, darker purpose that first attracted the attention of the government to the issue. There were rumours of working-class women leaving their babies at a communal proto-crèche where they were doped to make them docile. These reports of wide-scale use of opium on helpless babies – potentially killing them – sparked hysteria in parts of British society. While statistics did point at higher infant mortality rates in these areas, the practice of using opium 'soothers' was common in upper-class households as well. Much like the middle-class Indian parent reaching for a tablespoonful of Benadryl to calm a crying child today.

But because the finger in this case could be pointed at the working-class populations of 'dreary, foggy, cloggy, boggy wastes' like the Fens around Norfolk and Cambridge, it caught the twisted imagination of the benevolent among British society.[7]

That isn't to suggest that euthanasia (or murder, if you prefer) of children through opium never took place. It undoubtedly happened in India and Britain but access to opium probably had little impact on the practice. It's important to note that this was at a time when laws mandated that ten-year-olds could do only ten hours of factory work a day. Only ten hours. They were employed as chimneysweeps and coal miners. They died of black lung and burns by the scores. It was less than 200 years ago but Britain of the nineteenth century was as barbaric a country for working-class people as anywhere on earth.

It was in the middle of this public backlash that Lord Shaftesbury brought up the matter again in 1857, in the middle of the Second Opium War. This time, he tried the legal angle. In the House of Lords, he argued that the monopoly was illegal and went against the Treaty of Nanjing. Eventually, legal opinion was sought. The resulting decree was that the opium trade didn't contravene any of the terms of the Treaty of Nanjing but it did go against its 'spirit and intention'. But Shaftesbury didn't have time to celebrate: the Second Opium War rendered the Treaty of Nanjing obsolete.[8] Later that year, a member of Parliament (MP) died suddenly from an overdose of laudanum. Amidst this scandal and fearmongering over infanticide, public perception against the opium trade was shifting drastically.

In the 1850s and 1860s, a series of badly needed laws tried to regulate the burgeoning British pharmaceutical industry. It wasn't just opium-based concoctions and pills that needed to be curbed. Dozens of what we now consider poisons could be bought over the counter. Each preparation was an irregular mix of ingredients based on the skill of the pharmacist or apothecary who prepared it. As these potential bills were debated, the twin motives of public safety and private profits battled it out – as they do today. In an 1857 bill, opium was demarcated as one of the drugs to be kept under lock and key. Every sale would have to be recorded and witnessed by a third party who knew both the buyer and the seller. That bill was never passed but even the proposal shows how dangerous some parts of the medical establishment considered opium at the time. By the time a comprehensive Pharmacy Act was passed in 1868, all mention of opium had been dropped. It was too profitable and popular to be tied down with such onerous rules. But there were dissenting voices: A government committee observed that the fact that regulating 'the sale of opium would interfere with the trade profits of druggists ... constituted the strongest ground for inserting opium in the list of poisons'.[9] Eventually, an amendment added opium to the law. But it only required that druggists label their opium products properly.

But while the law wrestled with commerce, science too was slowly advancing. Data around opium addiction was being collected and analysed for the first time. Scientists began to put forward the first theories of addiction as a disease rather than a moral failing. Slowly, research revealed hitherto unknown details about the human body's physiological reaction to opium-based substances. This was completely opposed to the kind of 'racial science' of the past century that had declared 'inferior races' as being more susceptible to addiction because of weakness of character or spirit. This was a huge boost for anti-opium agitators who tried to leverage this new data to bring up the issue in Parliament again.

The Society for the Suppression of the Opium Trade

In 1874, some of these agitators together formed what would be called the Society for the Suppression of the Opium Trade (SSOT) with Lord Shaftesbury appointed as the first president.

While Lord Shaftesbury was in a way the public face of the opium debate, the primary moral force behind the organization were the Quakers. The Quakers are a Christian denomination that started as a revolt against the bureaucratic Church of England in the seventeenth century. While they have always been a heterogeneous group with differing beliefs, over their long history, Quaker communities have been at the forefront of several moral and political struggles, including the abolition of slavery. Both the financial support and political leadership of the SSOT came from wealthy Quakers, including railway baron Edward Pease. Edward's son would become the first Quaker inducted as an MP. Quakers obeyed a religious restriction against making oaths of any kind. A special committee had to specifically waive the oath of office for him to join Parliament. This set a precedent and slowly a cohort of other Quakers – including Edward's grandson, Joseph Whitwell Pease – joined Parliament over the rest of the nineteenth century. In 1880, after the death of his grandfather, Joseph Pease became the major force behind the SSOT. He inherited both his family's reformist opinions and their great wealth. As one later satirical caricature captured it, 'He has established science classes among his workmen. He is President of the Peace Society ... He is very rich.'[10]

Becoming the president of the SSOT after the death of Lord Shaftesbury, Pease would spearhead the introduction of opium debates into Parliament five times in sixteen years between 1875 and 1891. Each time, the organization failed to win any concrete action. The British empire was too invested in opium. As Li Hongzhang, a high-ranking Chinese minister, would say in a letter to the secretary of the SSOT in 1881, 'opium is a subject in the discussion of which England and China can never meet on common ground. China views the whole question from a moral standpoint; England from a fiscal.'[11] And this seems to be broadly true – even among the anti-opiumists. Many of them felt that legitimate British goods like cotton fabrics would more than make up for the lost opium revenue. Many of these anti-opiumists had vested interests in those other 'legitimate British goods'. Of course, for many of them, the primary motivation was religious. They were horrified by the idea that the cause of Christianity was hurt by the opium trade. The drug was spoiling their mission to 'save the souls of the heathens'. The SSOT wasn't a radical organization and had no squabble with British colonialism. Rather, they just imagined a different, potentially more 'holy', colonialism. As the SSOT's journal stated, 'for all of the weak points of British rule, it is still obvious that India would be only 1/10th as rich without the British presence'.[12]

But, in 1892, there was a moment of hope for the organization. The Liberal Party, to which Joseph Whitwell Pease belonged, came to power. William Gladstone, the leader of the party and new Prime Minister, had attacked the opium trade viciously when he was in the opposition. When the First Opium War broke out, he had said, 'Our flag must not become a pirate flag protecting a godless and deeply sinful enterprise.'[13] And even during this campaign, he had declared he would do anything 'within the bounds of reason' to end the opium trade.[14] But now that he was in power, Gladstone predictably saw the question in a new light. This would not be the first or the last time that he could be charged with hypocrisy. Gladstone was a titanic figure in British politics. To his supporters, he was 'the greatest statesman that ever lived'.[15] But to his enemies, he was an 'unprincipled maniac'.[16]

A Most Royal Commission on Opium

When the question of a Royal Commission to investigate the opium trade was brought up, Gladstone employed a subtle sleight of hand. The original motion was for the Commission to study and report what had to be done to slowly phase out the empire's dependence on opium revenues. Gladstone's substitute motion replaced the 'what' with a 'whether'. His proposal was for the Royal Commission to explore if anything had to be done at all. There was an understandable uproar among the anti-opium faction. But Gladstone's substitute motion won by a large margin. They had won their Royal Commission but in a much broader, more ambiguous avatar. As Gladstone defined it, the Commission had to answer multiple questions, the chief of which was whether opium cultivation had to be stopped and whether it had a negative moral or physical effect on the people of India. It had become a fact-finding committee – which was strange because everyone knew the facts by now. But this wasn't simply a delaying tactic. Gladstone and his advisors had shifted the focus of the Commission from the general trade of opium to the production of opium in India. China had been completely eliminated from the equation. By limiting the Commission's purview to British India, Gladstone had ensured that the one group most opposed to the opium trade would never be consulted: the Chinese. This wasn't an accident. In many ways, the anti-opium crusaders lost their battle here. As if enacting a manoeuvre from *The Art of War*, the pro-opium forces had won a fight by not fighting (about China) at all.

That's not to say the Commission was now destined to be an eyewash. A thorough committee under a strong, far-sighted chairman could still embarrass the government – if not force their hand. So the next step was to ensure that such a group wasn't assembled. There would've been much wheeling and dealing in the backrooms and corridors of Parliament to decide the rest of the Commission's composition. Both the pro-opium and anti-opium factions looked to stack the deck but only one of those two sides held power. The anti-opium faction lobbied and succeeded in appointing two of their own: Henry Wilson, a Liberal Party MP and avowed radical, and Arthur Pease, a former MP and Joseph Whitwell Pease's brother. The pro-opium faction put forward Arthur Fanshawe, director general of the Indian Post Office, and James Lyall, who had recently returned to Britain after a long and distinguished career in India. The only two potentially undecided members were Robert Mowbray, another MP with all the right gentlemanly credentials, and William Roberts, a celebrated doctor and one of the most authoritative voices on contemporary medicine. As for the chairman, that honour went to Lord Brassey. Thomas Brassey was a large, thickset man. He was born the son of a railway magnate and had become a lawyer and then a Liberal Party MP. After losing an election and having nothing to do, he was made a baron. He spent most of his time indulging in an obsessive fascination for ships and navies through a publication he founded called the *Naval Annual*. Brassey was a proud man but he wasn't known for having strong convictions. He was an uncontroversial establishment figure but he was, at least superficially, unbiased. As far as the SSOT were concerned, this group was 'as fair-minded and impartial a tribunal as could have desired to hear our case'.[17] This is partially a damnation of the process for they knew that Brassey's businesses were involved with opium dens in Borneo.[18]

Last, and probably least, were the two Indian members for the Commission. They were nominated by the viceroy of India – another biased source. When the viceroy asked for recommendations from his subordinates, the response was muted. None of the typical high-profile Bengali intellectuals of the time were willing to participate, according to the viceroy's source. They were pro-opium but couldn't say so because they didn't want to alienate the anti-opium MPs who, after all, were potential allies on other issues. Eventually, the viceroy nominated Lakshmishwar Singh, the maharaja of Darbhanga, and Haridas Veharidas, a former minister of the princely state of Junagarh in Gujarat. Neither of them were directly involved in the opium trade. Singh's vast lands were free of the opium crop. Junagarh, though near Malwa, wasn't an opium-producing state. Singh was a supporter and patron of the nascent Indian National Congress (INC) but what tipped the scales in his favour were his many firm friendships with officers in the highest level of government.

While everyone played a role in the story of the Commission, there were two standout figures who were the champions of their respective, opposed factions: James Lyall and Henry Wilson. Wilson was the radical reformer who knew the odds were stacked against him. He was born into a political family. His father had been an anti-slavery campaigner. Wilson and his wife Charlotte entered politics when the British government passed what were called the Contagious Diseases Acts in the 1860s. These laws gave the police permission to arrest anyone suspected of being a sex worker and forcibly test them for venereal diseases. The Acts legalized an entire system dedicated to violating the basic human rights of women. Wilson and others like noted feminist Josephine Butler founded the International Abolitionist Federation to abolish such laws in England and elsewhere in the world.

James Lyall was the quintessential government man tasked with getting the result they wanted. He had spent more than thirty years in government service in India. He started in the Bengal Civil Service after the Mutiny of 1857, just shy of twenty years of age. He retired as governor general of Punjab, one of the most prestigious posts available. Based on the daily private diary he kept over the course of the Commission's investigations, it's clear that he devoted himself completely to moulding the Commission towards the government's purpose. Even before the

Commission arrived in India, Lyall was deep in correspondence with the viceroy of India, discussing strategies. The plan, in his own words, was to collect 'native opinion in particular, which will carry sufficient weight to enable the question to be shelved'.[19] The viceroy spread feelers through official and unofficial networks for pro-opium voices, especially Indians. They were not hard to find. People rushed to ingratiate themselves with the leader of the Indian government by parroting the party line. Wilson and the SSOT had a tougher time of it.

J.G. Alexander, the SSOT's secretary, travelled ahead of the Commission to scout out and solicit witnesses to speak on the ills of the opium trade. Alexander was a Quaker and came from a line of conscientious objectors. His great-grandfather gave up a job as a foreman in a naval dockyard because of his pacifist beliefs. His grandfather quit a job at a bank because he didn't want to participate in raising loans for war. His father was a committed abolitionist and organized anti-slavery meetings where freed slaves would speak. He also ran a depot for sugar and cotton that weren't produced by slave labour. Alexander himself would devote his life to fighting for a variety of causes, with the opium trade being the primary one. Unlike the British government in India, Alexander had no real existing network to leverage. But as a religious man, he could rely on missionaries and other 'temperance' groups to wrangle sympathetic candidates. He felt that missionaries understood the plight of the farmers and workers much more than the 'native gentlemen, who know little of the lot of the masses'. Most of the upper-class people he was introduced to in Bombay were Parsis. He quickly caught on to their bias in the matter. In a letter home, he would write that they 'take their cue from the officials in this bureaucratic country, where almost every position to which a man of ability and ambition can aspire is at the disposal of the Government, and those who run counter to its views thereby cut themselves off from most of the best positions'. But at the same time, he didn't dismiss their opinions. 'If India does not want protection from the opium habit, such as we possess at home,' he wrote, 'we don't wish to force it on her – to protect China is our great aim, and we are quite determined that in carrying out that aim India shall not be made to suffer.'[20]

Eventually, his witness gathering had limited success. At final accounting, they presented 20 per cent of the Commission's total witnesses. The rest were either neutral or staunchly status quo. This wasn't for lack of trying. They repeatedly faced government repression – which they gleefully documented, hoping to use it to gain popular support in Britain. When four potential witnesses were arrested, Alexander wrote, 'I am sorry for the poor men, but it will be a splendid thing for our cause, and will clearly show how little value is to be attached to the mass of pro-opium evidence received from the Native States generally.'[21]

The Beginning of a Saga

The Royal Commission was a titanic process. After a week of interviews in London, they travelled to India where they spent more than three months. They began in Calcutta – the beating heart of the entire debate. From there, members visited British-controlled Burma, Patna, Benares, Lucknow, Lahore, Delhi, Agra, Jaipur, Ajmer, Ahmedabad, Indore and, finally, Bombay. They saw more than 700 witnesses. It was a parade of wary government servants, crisply dressed army officers, spirited missionaries, bespectacled physicians, nervous zamindars, exuberant merchants and eager lawyers. There were hakims and vaidyas, journalists and editors, and even the odd schoolmaster. The Commission deigned to speak to actual farmers on one or two occasions. And they even swapped pleasantries with a group of Chinese men in Calcutta for approximately ten minutes. It was an exercise in opposites – simultaneously thorough and expansive as well as ludicrously short-sighted and superficial.

Even before the Indian members joined them, the Royal Commission began their investigations in London in September 1893. The first man to the stand was Joseph Whitwell Pease who, for hours, laid out the basic facts of the opium question, drawing upon the vast body of research that had already been accumulated by the British government on the subject over the years. These facts were well known. So well known that Pease and the SSOT had initially assumed they could be taken for granted before Gladstone's incisive amendment changed matters completely. Now, even the most basic information had to be restated for the record. After Pease, a flurry of missionaries – most of whom had worked in China – stepped forward to denounce the opium trade. One member from the London Missionary Society said that when he was in China, 'no respectable man could tell me of any good that opium had done, but every man had his own narrative of evils, deaths, suicides, misery, ruin, that it had produced'. The word of a priest had some weight in a society as religious as nineteenth-century Britain. But as with anyone who criticized opium, a skilled interviewer could reveal them to be well-intentioned but misguided. James Lyall might have been a cruel interlocutor but he was also a skilled one.

As he would do repeatedly over the course of the entire Commission, Lyall stepped in to seed one of the pro-opium faction's prepared counters. While priests might be respected, there was a reason they were never invited to parties. The temperance movements that argued against all the upper crust's favourite vices were led by priests, after all. So, Lyall brought up the question of alcohol. 'Would not the same ground of immorality,' he asked, 'then make it obligatory upon the English Government to stop the export of spirits?'[22] The person to whom he directed this question was Donald Matheson, who used to work at Jardine and Matheson but had quit over the immorality of the opium trade and become a missionary. Matheson spluttered quietly. 'There is no comparison,' he responded. But Lyall pressed on. 'We know that spirits have swept populations absolutely out of existence in various parts of the world,' he said, pointing out examples in Africa, Australia and New Zealand. With the disinterested air of the amoral debate student, Lyall essentially argued that past alcohol-driven genocides were evidence that the British couldn't intervene in an opium-driven one. Arthur Pease, clearly side-eyeing Lyall, stepped in to save the floundering Matheson. 'You are aware, I think Mr Matheson,' he said gently, 'that the English Government have recognised their responsibility by prohibiting the importation of spirits in Africa, as parties to the Brussels Anti-Slavery Convention?' It isn't clear if Matheson, a racist who thought Africans were a 'very low type', comprehended the help he was being offered but the interview mercifully ended soon after.

While the initial thrust of the evidence was going against him, Lyall had no reason to be flustered. His star witnesses had yet to arrive. One of the first was Sir John Strachey, another dyed-in-the-wool government man, who introduced another contentious thread that would run through the entire Commission. 'Among the Rajputs and Sikhs in particular the use of opium has always been common,' he said. 'They regard it almost as a necessary of life, and it is a notorious fact that these Sikhs and I may say the same of the Rajputs – are physically, I believe I might also say morally, but at any rate physically they are the very finest races in all India.' Strachey was making two points. One, if opium use was standard practice among Britain's finest Indian soldiers, then prohibition threatened the smooth running of the machine of empire. And two, if opium was so 'universally destructive', how were the qualities of the Rajputs and Sikhs to be explained?

Then, another star witness, H.N. Lay, who had worked for the British in China for more than a decade, gave testimony on the 'true nature' of the opium wars. While the anti-opium faction had declared that these wars were driven by fiscal concerns, Lay's version of events depicted an honourable and friendly Britain faced with a country full of 'hatred of the barbarian' who wanted to expel the British entirely from their lands. The Chinese mentality, to H.N. Lay, forced Britain's hands into conflict. They had no choice. 'The moment you prostrate yourself before a Chinese, his answer is the knife.'

This was seconded by another star witness, Sir Thomas Wade, who had served as Britain's envoy in Peking. In Wade's words, all that Britain wanted was 'relations'. Wade had been a part of the negotiating team that had drafted the Treaty of Tienstin after the Second Opium War and so was one of the most authoritative sources on Sino-British politics that could be found. He listed factoid after factoid as evidence that the British government had no interest in opium. And neither did China. According to Wade, the British government had offered the Chinese government friendly advice on how to manage the trade but China had never shown the slightest inclination to do anything about it. But, just as Lyall had come prepared to dismantle the other side's witnesses, Henry Wilson showed that he too had done his homework. He shuffled some papers around and began to pepper Wade with quote after quote from Wade's predecessor, Sir Rutherford Alcock, which directly contradicted what he was saying. Wade, who said that he was 'exceedingly unwilling to … disagree with a gentleman under whom [he had] served for very many years', had to content himself with mumbling about how Alcock's generalizations were just a tad too sweeping.

A Flawed Process

From the London leg of the Commission, the danger of allowing the conversation to focus on China became more and more apparent to the pro-opium faction. Luckily for them, as the Commission's members boarded a ship to India, they were moving to more friendly terrain. After they arrived in Calcutta, the Government of India circulated a notice explicitly disclaiming all responsibility to produce any anti-opium evidence whatsoever. They would later completely reverse their position and deny any charge of being 'a defendant'. They would go from being openly partisan to adopting the guise of neutrality. Their goal, they declared, was 'enabling the Commission to fully ascertain the actual facts'.[23] But by then, the situation was clear enough to anyone who was paying attention.

The large public halls where the Commission sat to hear evidence quickly filled to the brim with well-spoken pro-government witnesses. The first Indian to sit before the Commission was Sita Nath Roy, a banker and a zamindar, who thought it 'absurd to talk of abolishing the manufacture and sale of such an innocuous article of commerce as opium'.[24] Roy was all praise for the current system and cast suspicion on any Indians who would criticize it. 'Some of the very gentlemen who are now loudest in their declamations against opium', he said, would be the first to rush into the business if the government's monopoly ended. But upon Wilson's probing, other less noble reasons came tumbling out. Roy was the secretary of the Bengal Native Chamber of Commerce, an association of merchants and landowners. Some of the merchants were opium traders.

And all of the landowners feared the government would raise taxes if the opium revenue was to disappear. It was a similar case for the British Indian Association, the precursor to industry lobby groups like NASSCOM or FICCI, who described opium as having a 'a divine origin'. Its stoppage would bring 'misery, distress and discontent' especially – and this would become a painfully common refrain – because of 'the increased taxation which would be necessary to enable the government of the country to be carried on after surrendering of the opium revenue'. Their memorial to the Commission failed to note that they had petitioned the House of Commons in 1853 to end the opium monopoly because it interfered with the freedom of cultivators.[25]

Another Indian championing the status quo was Kailas Chander Bose, a senior doctor and the president of the Calcutta Medical Society. Bose declared that in his long years of experience he had 'not yet been able to trace out any injurious or deleterious effect of opium upon the habitual eaters'.[26] In words that took on an Orwellian tinge, he assured the Commission that 'altogether opium-eaters, as a rule, are a peaceful class of citizens'. While he might have simply meant that they were not particularly prone to crime, it's hard not to read these words as advice for social control, that is, 'opium-eaters don't rebel against the state'. Wilson, getting the last word in the interview with Bose, asked him if his views were those of the medical textbooks. Bose replied, 'I must say – and I am sorry to have to say – that my views are not supported by medical authorities at home.' This was Wilson's modus operandi for pro-government witnesses. He probed them for flaws, biases and conflicting interests, often in ways that were overtly rude – alienating him from his colleagues. When interviewing K.G. Gupta, an excise commissioner in Bengal who for obvious reasons had nothing bad to say of opium, Wilson asked him, 'If you had two or three sons growing up to maturity, would you regard with complacency their taking a daily dose of opium?' He wasn't a man to flinch from making a point.

On the other hand, Lyall and Fanshawe would undermine the testimony of witnesses by questioning their social standing. When interviewing a schoolmaster who gave anti-opium testimony, Fanshawe asked how much money the man made in a month. A naked attempt to demean him. The schoolmaster responded, 'I have no objection to answer the question; but may I ask whether you put that question to all the European witnesses who have been examined?' To which, Fanshawe only sniffed and insisted on an answer.

The Commission was dogged by repeated accusations of government interference. After Wilson and Alexander had visited potential witnesses in Gaya, the police came knocking on those same doors. When Wilson raised the matter before the Commission, the exchange between him and Lyall grew poisonous. The exact words of that conversation will never be known because they happened behind closed doors. But when the magistrate was brought in to explain the actions of the police, he profusely apologized. He explained that the government was simply looking to learn what allegations were going to be made so they could prepare the appropriate rebuttal. The chairman, Lord Brassey, was entirely sympathetic with the government, which, he felt, had a right to be 'naturally anxious'.[27] While Wilson didn't accept the apology, the matter was dropped. The SSOT's aggressive snooping did pay off when Wilson's son found evidence of a zilladar uprooting a farmer's potato crop to force him to plant opium in its place. This was an immediate embarrassment to the government who had insisted that no coercion was involved in opium production.

They promptly launched an investigation but its results only reached the Commission after the members had returned to England. To their credit, the report suggested a genuine inquiry and documented multiple instances of wrongdoing. While Lord Brassey seemed to take the matter seriously, it was written off as a unique incident – not as evidence of systemic coercion behind the entire Bengal monopoly.

When the Commission reached Bombay, the allegation of intimidating witnesses would come up again in a peculiar fashion.[28] The original incident had taken place some years ago. In 1891, an organization known as the Bombay Medical Anti-Opium Alliance circulated a petition among doctors in Bombay to call for a total ban on opium. The organizers had collected signatures from forty-nine well-respected Bombay doctors and then sent the petition to England where it was printed and distributed. And that seemed to be that. But two years later, with the Royal Commission set to arrive in India, the Alliance published a letter in the *Times of India* that repeated their call for a ban and gave the names of all the signatories. This came to the attention of a government official who promptly sent an inspector to each doctor to verify if they had really signed the petition. The results shouldn't be surprising. Eighteen doctors 'did not remember signing'; six said they had never seen the petition before. Only three people – other than the Alliance members – did not recant their signature in one form or another. This included a doctor who had signed in the direct presence of Alliance members.

On 4 January 1894, after more than thirty-five days of hearing witnesses, the Commission spoke to their first set of actual farmers in Patna.[29] All their names aren't recorded. Many of them had probably come to add to the strength of numbers behind their deposition. The names we do know are Tilangi, Imri Singh and

Poonit Singh. Speaking through an interpreter, they gave the Commission a picture of their life. They lost money every time they planted poppy and pleaded for the chance to grow 'any other crop'. When Wilson asked why they grew an unprofitable crop, Tilangi responded, 'Because we are poor people, and it is the order of the Government that we should cultivate poppy.' Poonit Singh described how the zilladar had uprooted his wheat crop and forced him to grow opium on his entire land. The Commission heard this – mostly in silence – and then just moved on. Another group the Commission didn't have much time for were people with addictions who volunteered to testify. One such person, Mehr Singh, declared that opium was 'worse than snake-poison'. To Mehr Singh, those who were 'entangled in this vice ... become powerless, and so they drag their miserable life and are cause of disgrace to society'.

Almost three weeks later, the Commission's secretary would reveal that he had received a number of petitions from farmers and had not submitted them as evidence yet. These petitions were brief letters addressed to the Commission and signed by dozens of farmers. The first few that were read out were fervent prayers for the abolition of the opium trade or, at the very least, that the rates paid to farmers be increased. One petition ends, 'Exempt us from poppy cultivation from next year, for which act of kindness we shall ever pray for your Honor's long life and prosperity.' Of these, the one with the highest number of signatures was signed by 200 people. Along with these, the secretary also introduced several other petitions – with larger signature counts – that asked for the opium trade to be left unchanged. The story of who organized these petitions isn't clear. It's likely that when they observed anti-opium activists trying to organize signature campaigns among farmers, the local authorities directed their agents to organize their own counter-petitions. That would potentially also explain why the secretary held them in abeyance so that they could all be read at once, revealing a clear majority to the pro-opium side. The same thing would happen in Bombay. A petition by Chinese residents of Burma complained of the debilitating effects of opium. It was read alongside a petition from opium consumers in Bombay who wished to present 'an ocular demonstration against the futility of the out-cry the anti-opiumists have raised'.[30]

In one of the appendices to the Royal Commission's eventual report, there is another interesting gem submitted by the Bombay government. It is a report of the collected testimony of a long list of the city's opium smokers. The inspector who aggregated these accounts helpfully appended a description of each speaker. This varied from 'Bava Sahilj Ismail, a fleshy, well-set-up man' to 'Cassum Abdoola, short, but securingly strong'. Most of those questioned, like Salu Mahomed Ismail who was 'thin, and not very bright', said some version of 'if I leave it off I shall suffer, and not be able to do my work'. Whether they were 'languid looking' or 'a spending specimen of his race', the resounding message from more than 200 interviewees was that an opium ban was the opposite of what the working class of Bombay wanted.

An Anti-Climactic Result

By the end of the Bombay leg, the Commission had spent more than eighty days collecting evidence. They had amassed thousands of pages of witness testimony, typed out verbatim by diligent secretaries. For all the voices decrying opium, the volume of those that had shouted its praises was far, far louder. Even then, when the Commission gathered during their last few days in Bombay to discuss their final report to the British government,

Lord Brassey proposed that the Bengal monopoly be ended. He argued that it instead become more like the Malwa system, where the trade was in private hands. Lyall was having none of it, as it would mean a sharp reduction in the government's revenue. He quickly began to lobby everyone else. Wilson wasn't there, having fallen ill. But everybody including Arthur Pease eventually came around to Lyall's counter to Brassey's proposal. When the final vote was called, Lyall's honeyed words not only carried the vote but also ensured that the chairman felt no ill will against him. The final report declared that there was broad support among the population of India for the opium trade. There was no call for prohibition and the Government of India was handling everything perfectly well. In short, nothing had to be done. Every member of the Commission signed the report, except for Wilson.

In his lone dissenting note, he pointed out how the anti-opium faction had 'desired the appointment of a Commission for a very different and more useful purpose than that which was finally recommended by the resolution of the House'.[31] He recorded the vast class disparity between the Indians who spoke for and against the opium trade. He rammed home the case that compulsion was widespread in Bengal and that the recently arrived results of investigation by the government bore him out. He noted that no guilty official had been punished for their involvement. He rejected the notion that alcohol and opium were comparable. In England, alcohol was as common as water. In India, opium was a rare commodity. 'In the one case we have a nation of consumers, in the other a nation of abstainers,' he wrote. He even alleged that, 'Two different Ministries, and two different Parliaments, were entirely misled as to the action of the Government of India.' There had been multiple declarations in Parliament that the area under cultivation had been decreasing but Wilson showed that the opposite was true. He refused to let the matter of China disappear from the conversation, reiterating that there was overwhelming evidence of the evils that opium had wrought there. It was a noble addendum to an ignoble exercise. But in the end, it had no effect at all.

Back home, various British commentators praised the report when it was published. One former East India Company official would gravely write,

> But had it been otherwise; had the Commission recommended the cessation of the traffic; and had the Home Government, in consequence, decreed its cessation, there can be no doubt – amongst those who really know the Indian people – that there would have been a general uprising, an uprising so universal, so inspired by the heart of the people, that it would have been impossible for Great Britain – that Great Britain which permits the sale of intoxicating spirits in all its streets of her cities, her towns, and her villages – to repress it. Every domestic servant would have been a conspirator. The form the disaffection would have taken would not have been modelled on the outbreak of 1857. In its conception and in its action it would have been more deadly than the massacre of St. Bartholomew, wider-reaching than the Sicilian Vespers.[32]

The massacre of St Bartholomew was a wave of religious violence in France in the sixteenth century. It lasted weeks; political assassinations and riots led to the death of thousands. The Sicilian Vespers was a rebellion in the island of Sicily in the thirteenth century where the locals rose up and spilled the blood of thousands of their French conquerors in their bid for freedom. Clearly, to some, opium was one of the substances that kept the Indian populace quietly in their place.

Notes

1. Medhurst, Walter Henry. *China: Its State and Prospects.* Crocker & Brewster, 1838, p. 77.

2. Medhurst, Walter Henry. *China: Its State and Prospects.* Crocker & Brewster, 1838, p. 82.

3. Winther, Paul C. *Anglo-European Science and the Rhetoric of Empire: Malaria, Opium, and British Rule in India, 1756–1895.* Lexington Books, 2003, p. 3.

4. Lodwick, Kathleen L. *Crusaders against Opium: Protestant Missionaries in China, 1874–1917.* University Press of Kentucky, 1996, p. 33.

5. Winther, Paul C. *Anglo-European Science and the Rhetoric of Empire: Malaria, Opium, and British Rule in India, 1756–1895.* Lexington Books, 2003, p. 36.

6. Berridge, Virginia. *Opium and the People: Opiate Use and Drug Control Policy in Nineteenth and Early Twentieth Century England.* Free Association Books, 1999, p. 36.

7. Berridge, Virginia. *Opium and the People: Opiate Use and Drug Control Policy in Nineteenth and Early Twentieth Century England.* Free Association Books, 1999, p. 45.

8. Owen, David Edward. *British Opium Policy in China and India.* Archon Books, 1968, pp. 230–33.

9. Berridge, Virginia. *Opium and the People: Opiate Use and Drug Control Policy in Nineteenth and Early Twentieth Century England.* Free Association Books, 1999, p. 120.

10. Frederick, Margaretta S. 'A Quaker Collects.' *Journal of the History of Collections* 18, no. 1 (1 June 2006): 62. https://doi.org/10.1093/jhc/fhi039.

11. Lodwick, Kathleen L. *Crusaders against Opium: Protestant Missionaries in China, 1874–1917.* University Press of Kentucky, 1996, p. 28.

12. Brown, J.B. 'Politics of the Poppy: The Society for the Suppression of the Opium Trade, 1874–1916.' *Journal of*

Contemporary History 8, no. 3 (1 July 1973): 106. https://doi.org/10.1177/002200947300800305.

13. Dormandy, Thomas. *Opium: Reality's Dark Dream*. Yale University Press, 2012, p. 135.

14. Richards, John F. 'Opium and the British Indian Empire: The Royal Commission of 1895.' *Modern Asian Studies* 36, no. 02 (May 2002): 386. https://doi.org/10.1017/S0026749X02002044.

15. Erikson, Erik H. 'The Strange Case of Freud, Bullitt, and Woodrow Wilson.' *New York Review of Books*, February 1967. https://www.nybooks.com/articles/1967/02/09/the-strange-case-of-freud-bullitt-and-woodrow-wils/.

16. Partridge, Michael. *Gladstone*. Routledge, 2003, p. 2.

17. Richards, John F. 'Opium and the British Indian Empire: The Royal Commission of 1895.' *Modern Asian Studies* 36, no. 02 (May 2002): 389. https://doi.org/10.1017/S0026749X02002044.

18. Brown, J.B. 'Politics of the Poppy: The Society for the Suppression of the Opium Trade, 1874–1916.' *Journal of Contemporary History* 8, no. 3 (1 July 1973): 97–111. https://doi.org/10.1177/002200947300800305.

19. Richards, John F. 'Opium and the British Indian Empire: The Royal Commission of 1895.' *Modern Asian Studies* 36, no. 02 (May 2002): 388. https://doi.org/10.1017/S0026749X02002044.

20. Alexander, Horace Gundry. *Joseph Gundry Alexander*. Swarthmore Press, 1921, pp. 66–67.

21. Alexander, Horace Gundry. *Joseph Gundry Alexander*. Swarthmore Press, 1921, p. 78.

22. *Minutes of Evidence*, Volume 1. Royal Commission on Opium, 1894, p. 59, Question 812.

23. *Minutes of Evidence*, Volume 2. Royal Commission on Opium, 1894, p. 274.

24. *Minutes of Evidence*, Volume 2. Royal Commission on Opium, 1894, p. 44, Question 2709.

25. Wright, Ashley. 'Not Just a "Place for the Smoking of Opium": The Indian Opium Den and Imperial Anxieties in the 1890s.' *Journal of Colonialism and Colonial History* 18, no. 2 (2017). https://doi.org/10.1353/cch.2017.0021.

26. *Minutes of Evidence*, Volume 2. Royal Commission on Opium, 1894, p. 87, Question 3785.

27. *Minutes of Evidence*, Volume 3. Royal Commission on Opium, 1894, p. 26, Question 11426.

28. *Minutes of Evidence*, Volume 4. Royal Commission on Opium, 1894, pp. 256–259.

29. *Minutes of Evidence*, Volume 3. Royal Commission on Opium, 1894, pp. 22–23.

30. *Minutes of Evidence*, Volume 4. Royal Commission on Opium, 1894, p. 221, Question 24848.

31. *Final Report*. Royal Commission on Opium, 1895, p. 137.

32. Gibbon, Luke. 'Opium, the British Empire and the Beginnings of an International Drugs Control Regime, ca. 1890–1910.' PhD thesis, University of Strathclyde, 2014, p. 12.

7

Opium and Independence

The Grand Old Man of India

In 1893, the anti-opium faction of the British Parliament was planning their resolution against the opium trade – the one that would eventually lead to the Royal Commission. The natural choice to deliver the resolution on the floor of the House was Joseph Pease, the president of the Society for the Suppression of the Opium Trade. But maybe for that very reason, they cast around for another candidate – someone who could signal that this wasn't a narrow or partisan cause. Eventually, they decided upon Alfred Webb, an Irish MP from an activist Quaker family. Webb wasn't a very accomplished speaker and this meant that he usually let others do the talking. But now, when his time came, Webb stood up and delivered a solid if uninspiring account of the evils of the opium trade. Once he was done, Joseph Pease seconded the motion. And then as we know, Prime Minister

William Gladstone introduced his amendments and the anti-opium faction quickly lost control of their proposal. Lord Curzon, who would soon become the viceroy of India, spoke after Gladstone and effusively praised his amendments – despite being a member of an opposing party. Then, another non-party member jumped up to add his voice in support of Gladstone. George Chesney, a veteran of the British Army in India, dismissed the anti-opium resolution, declaring that 'the first consideration was the feelings and wishes of the people of India themselves'.[1]

After Chesney, one of the people of India he seemed to care so much about stood up and voiced his feelings. He was a relatively new MP but his seniority was visible. Almost seventy years old, he sported an impressive grey beard and serious-looking circular glasses. In many ways, he had the most important view on the subject in the entire assembly.

Dadabhai Naoroji had become the first Indian member of the British Parliament in the previous year when he was elected from Central London. To the 'Grand Old Man of India', as he was sometimes called, this was a well-worn issue: he'd been intimately familiar with it for forty years. He 'could not believe in the sincerity' of those who questioned the 'curse' of the opium trade. But as far he was concerned, opium was only a fringe problem in India's long list and Britain seemed to be obsessed with tackling each fragment individually. Therefore, he asked Gladstone 'to enlarge his Amendment' so that 'the Royal Commission should inquire into the whole condition of India'.[2] He was promptly ignored. Nobody was surprised.

Webb and Naoroji were well known to each other and the Indian statesman was probably aware that the resolution was going to be tabled that day. But he had already made his views clear to the SSOT a few years earlier at one of their conferences when he said,

> There is a great fear that if the opium revenue were to cease, the people of India would be utterly unable to fill up the gap in the revenue. They feel aghast at the very suggestion of it, and they go so far as to say that the opium revenue cannot be dispensed with … [Y]ou have not the complete sympathy of the natives of India in this matter.[3]

Regardless, after Webb's speech, the SSOT's secretary, J.G. Alexander, approached Naoroji to join a deputation to refocus the opium investigation on China rather than India. But Naoroji declined politely, saying,

> As the Indian National Congress has not spoken yet, the views I express are only my own. You know already that I am in full sympathy with the moral object of the Society, and I have made some sacrifice for it. You also know that according to my view the Society unfortunately does not realize the real source of the disease and of all our other woes.[4]

Dadabhai Naoroji was Parsi with family roots in the same town where Jamsetjee Jejeebhoy was born. Like Jejeebhoy, his father died when he was still a child. But he was lucky enough to receive a quality education, earning a scholarship to the institution that would become Elphinstone College. Then he joined the same college as an employee, and by 1850, he became the first Indian to break the colonial glass ceiling and become a professor. He would eventually try his hand at business, quitting teaching to become a partner in a Parsi firm. The firm, Cama & Co., wanted to be one of the few Indian firms to boast of a branch in Britain. According to his biographer, R.P. Masani, one of Naoroji's key motivations was the chance to lay the groundwork, not just for the success of the firm, but for 'the business enterprise of Indians generally'.[5] Cama & Co., as was typical of Bombay firms of that time, traded in both liquor and opium. But Naoroji refused his share of profits from any deals that involved either. His partner, feeling unfairly judged, wrote to him,

> Will you tell me from what sources Government get funds for the payment of salaries to professors of colleges and other officers? ... If you retire from business and revert to Government service, will you not once more live on the tainted revenue obtained from the same business that stinks in your nostrils? If our firm ceases dealing in opium, will it put a stop to the traffic in that commodity?[6]

To his credit, Naoroji stood his ground. But while his nascent political career would blossom, his business career collapsed. He had started his own firm, Dadabhai Naoroji & Co., but had to shut it down soon. He returned to Bombay which, as the nineteenth century progressed, was becoming a very different place. The city was politically effervescent. New organizations of every cause and stripe were cropping up in the oddest of places. Like so many well-intentioned causes, many would disappear soon enough but some would display surprising staying power, finding unlikely allies.

In 1887, William S. Caine, a Liberal MP, would visit Bombay as a part of a world tour. Caine was a temperance activist and member of numerous bodies in Britain that agitated against the 'scourge of drink'. Naoroji and several other Bombay luminaries paid him a visit and proposed an organization to collaborate on the cause of temperance in Britain and India. Thus was formed the Anglo-Indian Temperance Organization (AITA), which became a bastion of the long-lived temperance movement in India. And these temperance activists, though they were focused on drinking, had a very clear picture of what the British empire could do in India if allowed to freely peddle their vices: what they did in China. One Maratha journal declared that drinking was becoming a 'national vice in India' much like opium was in China.[7]

The Congress and the Temperance Movement

In 1886, Naoroji was part of another group of people who came together and founded another organization that might seem familiar, the Indian National Congress. But the Congress at its time of formation was a very different entity from what it is today or during the decades just before Indian independence. In one of its early reports, one of the founders wrote,

> the principle on which the Indian National Congress is based is that British Rule should be permanent and abiding in India and that, given this axiom, it is the duty of educated Indians to endeavour to the best of their power to help their rulers so to govern the country as to improve her material prosperity and make the people of all classes and communities happy and prosperous and contented as subjects of the British Empire.[8]

This wasn't a passionate party fighting for their vision of the future. It was mostly, as one historian puts it, 'a noble idea which took concrete form for several days at the end of each calendar year before dispersing until the next annual meeting'.[9] Nationalism, for the early Congress at that time, meant fighting for better governance of India. And that better governance would be achieved by the admission of young, bright, upper-class, upper-caste Indians into civil service of all types. This isn't to say that the early Congress was an entirely self-serving group. Many of their leaders cared deeply about the country, especially the systemic poverty that afflicted so many citizens. But their proposals – while potentially noble in intention – were always representative of their position in society.

Temperance and nationalism grew hand in hand in British India over the mid nineteenth century. In many ways, temperance agitation opened the door for nationalist agitation. Unlike nationalist agitation which was seditious, temperance agitation was noble – and more than that, it was *possible*. It was a complicated issue for the British in a way that independence would not have been. As one historian put it, 'Protesting liquor sales was a particularly effective critique of colonial rule because it was culturally-translatable, fitting within British understandings of justifiable resistance as "rightful dissent" and with the Indian idiom of "Dharmic protest".'[10] But to engage in these 'successful' temperance protests, the upper-class, upper-caste leaders of the burgeoning nationalist movement had to invent a precolonial India that didn't drink. They had to make alcohol synonymous with British culture so they could protest colonialism through the guise of alcoholism. But this image of a once great country of teetotallers that these activists portrayed never existed. One of the rare voices to question this narrative was B.R. Ambedkar. In his budget debates, he argued that while drinking might be an evil, it wasn't a problem in India and it definitely wasn't an urgent problem.[11]

Caine and the AITA started a journal called *Abkari*, named after the tax on alcohol, which maintained a circulation of around 3000 copies across India. In the pages of *Abkari*, there was essay after essay that denounced British rule by way of criticizing their alcohol policies. In one issue, they wrote that the 'greatest lawbreakers in India were the law makers'.[12] In this way, the temperance movement smuggled nationalism into the public sphere while the conflicted British debated what constituted an appropriate response.

Through the common cause of temperance, the AITA forged alliances with socio-religious organizations like the Brahmo Samaj and the Arya Samaj. The Brahmo Samaj was the social wing of Brahmoism, a Hindu reformation movement. In 1870, Keshub Chandra Sen, who had started his own breakaway Brahmo sect, had asked for the abolition of 'that iniquitous opium traffic which kills thousands of the poor Chinese people'.[13] Sen is a controversial figure who many see as a hypocrite, especially with regard to women's rights. But his strange mix of Christianity, mysticism and social reform made him a popular figure in British temperance circles for a while. Several members of the Brahmo Samaj also appeared before the Royal Commission when they visited Lucknow. All of them gave evidence against opium based on their personal experiences and called for its prohibition. One witness narrated the story of his brother's death when still a baby due to an accidental overdose of opium. In Calcutta, Dwarkanath Ganguly and K.K. Mitra, both Brahmos, even took members of the Commission to an opium den so they could see it with their own eyes. When they arrived at the corner of College Street and Bowbazar Street, it was locked up. Mitra and Ganguly wrangled their way inside and showed the two British men 'a dirty squalid place' separated from a brothel by 'a mat wall'.[14]

In 1893, Caine demonstrated how temperance and proto-nationalism were complementary in a proposal to the INC. His resolution called for the government to 'suppress the common sale of alcohol, opium, hemp drugs, and other intoxicants, and so cease to derive any portion of its revenues from the vice, degradation, and misery of the people' and make up for the lost revenue by 'the wider employment of Indians in the civil and military service of the Empire'.[15] Alongside Naoroji, G.K. Gokhale, Romesh Chandra Dutt and Lala Lajpat Rai were also frequent attendees of AITA meetings. Bipin Chandra Pal was a paid lecturer hired by the AITA to travel the country and speak at rallies to educate and build popular support for the cause. Caine and the AITA consciously intertwined themselves with the INC. They boasted that half of their membership were the same. The AITA and the broader British-led temperance movement in India gained legitimacy through the Congress while the Congress gained access to British political influence and support. Naoroji and Caine would, alongside others, found a British wing of the Congress and publish a paper called 'India' with the intention of raising awareness of Indian issues in England. Caine was originally chosen by the SSOT to be on the Royal Commission but was replaced by Henry Wilson after he fell ill, much to the relief of the British government in India. When the Commission was in India, the Congress sent no official representatives. Even if they were so inclined, the presence of one of their major financial supporters on the Commission, the maharaja of Darbhanga, would probably have scared them off.

In 1896, the Congress wanted a British MP to preside over their annual conference. While most presidents had been Indian, the Congress had chosen British men to be president twice before. But this time they were looking for someone who might raise the profile of their concerns – someone who would spark conversation in England and elsewhere in the world. Naoroji felt it should be someone from the Irish Parliamentary Party. The Irish, who like India were fighting for home rule, had been Naoroji's greatest allies in the British Parliament. They had helped him get elected in the first place. After first considering four or five other candidates who were ruled out for various reasons, Naoroji invited Alfred Webb. Webb wasn't a prominent figure. The resolution that led to the Royal Commission was the only one he ever introduced in Parliament. But he was delighted to be asked to preside over the Congress so he agreed. While the president's role is minor, Webb did take the opportunity to – in a slightly patronizing tone – bring up his three major interests in his opening speech. He criticized the Cantonment Acts, the liquor policies and the opium trade.

> To Opium, I find little reference in your proceedings ... I cannot here initiate discussion upon it. Your business for this session is already planned and cannot be altered. However, at some time, your knowledge and advice would be helpful to those of us in the United Kingdom, who desire to do our duty in this matter.[16]

In those early days, the Congress remained firmly in the grip of Allan Octavian Hume. Hume was a career government servant with an obsessive interest in Indian ornithology who left behind a controversial and complicated legacy. He flirted with the mystical – charmed by kooks like Helena Blavatsky, founder of the Theosophical Society. He believed that British rule was a good idea in theory but lacked in practice. Hume held multiple positions over his career, including being a district officer in charge of collection revenues from liquor. But even as he collected it and reported his success to his bosses, he complained that, 'To me however the constant growth of the Abkaree revenue is a source of great regret.'[17] This didn't make him very popular, and eventually, he was unceremoniously ejected from the government.

He was general secretary of the Congress till 1906 – almost two decades. Hume directed the early Congress with a 'loving and lovable despotism'.[18] While the lovable nature is arguable, the despotism is clear. Initially, the resolutions to be tabled were decided in advance by a meeting in Hume's bungalow; this stopped when other members who weren't invited to these meetings protested. While he was much more inclusive and visionary than most of the elitist Congress cohort, this also made him condescending and patronizing – like a parent mothering lazy children.

In the end, the Congress passed their first resolution against opium in 1924 – almost forty years after their founding. In the words of M.K. Gandhi, they declared that 'the opium policy of the Government of India is altogether contrary to the moral welfare of the people of India and other countries', adding that 'the people of India would welcome the total abolition of the opium traffic'.[19]

The historian Bipan Chandra saw most Congress leaders as torn between two good impulses. In his words, they had to 'choose between national self-interest – which was their guiding factor in most other respects – and humanitarianism and philanthropy – on the basis of which they usually appealed to the British people and government to grant them economic and political concessions'.[20] Unlike the case with alcohol, the conversation around opium for those four decades of silence in Congress circles remained firmly rooted in economics. Romesh Chunder Dutt, one of the finest economic minds of his time, dismissed the idea that the government's revenue came from China and not India. He argued that because the money accrued to the state treasury and not to Indian hands, it was essentially an invisible tax. In his monumental *Economic History of India*, he wrote,

No sound economist will, we think, deny that a Government monopoly, which excludes the people from a profitable industry, and stops cultivation, manufacture and trade in a paying article, is a tax on the people, in the truest sense of the word. No impartial historian has defended Lord Palmerston's wars in China in order to force the Chinese to admit Indian opium into their ports against the wishes of their Government. And no sober statesman desires to keep up the Government monopoly in this article, if it can be safely dispensed with.[21]

But even he was proposing an end to the monopoly – not to the production.

A large majority of the Congress supporters disliked the anti-opium agitations going on in England. They wholeheartedly agreed with pro-opiumists who felt that the SSOT were trying 'to have all the glory and honour of the crusade against opium, but the mild Hindoo is to pay the bill'.[22] They were happy to ignore every part of the moral question, blinkered by the threat of new taxes that might arise to fill the gap in revenue. Dozens of editorials in Indian journals and newspapers were vociferous in their defence of opium. In 1889, *The Hindu* wrote, 'Opium may be a great evil, but national bankruptcy is a greater evil.'[23] In 1908, the *Times of India* would assert that 'sacrificing a large portion of Indian revenue to meet the wishes of China in respect to the opium traffic' would be 'Quixotic'.[24] Another editorial, in *Amrita Bazar Patrika*, declared, 'To abandon such a source of revenue and then make good the gap by ruinous taxes wrung from the life-blood of an already impoverished nation would be … in the highest degree immoral.'[25] That isn't to say moral counter-arguments were non-existent. An editorial in *Anand Bazaar Patrika* argued, 'as well might a robber justify his acts by pleading necessity, and a murderer by remarking that the person whom he had murdered would have certainly died someday, though not by his hands'.[26] And Gandhi himself almost exclusively used moral arguments. 'I do not want India to rise on the ruin of other nations,' he would write in *Young India*. He felt that a free India would share with 'the world her treasures of art and health giving spices, but ... refuse to send out opium or intoxicating liquors although the traffic may bring much material benefit'.[27] Jawaharlal Nehru also felt that opium was an issue worth fighting. He urged a fellow Congressman to raise the issue 'continually both in the assembly and in outside agitations' in a letter.[28] Clearly, some of these figures felt they had to keep silent on the controversial issue. In 1907, when the opium trade was set to end, Gopal Krishna Gokhale confessed he had 'always felt a sense of deep humiliation at the thought of this revenue, derived as it is practically from the degradation and moral ruin of the people of China'.[29]

Charles Freer Andrews in Assam

Gandhi believed alcohol degraded people. They needed to be purified and kept safe as well from all other forms of moral corruption. In *Young India*, he wrote, 'Drugs and drink are the two arms of the devil with which he strikes his helpless slaves into stupefaction and intoxication.'[30] Elsewhere, he added,

> The criticism leveled against alcohol applies equally to opium, although the two are very different in their action. Under the effect of alcohol a person becomes a rowdy, whereas opium makes the addict dull and lazy ... Thousands have fallen victim of this intoxicant ... They give one the impression on living on the verge of death.[31]

His plan to gain freedom relied on building a citizenry that was physically and spiritually strong enough to throw off the shackles of colonialism. This was a project that he believed would require a mastery of both body and mind.

But if there was someone who seemed to care more about temperance than Gandhi did, it was Charles Freer Andrews. Andrews once said to Gandhi, 'When you settled upon the threefold programme of untouchability, Hindu–Muslim unity and khaddar, and left out the question of drink it struck me as a sad omission … it has become impossible to get the people to take interest in the opium question.'[32] Andrews was an English missionary who came to India to be the principal of St. Stephen's College in Delhi. He was a close confidant of both Gandhi and Rabindranath Tagore. Andrews was possibly the only person in the world who called Gandhi by his first name, Mohan.[33] Surrounded by unrepentant colonizers, for both Gandhi and Tagore, Andrews was a symbol of hope: an Englishman with a conscience. Tagore, just before his death, would say that men like Andrews would have to 'save British honour from shipwreck'.[34] Drawn into the freedom struggle, he realized – radical for an Englishman – that the best future of the average Indian was without British rule. So as the Congress began to take the opium problem seriously, they tasked him with forming a committee to investigate reports of an opium epidemic in the plantations around Assam.

Colonial Assam was built on the abuse and exploitation of plantation workers – a tradition that proudly continues through independent India till the current day. British administrators turned Assam into the ideal site for tea plantations. As early as 1788, Joseph Banks, naturalist and president of the Royal Society, had written that eastern India had the right climate for tea. This was the beginning of a long struggle to reduce

Britain's dependence on China. Administrators believed that if they could manufacture tea in India, they could potentially double the country's exports. In the 1820s, various explorers found that tea was naturally growing in Assam – shattering the myth that it was unique to China. It was an ordinary part of the life of communities like the Singphos and the Khamtis. Those same early colonialists also pointed out the abundant swathes of poppy. The two crops would develop a twisted relationship. In 1827, Assam was taken over by Company rule and the Assam Tea Company was set up in 1839 – just as the First Opium War broke out. While poppy was initially promoted as a commercial crop, British administrators began to complain about the effect of the drug on their workforce. Apparently, Assamese workers with opium addiction were hindering their great colonial expansion. Charles Bruce, who was tasked with the supervision of the tea plantations by the East India Company, would fervently declaim to his superiors,

> Would it not be the highest of blessings, if our humane and enlightened government would stop these evils by a single dash of the pen and save Assam and all those who are about to emigrate into it as tea cultivators, from the dreadful results attendant on the habitual use of opium. We should in the end be, richly rewarded by having a fine healthy race of men growing up for our plantations, to fell our forests, to clear the land from jungle and wild beasts, and to plant and cultivate the luxury of the world. This can never be effected by the enfeebled opium-eaters of Assam, who are more effeminate than women.[35]

When the Royal Commission on Opium spoke to witnesses about opium use there, horrifying stories came tumbling out.

The government moved to quickly deny or cover them up. Tea plantation owners were selling opium directly to the workers because, as one planter declared, 'those who take opium invariably do more work than the non-consumer'.[36] The planters were quite happy to inform the Commission that opium was essential to workers who needed it to survive their hours of back-breaking labour. One particularly repulsive witness told the Commission that if the drug was banned, the Assamese would revolt and then he would lose all his 'local labour' because 'the people would die out'.[37] This wasn't unique to just tea planters: indigo planters and others also shamelessly told the Commission that opium was essential to their workers. They argued that it kept hunger at bay – ignoring, of course, that they were the ones starving their employees in the first place.

When Andrews and the Congress investigated Assam, they found that 'there were nearly the same number of [government-licensed opium] shops as there were villages'.[38] Andrews called out the government of Assam as an 'Opium government' that hid a multitude of sins under their trite official maxim of 'maximum of revenue with minimum of consumption'. He, like others of his time, subscribed to the patently false, racialized view that the Assamese were inherently more susceptible to the drug. But at the same time, in his report, Andrews would say, 'We do not think that human nature in the East is different from human nature in the West.' Based on this fundamental equality, he wrote, 'If opium, as a poison, is regarded as a dangerous drug in the West, it should equally be regarded as a dangerous drug in the East.'[39]

Soonderbai Powar

In 1889, Soonderbai Hanna Powar, a social activist and Christian missionary, toured England to preach against opium. Powar was an associate of Pandita Ramabai, the feminist scholar and activist who has been described as 'the most controversial woman of her times'.[40] Powar and Ramabai were both connected to the American-led temperance movement. Just as Ramabai had successfully toured the USA, Powar was invited to do a speaking tour of England by one of the owners of a newspaper published in India and Britain. Wilbur Craft, an American priest who would have a major role to play in the USA's anti-opium movement, attended one of her speeches. He would later write down his impressions, remarking on the messages that Powar carried from India:

> One of these messages from a mass meeting of Mohammedan women in Lucknow was: 'We will thank the government to take the sword and kill the wives and children of opium smokers, so as to rid us of the agony we suffer!' When these bitter cries from outraged heathen women were repeated to Christian England the verdict of 'shame! shame!' was heard again and again, but will public sentiment be strong enough to induce the British government to forego this blood money which swells her revenues?[41]

In another speech, Powar recounted a woman saying to her, 'Tell the English Government that if they will stop the Opium curse, I and other women in India will willingly take off the skin of our bodies to make shoes for the English Government and people.'[42] As she travelled to give these speeches in towns across England, the press followed her, covering her events more than a hundred times. Her speeches were collected into a pamphlet titled *An Indian Woman's Impeachment of the Opium Crime of the British Government: A Plea for Justice for her Country People*.

Powar was born a Christian into a traditionally wealthy upper-caste family. She was the founder of the Zenana Training

Teacher's School in Pune, which was a space for Christian women interested in taking the religion into zenanas that were closed from men. As a missionary, she differed widely from Western missionaries of her time, but she was able to employ her knowledge of Christianity to translate the plight of Indian women to Western audiences. Her book *Hinduism and Womanhood* criticized religion, social practices and men for their role in reducing Indian women to states of slavery and bondage.[43]

The Tagore Family

Rabindranath Tagore had great affection for China and its people, and established an institute for Chinese studies in Santiniketan. When he was just twenty years old, Tagore published an essay in Bengali titled '*Chine Maraner Byabasay*' ('The Death Traffic in China' or 'The Commerce of Killing People in China'). In the essay, Tagore wrote, 'Both the hands of China were tightly bound. Opium was forced down China's throat with the help of guns and bayonets, while the British merchants cried, "You have to pay the price of all the opium you take from us."'[44] Forty years later, he would revisit the issue in the Bengali magazine *Kalantar*, writing that the Europeans had fired 'cannon shells and opium … at the very heart of China. None had seen such an apocalypse in history.'[45] But Tagore's family had a long historical involvement in the opium trade he so despised.

Tagore's family were Bengali Brahmins who had been landowners for centuries. The extended Tagore family had multiple financial interests in the opium trade at its peak. When his grandfather, Dwarkanath Tagore, was twenty-eight, he left the day-to-day management of the estate in the hands of European managers and took a posting in the salt department of the Board of Customs, Salt and Opium. Over the next few decades, Dwarkanath would grow into one of Calcutta's foremost business leaders, coinciding with the height of the opium trade.

His firm, Carr, Tagore and Company, was one of the first to have both European and Indian directors. As a shipping agent, it handled a lot of opium. Dwarkanath also owned half of the opium clipper the *Waterwitch*, which was the third clipper to be built in Calcutta after the *Red Rover* (co-owned by Jardine and Matheson) and the *Sylph* (owned by a Parsi merchant). As discussed before, these clippers transformed the opium trade because they could sail against the monsoon and carry opium to China even in the 'off-season' when demand was highest. In 1838, the *Waterwitch* set a record when it sailed from Canton to Calcutta in twenty-five days.[46] During the First Opium War, when the speed of communication was key, the clipper was deployed to carry mail for the British from India through the Suez Canal.

Through his companies, Dwarkanath operated coal fields that supplied coal at very profitable rates to the government. When the First Opium War broke out, the government was in desperate need of fuel for their ships. A dozen steamships needed almost 200 tons of coal per day. Dwarkanath's firms had a near monopoly and were happy to gouge them on price, even selling them inferior quality coal on repeated occasions. Tagore was also deeply involved with the tea plantations of nearby Assam. Dwarkanath was one of the largest Indian shareholders in the Assam Tea Company. His ship, the *Waterwitch*, transported G.J. Gordon, an opium trader, on his mission for the government to smuggle tea seeds and saplings out of China. Gordon's smuggled prizes would seed the Assam plantations.

In this way, Dwarkanath was enmeshed in almost every profitable colonial project of his time. His vision for the country was one where Englishmen and westernized Indians worked together in mutual respect. While he never got to see this, he was, in many ways, the British Raj's ultimate success story. He was the Indian they had liberated – the gentleman they had created through their 'civilizing' mission in India. When Dwarkanath visited England, he was feted by the British high society for months. He even shook hands with the queen.[47]

The League of Nations

After the First World War, the nations of Europe formed the League of Nations. Surprisingly, after much debate, India was admitted as a member despite the fact that it wasn't an autonomous nation. It was the only non-self-governing colony that was allowed to join.[48] This was a fantastic platform for nationalists to raise issues but the government naturally controlled which representatives would attend. Inevitably, the government chose people who would defend their policies and the group was always led by a non-Indian. This policy was heavily criticized in the Indian press. V.S. Srinivasa Sastry, a member of the Indian Liberal Party, was chosen by the government and spoke before the League in 1921. He did his job and defended the status quo.

In 1924, the League organized another conference on the opium issue in Geneva. Horace Alexander, son of J.G. Alexander, wrote a letter to C.F. Andrews from Geneva, saying, 'I wish it had been possible for you to send a representative of the real India to Geneva: I wish too, that I had a message direct from Mr. Gandhi to deliver here. But these are vain wishes: it is too late.'[49] But he spoke too soon because for the first time, the Congress had decided to approach the League directly. Gandhi and Tagore submitted statements asking the government to 'adopt measures adequate for total extirpation of the plants from which these drugs originate, except as found necessary for medicine and science'.[50] When it was read out, the official government representative jumped to his feet in protest.

When the Government of India's delegation rejected the proposals of the Geneva conference, Andrews would write, 'Never perhaps before in recent times has the complete political subjection of India been so shamefully exposed before the civilised world as at Geneva.'[51] The fact that the Congress's message and the government message differed was touted in international circles as evidence that the government didn't really represent the people any more. Nationalists like Tarak Nath Das worked with journalists like Ellen La Motte to spread the news in the USA where anti-opium moral feeling was strong. The British were nonplussed. They didn't understand why the nationalists suddenly cared about the opium question. As far as they were concerned, 'the Indian National Congress discovered this opium question only last year'.[52]

Notes

1. Hansard, H.C. Deb. *Indian Opium Revenue*, vol. 14, cols. 591–634, 30 June 1893. https://api.parliament.uk/historic-hansard/commons/1893/jun/30/indian-opium-revenue#S4V0014P0_18930630_HOC_167.

2. Hansard, H.C. Deb. *Indian Opium Revenue*, vol. 14, cols. 591–634, 30 June 1893. https://api.parliament.uk/historic-hansard/commons/1893/jun/30/indian-opium-revenue#S4V0014P0_18930630_HOC_167.

3. Naoroji, Dadabhai. *Speeches and Writings*. G.A. Natesan and Co., 1918, p. 193.

4. Masani, Rustom Pestonji. *Dadabhai Naoroji: The Grand Old Man of India*. Allen and Unwin, London, 1939, p. 361.

5. Masani, Rustom Pestonji. *Dadabhai Naoroji: The Grand Old Man of India*. Allen and Unwin, London, 1939, p. 73.

6. Masani, Rustom Pestonji. *Dadabhai Naoroji: The Grand Old Man of India*. Allen and Unwin, London, 1939, p. 84.

7. Colvard, Robert Eric. 'A World without Drink: Temperance in Modern India, 1880–1940.' PhD thesis, University of Iowa, 2013, p. 59.

8. Johnson, Gordon. *Provincial Politics and Indian Nationalism: Bombay and the Indian National Congress, 1880 to 1915*. University Press, 1973, p. 14.

9. McLane, John R. *Indian Nationalism and the Early Congress*. Princeton University Press, 2015, p. 91.

10. Colvard, Robert Eric. 'A World without Drink: Temperance in Modern India, 1880–1940.' PhD thesis, University of Iowa, 2013, p. 3.

11. Ambedkar, B.R. *Dr Babasaheb B. Ambedkar: Writings and Speeches, Vols. 1–9*. Edited by V. Moon. Dr Ambedkar Foundation, Ministry of Social Justice and Empowerment, Government of India, 2014, p. 27.

12. Brown, J.B. 'Politics of the Poppy: The Society for the Suppression of the Opium Trade, 1874–1916.' *Journal of Contemporary History* 8, no. 3 (1 July 1973): 105. https://doi.org/10.1177/002200947300800305.

13. Chandra, Bipan. *The Rise and Growth of Economic Nationalism in India: Economic Policies of Indian National Leadership, 1880–1905*. Har Anand Publications, 2010, p. 506.

14. *Minutes of Evidence*, Volume 2. Royal Commission on Opium,1894, p. 260.

15. Carroll, Lucy. 'The Temperance Movement in India: Politics and Social Reform.' *Modern Asian Studies* 10, no. 3 (July 1976): 422. https://doi.org/10.1017/S0026749X00013056.

16. Report of the Tenth Indian National Congress.

17. Wedderburn, Sir William Bart. *Allan Octavian Hume, C.B. 'Father of the Indian National Congress,' 1829 to 1912*. Unwin, 1913, p. 21.

18. Johnson, Gordon. *Provincial Politics and Indian Nationalism: Bombay and the Indian National Congress, 1880 to 1915.* University Press, 1973, p. 43.

19. Gandhi, M.K. *Young India: 1924–26.* S. Ganesan & Co., 1927, p. 352.

20. Chandra, Bipan. *The Rise and Growth of Economic Nationalism in India: Economic Policies of Indian National Leadership, 1880–1905.* Har Anand Publications, 2010, p. 506.

21. Dutt, Romesh Chunder. *The Economic History of India in the Victorian Age.* Vol. 2. Kegan Paul, 1904, p. 155.

22. Brown, J.B. 'Politics of the Poppy: The Society for the Suppression of the Opium Trade, 1874–1916.' *Journal of Contemporary History* 8, no. 3 (1 July 1973): 103. https://doi.org/10.1177/002200947300800305.

23. Chandra, Bipan. *The Rise and Growth of Economic Nationalism in India: Economic Policies of Indian National Leadership, 1880–1905.* Har Anand Publications, 2010, p. 508.

24. Rimner, Steffen. *Opium's Long Shadow: From Asian Revolt to Global Drug Control.* Harvard University Press, 2018, p. 219.

25. Chandra, Bipan. *The Rise and Growth of Economic Nationalism in India: Economic Policies of Indian National Leadership, 1880–1905.* Har Anand Publications, 2010, p. 508.

26. Chandra, Bipan. *The Rise and Growth of Economic Nationalism in India: Economic Policies of Indian National Leadership, 1880–1905.* Har Anand Publications, 2010, p. 510.

27. Gandhi, M.K. *Young India: 1924–26.* S. Ganesan & Co., 192, p. 665.

28. Siegel, Benjamin. 'Beneficent Destinations: Global Pharmaceuticals and the Consolidation of the Modern Indian Opium Regime, 1907–2002.' *The Indian Economic & Social History Review* 57, no. 3 (July 2020): 11. https://doi.org/10.1177/0019464620930886.

29. Rimner, Steffen. *Opium's Long Shadow: From Asian Revolt to Global Drug Control.* Harvard University Press, 2018, p. 118.

30. Gandhi, M.K. *Young India: 1924–26.* S. Ganesan & Co., 1927, p. 765.
31. Gandhi, M.K. *Key to Health.* Navajivan, 1948, p. 25.
32. Gandhi, M.K. *Young India: 1924–26.* S. Ganesan & Co., 1927, p. 120.
33. Guha, Ramachandra. 'His Faith, Our Faith.' *Hindustan Times*, 29 January 2008. https://www.hindustantimes.com/india/his-faith-our-faith/story-sdpOimN69y2gTuSJs1SltI.html.
34. Guha, Ramachandra. 'Searching for Charlie – A Real Christian and a Gentleman.' *The Telegraph*, 28 February 2009. https://www.telegraphindia.com/opinion/searching-for-charlie-a-real-christian-and-a-gentleman/cid/503564.
35. Kour, Kawal Deep. *History of Intoxication: Opium in Assam, 1800–1959.* Indian Institute of Technology, 2013, http://gyan.iitg.ernet.in/handle/123456789/442.
36. *Minutes of Evidence*, Volume 2. Royal Commission on Opium,1894, p. 291.
37. *Minutes of Evidence*, Volume 2. Royal Commission on Opium,1894, p. 294.
38. *Assam Congress Opium Enquiry Report.* Indian National Congress, 1925, p. 22.
39. *Assam Congress Opium Enquiry Report.* Indian National Congress, 1925, p. 4.
40. Khan, Aisha. 'Overlooked No More: Pandita Ramabai, Indian Scholar, Feminist and Educator.' *New York Times*, 14 November 2018. https://www.nytimes.com/2018/11/14/obituaries/pandita-ramabai-overlooked.html.
41. Rimner, Steffen. *Opium's Long Shadow: From Asian Revolt to Global Drug Control.* Harvard University Press, 2018, p. 89.
42. Rimner, Steffen. *Opium's Long Shadow: From Asian Revolt to Global Drug Control.* Harvard University Press, 2018, p. 92.
43. Anagol-McGinn, Padma. *Women's Consciousness and Assertion in Colonial India: Gender, Social Reform and Politics in*

Maharashtra, c.1870–c.1920. School of Oriental and African Studies, University of London, 1994, p. 26.

44. Rimner, Steffen. *Opium's Long Shadow: From Asian Revolt to Global Drug Control.* Harvard University Press, 2018, p. 107.

45. Sen, Amartya. 'Tagore and China.' In *Tagore and China*, edited by Tan Chung, Amiya Dev, Wang Bangwei and Wei Liming, Sage Publications India, 2011, p. 411.

46. Kling, Blair B. *Dwarkanath Tagore and the Age of Enterprise in Eastern India.* University of California Press, 1977, p. 91.

47. Kling, Blair B. *Dwarkanath Tagore and the Age of Enterprise in Eastern India.* University of California Press, 1977, p. 169.

48. Framke, Maria. 'Internationalizing the Indian War on Opium: Colonial Policy, the Nationalist Movement and the League of Nations.' In *A History of Alcohol and Drugs in Modern South Asia: Intoxicating Affairs*, edited by Harald Fischer-Tiné and Jana Tschurenev, Routledge, 2014, pp. 155–172.

49. Nag, Susanta. 'Andrews and the Opium Evil in India.' In *C.F. Andrews Centenary Volume, 1871–1971*, Deenabandhu Andrews Centenary Committee, 1972, p. 149.

50. Framke, Maria. 'Internationalizing the Indian War on Opium: Colonial Policy, the Nationalist Movement and the League of Nations.' In *A History of Alcohol and Drugs in Modern South Asia: Intoxicating Affairs*, edited by Harald Fischer-Tiné and Jana Tschurenev, Routledge, 2014, p. 162.

51. Framke, Maria. 'Internationalizing the Indian War on Opium: Colonial Policy, the Nationalist Movement and the League of Nations.' In *A History of Alcohol and Drugs in Modern South Asia: Intoxicating Affairs*, edited by Harald Fischer-Tiné and Jana Tschurenev, Routledge, 2014, p. 163.

52. Framke, Maria. 'Internationalizing the Indian War on Opium: Colonial Policy, the Nationalist Movement and the League of Nations.' In *A History of Alcohol and Drugs in Modern South Asia: Intoxicating Affairs*, edited by Harald Fischer-Tiné and Jana Tschurenev, Routledge, 2014, p. 164.

8

Endings and Legacies

The Boxer Rebellion and America's Entry on to the Stage

In 1894, after his disappointing experience with the Royal Commission in India, J.G. Alexander, the SSOT's secretary, travelled to China. Alexander wanted to cultivate allies for the organization in China. Apart from missionaries and members of Chinese anti-opium groups in settlements across the country, he reached out to members of the government. At Peking, he met Chang Yin-huan, who had been an ambassador to the USA recently. Alexander had a proposal for Chang, who was now the president of the Board of Revenue. He and the SSOT believed that if China pushed for it, the opium trade could be ended through 'concurrent action in India and China, gradually reducing the area of poppy growth over a period of ten years'. Chang replied, 'We did stop it once, and it caused a war.'[1]

Alexander would later say that his 'plan of gradual and concurrent suppression is quite knocked on the head; the Chinese statesmen all asked for stoppage of the import from India.' Li Hongzhang, a minister who had written letters to the SSOT before, told him, 'You may be sure that if you cease sending our people poison, we shall prevent them from providing themselves with it.'[2] The simple fact of the matter was that China was under obligation to trade opium with Britain and they didn't want to break that treaty. Because they knew the consequences and they simply had too many other problems, including the ominous echoes of the brewing Boxer Rebellion.

Soon after the Second Opium War, the Xianfeng emperor died. His son was crowned the Tongzhi emperor but he was only a boy, just five years old. The empire had to be ruled by regents till he came of age. The Tongzhi emperor's mother was now elevated to the position of empress dowager and took the name Cixi. Empress Dowager Cixi turned out to be a shrewd politician and was soon the real power behind the throne – the only woman to ever rule China. But the empire she ruled was crumbling: they were surrounded by enemies, laden with debt, riven with insurrection. The Boxer Rebellion was only the latest. For years, there had been growing attacks on missionaries and Christian converts, especially in Shandong province. Over time, these attacks became more coordinated and a cohesive rebel militia developed. Their aim was to purge the empire of any foreign presence before it was too late. This anti-foreign, anti-Christian uprising came to be known in the West as the Boxer Rebellion because the rebels were thought to practise martial arts or 'Chinese boxing'. As the Boxers marched on Peking in 1900, there was tangible panic in the capital; the fear was that the rebels blamed the Qing government and would attack the city. The Empress Dowager Cixi – with little choice in the matter – declared her support for their cause. When the Boxers reached the city, they laid siege to the foreign quarters where all of Peking's European residents resided.

The uproar in the West was immediate. In response, an alliance of eight nations including Britain, USA, Russia and Japan invaded China. Much of the British troops were Sikh and Rajput soldiers from India. This combined army marched to Peking and attacked the empress dowager's army and the Boxer militia. The alliance forces were victorious. Their armies marched into a shattered Peking. After widespread violence against civilians and looting with soldiers grabbing and running with whatever they could, the empress dowager was forced to sign a treaty to pay war reparations. The amount would be approximately Rs 70,000 crores today and had to be paid over the course of the next forty years. This was greater than the entire annual revenue of the empire at the time. In many ways, this was the happier outcome. If Kaiser Wilhelm II, the ruler of Germany, had his way, his army would've 'razed [Peking] to the ground'. The kaiser wanted a large-scale massacre of the Chinese. 'No quarter will be given! Prisoners will not be taken! Whoever falls into your hands is forfeited,' he said in a speech to his soldiers.

> Just as a thousand years ago the Huns under their King Attila made a name for themselves, one that even today makes them seem mighty in history and legend, may the name German be affirmed by you in such a way in China that no Chinese will ever again dare to look cross-eyed at a German.[3]

But the other nations in the alliance ended the battle before the German forces could even arrive. Once the Germans were there, they stayed for a year, viciously attacking alleged 'Boxer outposts'.

Back in India, the nationalists were sympathetic to what they saw as a war for independence – the Chinese equivalent of the Indian events of 1857. Tagore would write:

The century's sun has set in blooded clouds.
There rings in the carnival of violence
from weapon to weapon, the mad music of death.[4]

For the British administration, it was a sign that they had to be even more vigilant in their control of India.

The empress dowager, scrambling to find sources of income to pay off the reparations, raised taxes on domestic and imported opium. The drug was becoming more entrenched, not less. The anti-opium movement stuttered. In Britain, Liberal MPs kept the issue alive on the floor of the House of Commons but no real progress was being made. This would change only when a new participant took control over the issue. In 1906, J.G. Alexander received a letter from an American priest, Rev. Wilbur Crafts. Crafts was a loud voice in American politics at that time, fighting numerous (sometimes bewildering) causes that he felt threatened the moral fabric of the country. He was also the same priest who had heard Soonderbai Powar speak about opium during her tour of England. Crafts told Alexander that America had decided that the opium trade must end – for the good of the human race. The USA Secretary of State had told Crafts, 'I am with you and the government is with you … My part is diplomacy, your part is agitation.' While Alexander was cautiously optimistic about support from the USA, he didn't have much hope. He felt that it would be too much of a 'delicate thing' for the USA to pressure Britain on this matter.[5] But the next few years would prove him very wrong.

As the twentieth century progressed, the USA was reinventing itself as a 'moral empire'. It hadn't yet declared itself a putative 'leader of the free world' but the time wasn't far off. But right then, after putting down their own armed insurgency in the Philippines, American colonialism was under attack. American missionaries, among others, accused the US government of being more regressive than other colonial powers. At the same time, Protestant reformers were at the head of global and domestic temperance movements as alcoholism and drug addiction rates soared in the USA. These forces intersected with the question of the opium trade. The Philippines was one of the major destinations after China for Indian opium. At the start of the twentieth century, they were importing 30 metric tonnes per year.[6] The US President Theodore Roosevelt, after political pressure from reformers like Crafts, directed an investigation into the opium problem in the Philippines. Roosevelt appointed Charles Brent, a bishop in the Philippines and a fierce opium critic, as the head of the committee. After their investigation, Brent and the committee submitted a report with recommendations that closely followed Japan's policy in Taiwan (then Formosa). They called for complete prohibition in three years, during which time opium would be a government monopoly. The only opium to be available was for medical purposes and for the use of people with addictions in their treatment process. The report had immediate global ramifications. As the complete opposite of the Royal Commission, it was a moral slap in the face for the British empire. America was branding itself as a country that was willing to do the right thing, regardless of what it cost.

The fact that men like Brent and Crafts held Japan as a model to be replicated should trigger a certain scepticism. They praised Japan's 'superiority ... in energy and progress' that allowed their 'successful prohibition of opium'.[7] It is true that Japan had successfully resisted a domestic opium crisis through a combination of pre-emptive policy and harsh punishment. They had also gradually phased opium out of their colony, Taiwan, where it had sunk its teeth. But by claiming Japan as the premier example for 'Asiatic' self-governance, the USA was revealing what they were willing to ignore. Where Japan had invaded and conquered territory in China, they maintained opium policies, using it as a means of generating revenue and ignoring the damage done to their subjects. After the First World War, Japan also became a centre for morphine production. They bought raw opium from Britain and refined it into morphine and then exported the pills to China in huge quantities.[8] In many ways, the acknowledgement of Japan's potency in Asia was just one imperialist power recognizing another.

The Opium Edict

In 1906, Empress Dowager Cixi issued an edict declaring that China was to put an end to opium production and consumption. Bishop Brent would claim his report was the 'immediate cause'.[9] 'It is hereby commanded,' the edict read, 'that within a period of ten years the evils arising from foreign and native opium be equally and completely eradicated.'[10] It then listed ten regulations. The very first one was an acknowledgement that they had to end cultivation if they wanted to 'eradicate the evil'. At the time, domestic production of opium in China was at an all-time high. In 1906, the country had generated more than 35,000 metric tonnes of opium.[11] This was despite the fact that growing opium in China had been illegal for the last twenty years. The various rebellions had specially stimulated the shift towards domestic production. The putative freedom fighters needed money to finance their wars and opium was an easy and effective source. No longer was opium a problem with an external cause. It had sunk roots deep into Chinese soil. The road to prohibition would not be easy.

China wrote to the British and asked for their cooperation with this new edict. It could've been easily dismissed but the British regime that received their message looked very different from the ones that had come before. While the Liberal Party was in power, Gladstone was now dead and Palmerston was a painting on the wall. The secretary of state for India was John Morley and the foreign secretary was Edward Grey, both of whom had voted for Joseph Pease's 1891 resolution that declared the opium trade 'morally indefensible'.[12] Anti-opium sentiment was widespread among the public. The opium trade's share in British India's revenue had been consistently declining over the years. While still a large sum of money in absolute terms (running into crores of rupees), it was now a fraction of the state's total revenue. The ruling Cabinet had given Morley permission to handle the opium trade as he saw fit. And he sympathized with members of the SSOT. He would write that it was his 'lifelong way … not to be afraid of either of two words: "philanthropist" is one, and "agitator" is the other. Most of what is decently good in our curious world has been done by these two much abused sets of folk.' Morley genuinely believed that times had changed. In his words, 'the opinion of the civilized world and … this island [meaning Britain]' had moved on.[13] The Philippines report had made an impression on him as well. The USA had 'recognized the use of opium as an evil for which no financial gain could compensate' and he knew that Britain couldn't be seen to be lagging behind. But the government in India weren't as keen.

India was more and more looking like an outlier. The British administration in Sri Lanka (then Ceylon) directed a commission to investigate opium on the island. The resulting report was a complete volte-face from the recommendations of the Royal Commission in 1893. It wholeheartedly approved the logic of the American report from the Philippines. Rather than treating it as an embarrassment, the British leveraged the report to show they were keeping up with the times.[14]

But when they heard of China's request to stop the trade, several senior officials were sure it was a ploy. In their head, China was trying to eliminate opium imports so they could boost their own domestic production. They argued that despite their bombastic claims in the edict, the Qing administration was too weak to put an end to domestic opium production. So, they claimed, even if India stopped opium, it wouldn't help the Chinese at all. The only thing that would happen, they claimed, was a hit to India's revenue.

So, when Britain eventually responded to China's plea, their acceptance came laden with paternalistic conditions. And China, with no power to manoeuvre, had to accept. The British agreed to reduce the annual export of opium from India by 10 per cent every year for ten years – if China did the same thing with their domestic production. They also appointed their own official to travel through China and verify that production was being suppressed. In return, a Chinese official could live in Calcutta and ensure that the British stuck to their export limitations. The most striking thing about this agreement was that it did not focus on ending the opium trade between India and China. It was an agreement to end the opium trade from India to anywhere. This was detrimental to China in the short term. Because the British could chose to end exports to other countries first before limiting their exports to China.

The Shanghai Commission

But even before they could sign their agreement with China in 1907, the American government and the head of the Philippines committee, Bishop Brent, invited Britain to a meeting in Shanghai that would be the first of its kind. Shanghai's opium history runs deep. Before it became a treaty port after the First Opium War, it was one of the destinations for enterprising smugglers. After it was opened up to European powers, it replaced Canton as the premier centre for opium. Soon, more than 60 per cent of China's entire opium imports came through the city.

The Shanghai that emerged in the nineteenth century was a city of extremes – both in business and pleasure. And its economy was singular in China in using opium not only 'as commodity but also as currency'.[15] You could buy opium everywhere – from tea houses to parks to brothels. Loans to opium traders were the bedrock on which the city's entire financial infrastructure was built. If the trade suddenly collapsed, the entire city could come to ruin. Shanghai's wealth led to the most luxurious avatar of opium culture in the empire. The city's opium dens weren't seedy houses of ill repute but rather refuges for the fortunate after a day of wrestling with life's vicissitudes. To differentiate themselves from the masses, the Shanghai cognoscenti had elevated (or perhaps reinstated) opium smoking to a beautiful, tasteful indulgence. Certain opium dens were cultural landmarks marked by their ornate woodwork and comfortable cushions, tasteful art adorning the walls, large mirrors that glimmered in lantern light, and an extravagance of hospitality. According to one Chinese poet, they were 'a world of glass, a cosmos of pearls and jade, that dazzles the eye and sets the heart racing'.[16]

Shanghai was also the base of the Anti-Opium League, a broad coalition of missionaries trying to raise international awareness of the crisis. In 1909, the International Opium Commission, as the conference was called, was the first international commission to investigate the opium problem. It was held at the Palace Hotel where, a few years later, Sun Yat-Sen, China's first President, would celebrate the founding of the republic. Representatives from more than a dozen countries were invited. Apart from European nations like France and Germany, the Commission included Japan, Russia, Siam and Persia. But, of course, all eyes remained on the three key players: Britain, China and the USA. While John Morley was clear that Britain had to attend, his colleagues in India were slightly suspicious, sensing an ulterior American motive. And they were right.

At the head of the US delegation was someone who typified the hypocrisy of the American moral crusade: Hamilton Wright. Wright was a surgeon by profession but had found his calling in anti-drug scaremongering. Anti-opium policy in America had always been based on racism. The anti-opium laws passed in the late nineteenth century directly targeted Chinese immigrants but were only amongst a swathe of laws that limited their rights to marry and own property as well as what jobs they could take. Racist 'Yellow Peril' style campaigns around Chinese immigrants weren't seen as a problem to be counteracted; they constituted officially promoted xenophobia. This led to widespread discrimination and sometimes death. In 1871, one of the largest mass lynchings in American history took place when a mob of hundreds of predominantly white Americans murdered around twenty Chinese men in Los Angeles. Wright extended that racist messaging to other groups. He worked with billionaire and newspaper magnate William Randolph Hearst to launch hate-driven campaigns against African Americans, emphasizing their threat to white women.[17] This was the man who became the opium commissioner of the USA and official delegate to the International Opium Commission.

The Americans had been secretly coordinating with China and had come to ambush the British during the Commission. They had a plan to shame the British and force them to renegotiate their agreement with China. This included British India's domestic opium regulations, which were now partially based on that agreement. Instead of a long-drawn ten-year timeline, China wanted the opium trade to end as soon as possible. Predictably, Britain didn't like being ambushed. They thought they were there to share notes about the opium problem in Asia and agree on some vague non-binding resolutions. Despite Brent trying to keep the discussions productive, Wright harangued the British about their moral flaws while proudly and incorrectly holding up America as a country that had never profited off opium. In response, the British representatives vociferously refused to discuss their existing agreement, arguing that the conference wasn't a diplomatic meeting.

It seemed that nothing tangible came out of the Shanghai meeting but it was a milestone on the road to grand, sweeping changes. A few years later, China and Britain negotiated a new agreement to replace their earlier one. They sped up the rate at which exports would stop and brought forward the intended termination date. The end of opium trade was in sight. In India, the government shut down the Patna factory and drastically decreased poppy cultivation in Bihar. The area under cultivation reduced by almost two-thirds.[18]

The Hague Conference

In 1911, the USA organized another conference in The Hague in the Netherlands. At this conference, countries drafted binding resolutions on opium. Britain made it a condition that they would not participate unless morphine and cocaine were included in the agenda. At first, there was resistance from countries like Japan and Germany who were major manufacturers of these drugs. Even the US was hesitant, as they knew this would complicate matters. Whether this was hypocrisy or just short-sightedness is a matter of interpretation. Already by this time, the early twentieth century, morphine pills and cocaine were being used as a substitute for opium smoking. As opiates, they differed from each other in terms of their effects but they shared a destructive addictiveness. In various parts of British India, colonial officers had complained about the infiltration of morphine and cocaine and the damage they were doing. People with opium addictions were often shifting to these drugs – and in the process, being labelled as 'cured'. Morphine, derived from opium, was considered a medical marvel. Doctors around the world were actively using it to 'wean' people with addictions away from opium.

Some historians have cast Britain's stubbornness as a ploy. But it's not clear what the ploy was – other than finding a way to position themselves as moral leaders where previously they were undoubtedly not. If that was the case, the stratagem was partially successful. Unlike in Shanghai, the conference at The Hague was a meeting of diplomatic envoys with representative powers. These resolutions were meant to become part of the League of Nation treaties and ratified by the home countries. This wasn't a quick process. The nations met three times, the last meeting occurring in 1914, two years after the first. At this final meeting, most of the attendee nations ratified the (repeatedly watered down) resolutions. But even as Britain did so, British India did not. This meant that despite Britain signing a binding international resolution, its colony – albeit technically an autonomous one – did not sign or implement it. The excuses for this were no different from the ones parroted for a century. The government claimed they were being sensitive to the sentiments of the people for whom opium was a part of their culture and that banning opium would place a burden on the princely states. And finally, they feared banning opium would push people towards even more dangerous drugs like morphine or cocaine. None of these reasons survive a close scrutiny. While they didn't immediately sign The Hague convention, they did fulfil their obligation as per their agreement with China. In 1913, even earlier than agreed, the last cargo of opium from India reached China. The Chinese received the shipment and then set it on fire. As the smoke rose into the air, the Indo-China opium trade was – at least, officially – over.

It was the end of an era – the result of a long, complicated process with participants from all over the globe. As historian Steffen Rimner put it, 'Qing diplomats found unexpected support among European journalists; British social reformers among Hindu widows; colonial publicists among nationalist revolutionaries and medical drug experts. Chinese antiopium activists joined forces with Indian colleagues; Dutch critics with American crusaders; British liberals with Chinese Confucianists.'[19] And while this wasn't the end of the story of opium, one chapter at least was finally closed.

Opium's Legacy in Asia

While the last shipment of opium had sailed from India to China, opium was still being produced all over Asia. British India could still export the drug to other countries. And China was still trying to regulate the drug within its own borders. The Americans and Japanese had already taken measures in the Philippines and Taiwan, as we have seen. Most other colonies in

South East Asia saw little change. In French-occupied Vietnam and Dutch-occupied Indonesia, the governments followed the letter of The Hague convention and converted opium into a government monopoly – purportedly with an eye to total prohibition. But taxes on opium were vital to both these colonies and they dragged their feet on abolishing the monopoly for as long as they could. And then there were the British-controlled territories in South East Asia called the Straits Settlements, which included Singapore and British Malaya.

Singapore arose from the swamps of the opium trade. In 1818, Thomas Stamford Raffles, a minor British governor in the region, feared for the safety of British trade in Asia. At the time, the Dutch controlled the Strait of Malacca, the vital sea link from India to China. With the permission of local rulers, they maintained a navy that patrolled these sea lanes. The British government were reluctant to antagonize them, given that they were already in the middle of a war with the French. Raffles convinced one of the founders of the British empire in India, Lord Hastings, to give him permission to set up a trading post somewhere near the mouth of the strait. This port would provide ships a vital stopping point on the journey between India and China. Raffles and his aides negotiated with local powers and obtained on lease some land at the mouth of the Singapore River, a location with a natural protected harbour and ample drinking water. But so little support was given to the nascent trading post that the city's governor legalized gambling, arrack and opium to generate revenue. The system was a huge success. It's not an exaggeration to say that in the nineteenth century, Singapore 'literally lived on the back of the opium-smoking Chinese coolie'. The city derived half of its revenue from opium.[20]

The system used in Singapore and British Malaya was roughly the same. The government sold licenses for taxes to be collected

182 \ Opium Inc.

on their behalf. The tax farmers paid them a fixed sum of money and had the right to keep any amount of money they collected above that fixed rent. Each license was usually for a particular commodity or 'vice' – such as opium, liquor, pork, gambling or prostitution. So while nobody was directly taxed, every time they spent their money on these goods or services, they were paying an indirect tax to the government. This was the basis for a much more insidious process whose effects still mark South East Asian society.

In Singapore, Chinese merchants bought the opium licenses to set up farms and then consciously propagated the drug among Chinese workers. The rural lands around Singapore in the mid nineteenth century were plantations that grew pepper and gambier (an ingredient used in tanning and dyeing). Just as in the plantations of Assam, opium became a tool to capture this labour force and hold them to ransom. The workers were addicted to opium whose price was fixed at a sum higher than their wages. They were thus 'permanently trapped by opium in the cycle of labor, indebtedness, addiction and ultimate death'.[21] While these workers were paid a wage on paper, most of the time this money never reached them. They had already 'spent' their wages by consuming what their bosses provided. And this made Singapore's exports more competitive which resulted in greater profits flowing into the city. When urban Singapore expanded and plantations faded away, the opium farms moved to serve the influx of informal workers employed as porters, tradesmen and labourers across the city.

This was the same situation in British-controlled Penang, an island in current-day Malaysia situated at the northern tip of the Strait of Malacca. The British had demarcated it as a 'free port' and didn't change any duties on trade. This meant they had no sources of revenue except their income from tax farmers. At one point, opium provided more than half of Penang's meagre revenue.[22] All of this was possible because of Chinese migration and the standardized practices of exploiting them. The repercussions of the resulting class system can still be felt today.

Singapore was also a vital part of the opium systems of other countries who used its industrial infrastructure. In May 1930, a reporter for a Singaporean newspaper visited the Opium Packing Plant in the city's Pasir Panjan neighbourhood. This area, which was sometimes called Bukit Chandu, meaning 'opium hill' in Malay, was the site of a battle with the Japanese during the Second World War. Today, a renovated colonial bungalow houses a museum that commemorates the battle though little is said of the opium that inspired the name. The 'House of Tiny Tubes', as the journalist called it, had just come 'into fully swing'.[23] It packed chandu (one preparation of opium) into round tin tubes of two sizes, the bigger one about ten times larger than the smaller. The journalist was wowed by the vast machinery used in the process, calling one gadget 'the cutest piece of work imaginable'. But while he lovingly described the technical apparatus, no sympathy was extended to the workers there. The plant employed 75 men, 200 women and 100 'girls'. In an illustration of the gross human rights abuses that would be brushed aside during Singapore's rise to economic power, the journalist wrote that it was 'amusing to recall that when minor accidents (such as cuts to or squeezing the fingers) occurred at the beginning, they abandoned the machines as being possessed by the devil'. The plant could produce 450,000 of the smaller tubes daily. And Singapore, alone, consumed 40,000 per day. The rest was sent to other countries, such as Thailand and Malaysia.

Thailand, or Siam at the time, is one of the few countries in the Global South to have never been colonized. Siam was essentially a city-state, Bangkok, ruled by a king who held partial power and influence over a large hinterland. Almost all of their trade was with China. Opium was illegal in Siam but the drug was still smuggled into the kingdom, regardless of the government's efforts. Eventually, after a new king came to power, Siam legalized the production of opium and began selling farming licenses to Chinese merchants to raise revenue. Justifying his actions, the new king would write, 'Even though opium has been forbidden in Siam over a hundred years, its use has not been stopped; we have to give up ...'[24] It was reserved for Chinese immigrants and still illegal for local Siamese to consume opium. If local residents were caught using opium, they were either killed or forced to declare themselves Chinese and give up their Siamese identity.

But while it was essential for state revenue, opium was never an important trade commodity. The limited amount that came in was imported by Chinese merchants to be sold to Chinese labourers who were working in the mines and jungles. In the tin mines, the death rate amongst the miners was astronomical. One British engineer estimated it to be around 60 per cent. He was told by a miner that opium was 'more essential to the maintenance of order than even rice', allowing them to numb the pain of the day's labour.[25] When denied their daily opium ration, whole crews of miners had been known to desert.

Opium and Hong Kong

When the British first retreated from Commission Lin's onslaught to Hong Kong, they described it as an inhospitable, barren rock. In the second half of the nineteenth century, more than half of the India–China trade passed through Hong Kong.

As that money poured in, the island flourished. Apart from the standard commercial establishments to complement trade – banks, clearing houses, docks, etc. – the city also came to house a number of unique attractions. Historian Julia Lovell writes of 'a casino with a damp Venetian facade, theatres and a performing orangutan called Gertrude, on daily display to the public between midday and one o'clock, taking her dinner, sitting on a chair at a table, using spoons, knives and forks, wiping her mouth with a towel'. The orangutan would 'open a bottle of wine and drink to the health of the spectators' and then 'smoke a cigar'.[26]

As far as its domestic policy was concerned, Hong Kong too maintained an opium licensing system. Its governors pointed at Singapore's success.[27] Again, the targets of the opium policy were migrants from the mainland who were moving en masse to this bustling port in search of work. As in Singapore, the administrations left the exploitation of the Chinese workers to Chinese merchants who did an excellent job of it. In 1883, there were approximately 160,000 residents in Hong Kong but the island consumed enough opium for maybe 40,000–60,000 heavy users.[28] As the century drew on, Hong Kong became the base for exports to California and Australia where large Chinese populations emerged. When China began cutting back on opium production after their edict in 1907, the British government ordered all the opium dens in Hong Kong shut down. Scared of being shamed, they had no choice but to meet 'the standard set by the Chinese Government'.[29]

The Hong Kong government relied on opium revenue for decades. Even after The Hague convention, when the British government took over the monopoly with the aim of full prohibition, Hong Kong still raked in huge profits. In 1918, the government made a record $8.5 million from opium as prices rose because of opium suppression in other countries. This was true across South East Asia. Eventually, the post–First World War 1925 Geneva Conventions declared a fifteen-year timeline for opium-producing nations to completely end all production. But this meant that even in 1939, on the eve of the Second World War, the opium monopolies of British Malaya, Burma, French-occupied Vietnam, Dutch-occupied Indonesia, Hong Kong and Siam, among others, still existed. The opium monopoly in Hong Kong only ended when the Japanese invaded and occupied the island during the Second World War.[30]

Notes

1. Lodwick, Kathleen L. *Crusaders against Opium: Protestant Missionaries in China, 1874–1917*. University Press of Kentucky, 1996, p. 59.
2. Alexander, Horace Gundry. *Joseph Gundry Alexander*. Swarthmore Press, 1921, p. 95.
3. Johannes Prenzler, ed. *Die Reden Kaiser Wilhelms II*. [The Speeches of Kaiser Wilhelm II]. 4 vols. Leipzig, n.d., 2. pp. 209–12. http://ghdi.ghi-dc.org/sub_document.cfm?document_id=755.
4. The lines are from the Bengali poem, 'Sunset of the Century'. The specific translation is from Bayly, C.A. 'The Boxer Uprising and India: Globalizing Myths'. In *The Boxers, China, and the World*, edited by Robert Bickers and R.G. Tiedemann, pp. 147–156. Rowman & Littlefield Publishers, 2007.
5. Tyrrell, Ian R. *Reforming the World: The Creation of America's Moral Empire*. eBook, Princeton University Press, 2010.
6. Haq, M. *Drugs in South Asia: From the Opium Trade to the Present Day*. Springer, 2000, p. 45.
7. Tyrrell, Ian R. *Reforming the World: The Creation of America's Moral Empire*. eBook, Princeton University Press, 2010.

8. Goto-Shibata, Harumi. 'The International Opium Conference of 1924–25 and Japan.' *Modern Asian Studies* 36, no. 04 (October 2002): 969–991. https://doi.org/10.1017/S0026749X02004079.

9. Tyrrell, Ian R. *Reforming the World: The Creation of America's Moral Empire.* eBook, Princeton University Press, 2010.

10. Lodwick, Kathleen L. *Crusaders against Opium: Protestant Missionaries in China, 1874–1917.* University Press of Kentucky, 1996, p. 117.

11. Bauer, Rolf. *The Peasant Production of Opium in Nineteenth-Century India.* Brill, 2019, p. 50.

12. Lodwick, Kathleen L. *Crusaders against Opium: Protestant Missionaries in China, 1874–1917.* University Press of Kentucky, 1996, p. 122.

13. Gibbon, Luke. 'Opium, the British Empire and the Beginnings of an International Drugs Control Regime, ca. 1890–1910.' Phd thesis, University of Strathclyde, 2014, p. 80.

14. Haq, M. *Drugs in South Asia: From the Opium Trade to the Present Day.* Springer, 2000, p. 72.

15. Des Forges, Alexander. 'Opium / Leisure / Shanghai: Urban Economies of Consumption.' *Opium Regimes: China, Britain, and Japan, 1839–1952,* edited by Timothy Brook and Bob Tadashi Wakabayashi. University of California Press, 2000, p. 168.

16. Des Forges, Alexander. 'Opium / Leisure / Shanghai: Urban Economies of Consumption.' *Opium Regimes: China, Britain, and Japan, 1839–1952,* edited by Timothy Brook and Bob Tadashi Wakabayashi. University of California Press, 2000, p. 170.

17. Wright referred to the threat of 'negro cocaine peddlers' and 'cocainized n****r rapists'. As quoted in Buxton, Julia. 'The Historical Foundations of the Narcotic Drug Control Regime.' *Innocent Bystanders: Developing Countries and the*

War on Drugs, edited by Philip Keefer and Norman Loayza. The World Bank, 2010, p. 73.

18. Haq, M. *Drugs in South Asia: From the Opium Trade to the Present Day*. Springer, 2000, p. 76.

19. Rimner, Steffen. *Opium's Long Shadow: From Asian Revolt to Global Drug Control*. Harvard University Press, 2018, p. 2.

20. Courtwright, David T. *Forces of Habit: Drugs and the Making of the Modern World*. Harvard University Press, 2001, p. 136.

21. Trocki, Carl. *Opium, Empire and the Global Political Economy: A Study of the Asian Opium Trade 1750–1950*. Routledge, 2012, p. 133.

22. Buxton, Julia. 'The Historical Foundations of the Narcotic Drug Control Regime.' In *Innocent Bystanders: Developing Countries and the War on Drugs*, edited by Philip Keefer and Norman Loayza. The World Bank, 2010, pp. 61–94.

23. 'House of Tiny Tin Tubes.' *The Singapore Free Press and Mercantile Advertiser*, 7 May 1930. https:// eresources.nlb.gov.sg/newspapers/Digitised/Article/ singfreepressb19300507-1.2.65.

24. Stringer, Nathan O. 'British Opium in Siam: From Grievance to Habit, 1819–92.' MSc thesis, London School of Economics and Political Science, 2013, p. 26.

25. Stringer, Nathan O. 'British Opium in Siam: From Grievance to Habit, 1819–92.' MSc thesis, London School of Economics and Political Science, 2013, p. 25.

26. Lovell, Julia. *The Opium War: Drugs, Dreams, and the Making of Modern China*. eBook, Abrams, 2011.

27. Munn, Christopher. 'The Hong Kong Opium Revenue, 1845–1885.' In *Opium Regimes: China, Britain, and Japan, 1839–1952*, edited by Timothy Brook and Bob Tadashi Wakabayashi. University of California Press, 2000, pp. 105–126.

28. Munn, Christopher. 'The Hong Kong Opium Revenue, 1845–1885.' In *Opium Regimes: China, Britain, and Japan, 1839–*

1952, edited by Timothy Brook and Bob Tadashi Wakabayashi. University of California Press, 2000, pp. 105–126.

29. Rimner, Steffen. *Opium's Long Shadow: From Asian Revolt to Global Drug Control.* Harvard University Press, 2018, p. 217.

30. Munn, Christopher. 'The Hong Kong Opium Revenue, 1845–1885.' In *Opium Regimes: China, Britain, and Japan, 1839–1952*, edited by Timothy Brook and Bob Tadashi Wakabayashi. University of California Press, 2000, pp. 105–126.

9

Opium, Cotton, Sugar, Slavery

axmichand Motichund saw the coasts of Africa as a young boy. He was a Gujarati bania, the latest apprentice in a family firm that traded all over the Indian Ocean. As he grew older, he impressed his family enough to be promoted to the firm's main agent in Mozambique, a country on the southeastern coast of the African continent, just above modern-day South Africa. Despite being separated by the vast blue expanse of the Indian Ocean, the eastern coast of Africa and the western coast of India have been connected by trade for hundreds of years. Through these trade networks, silk from China and spices from South East Asia travelled to the gold-rich kingdoms in North and West Africa. Muslim and Gujarati merchants dominated the trade, harnessing the regular monsoon winds and the peaceful political climate to build a system that prospered for centuries. In the 1780s, when Laxmichand lived in Mozambique, his primary interest was in ivory. Ripped from the mouth of the

African elephant and polished till it shone, ivory was a coveted luxury. But there were two other commodities that were central to Laxmichand's trade. The first was cotton, the soft, smooth fabric that adorned shoulders and waists all across Africa and South East Asia. The second was people. Slaves. In exchange for cotton, Laxmichand purchased ordinary African men and women and then transported them to Mauritius where they would spend their lives trapped in endless labour on the island's sugar plantations.[1]

So far, this book has followed the thread of opium through history. But history isn't a spool of thread to unwind. It's a tapestry, and while following a single thread through a tapestry can take you to interesting places, at the same time it remains just one thread. It might be enjoyable but it is also inherently narrow. The story of opium is only one small pattern in the global history of capitalism and colonialism and how they intertwine. There are so many other threads, weaving through one another in subtle and fascinating ways. This book has alluded to how opium connects to tea: one was a means to an end, the other was the end in itself. As Britain's hunger for tea fuelled the opium trade in Asia, it also fuelled another commodity with a blood-soaked past: sugar. The story of tea is also the story of the secret ingredient that was the source of its popularity. For Europeans, tea was an energizing beverage but sugar transformed it into a pleasure. Over the sixteenth and seventeenth centuries, sugar went from being a pricey luxury good to cheap household item. But this affordability was only possible because of one institution: slavery. The atrocities of the Atlantic slave trade built Western society as we know it today. It built the pedestal the world now places them on.

But it isn't sugar that is often associated with slavery; it is another crop – one that brings us back to India. Cotton. If there is one crop that weaves together every corner of the world and every epoch of humanity, it's probably cotton. Even as the story of opium unfolded, cotton tied together Britain and India and Africa in another way. And as slavery was abolished over the nineteenth century, millions of Indian and Chinese men and women emigrated – voluntarily and involuntarily – to work on cotton and sugar plantations. These were the decades of the 'coolie trade'. And that brings us back to opium, which often travelled with these putative plantation workers – as entertainment and medicine but also a weapon in the hands of their masters. These workers were technically free. Addiction was one way of massaging that technicality. And, of course, underneath all of this, there is the other layer – that of currency, of gold, silver, letters of credit and other more ephemeral mediums of exchange.

The Bittersweet History of Sugar

Sugar cane is a crop that has been grown in India and China for thousands of years. The techniques of manufacturing sugar have been traded back and forth between the two countries. The Hindi word for the fine polished sugar, cheeni, attests to that connection. But when sugar first circulated in Europe, it was a niche ingredient. Till the fourteenth century, it was absurdly expensive and primarily a way of making bitter medicines go down easier, a la Mary Poppins. But as sweetness came to be appreciated for its own sake, the rich and the aristocratic refashioned sugar into a marker of power and wealth. In 1591, a merchant who needed to impress Elizabeth I, Queen of England, threw a 'sugar banquet'. It was so elaborate that some say it inspired the revelry in Shakespeare's *Midsummer Night's Dream*.[2] Hundreds of men paraded before the queen carrying sugary sculptures of castles and soldiers and swords as well as animals and birds and fish. Slowly, the fashion of sugary desserts trickled down from the aristocracy. But even as cookbooks flaunted sugary recipes that could bring this luxurious ingredient to the tables of the mercantile classes, the real sugar tsunami had not arrived on Britain's shores. The wave only struck with the introduction of the trifecta of bitter beverages: coffee, chocolate and tea.

Both coffee and tea were introduced to British culture as both medicine and refreshment. Coffee filtered in from Turkey. In the seventeenth century, when coffeehouses sprung up all over Britain, some referred to them as 'Turkish alehouses'. At first, they were exclusive spaces for the elite to meet and talk about worldly affairs over steaming, stimulating mugs. But soon, much like their modern avatars, they became a cheap place to socialize over a cup of black tea or coffee. For one contemporary source, they were a place to learn 'all Manner of News'. Their description paints a picture of a place of charm and ease: 'You have a good Fire, which you may sit by as long as you please: You have a Dish of Coffee; you meet your Friends for the Transaction of Business, and all for a Penny, if you don't care to spend more.'[3] Coffee and tea (like beer) were actually safer to drink at the time than regular water because the water used had been boiled. And unlike beer, they didn't invite a scolding from priests and other temperance activists.

You could also get a mug of chocolate at some of these establishments. Originally, this was an Aztec drink that their Spanish colonizers disdained for its bitterness till sugar and other warm spices like cinnamon or vanilla were mixed in. Unsurprisingly, now people couldn't have enough! Another drink that came out of the sugar production revolution was rum. Made from molasses, rum became a part of the Atlantic sailor's rations – half a pint per day in the seventeenth century. These various drinks became a part of the daily routine of

British life. By some estimates, over the eighteenth century, the average person's sugar consumption quadrupled.[4] And lockstep with this expansion, sugar's prices were falling rapidly. Over the seventeenth century, the price of sugar halved.

This new ubiquity of sugar coincided with another paradigm shift: the Industrial Revolution. As the old fabric of human lives was rewritten according to the new rules of industrialization, sugar became, as one historian put it, 'the general solace of all classes'.[5] They weren't the only solace: narcotic drugs like opium were also widely available at the time but, as we have seen, a burgeoning temperance movement was reclassifying them as sins and vices. Sugar, on the other hand, was aspirational – a former luxury reserved for the elites that was now available to the working class. It was integrated into factory life. In the middle of their hectic work schedule, factory workers were given a limited time to rest with some tea and sugar for a small boost of energy before they returned to work. Without sugar, there would never have been the 'tea break'.

On the Backs of Slaves

But behind the booming supply and falling prices was an insidious trend. Historically, European sugar came from the Mediterranean – a region that encompassed everything from Spain to Palestine. It was a hard crop to grow, intensive in terms of both land and labour. Colonization of the Americas solved their land problem. Sailing into the 'New World', Europeans committed genocide against the native inhabitants of those lands through war and disease. They labelled themselves 'discoverers' and described as 'virgin' or empty the lands they depopulated. But even with these new territories, there was no way to keep up with the demand without importing a whole new source of labour. And that is where they turned to mass enslavement. At first, these slaves were not necessarily African. In the late fifteenth century, the Portuguese colonized the island off the western coast of Central Africa that they christened Sao Tome. They turned it into a sugar plantation that, amongst various other abuses, 'employed' 2000 Jewish children, all under ten years old.[6]

Another infamous source was convicts. Plantation colonies petitioned courts and governments and soon prisoners were sent on ships to serve out sentences in distant lands doing hard labour. Magistrates in Bristol handed out longer sentences for minor crimes so that these 'criminals' could be sent to the plantations in the Caribbean. The seventeenth-century British mastermind Oliver Cromwell was said to 'barbadoe' his enemies, banishing them to sugar plantations in Barbados and elsewhere in the Caribbean. But there simply weren't enough prisoners to satiate the hunger for plantation workers. Slavery allowed for sugar prices to stay low, turning it into a mass-market commodity, that in turn stimulated demand for more sugar and, thus, more slaves.

From the fifteenth to the nineteenth centuries, more than 13 million Africans were kidnapped and sold into slavery. These men and women went through a process of calculated degradation to ensure that they were transformed from people into property. Their humanity was ripped away from them, slowly and meticulously. Many did not survive the process. Those who did were put to work.

They planted, watered, maintained, harvested. They crushed, boiled, carried. They built, repaired, tended animals, gathered food, cooked. And the entire time, they were assaulted, whipped and, often, murdered. In *Candide*, the French writer Voltaire would write about a slave from Surinam who lacked an arm and a leg. 'When we work in the sugar mills and we catch our finger in the millstone, they cut off our hand; when we try to run away, they cut off a leg; both things have happened to me. It is at this price that you eat sugar in Europe.'[7] Voltaire had a great love for free-wheeling discussions in coffeehouses where he drank large pots of his favourite beverage: coffee mixed with chocolate. This relationship between sugar and slavery is fundamental. It can still be seen in our language. Demerara, which is now used almost as a synonym for brown sugar, is the name of the Dutch colony that would later become British Guiana. It was the site of numerous slave rebellions, most famously in 1823 when more than 10,000 Afro-Caribbeans rose up and were brutally put down.

For centuries, European and American merchants built estates, legacies and institutions through this murderous traffic in human beings. According to historian Joseph Inikori, 'Taking together all the commodities produced for Atlantic commerce in the Americas, the proportion produced by Africans and their descendants grew from approximately 54% in 1501–50 to … a peak of 83% in 1761–80.' Even as late as 1850, this percentage was around 69 per cent.[8]

Cotton's Frayed History

It's easy to overlook that the Atlantic slave trade was, in fact, a trade. In return for the many thousands of men and women they bought, European traders exchanged a commodity that the slave ports and kingdoms of West Africa prized: Indian cotton. Traditionally, the fabric made its way to the lands in North and West Africa from the ports around the Indian Ocean. Over the hundreds of years of trade, there was a sophisticated internal market across Africa for all the subtle variations and styles produced in India. Different principalities coveted different weaves and dyes. This was the trade that the British usurped and profited from. In fact, Africa and the colonies in America were the primary destinations for British cotton exports in the eighteenth century. Around 94 per cent of all cotton was traded there.[9]

This is the key to another globe-spanning triangular trade where, in the words of historian Sven Beckert, 'the products of Indian weavers paid for slaves in Africa to work on the plantations in the Americas to produce agricultural commodities for European consumers'.[10] At each stage, Britain profited. When they sold cloth in Africa, they profited. When they sold African slaves in the Americas, they profited. When they sold the cotton from America, they profited for a third time on essentially the same cycle of transactions.

Cotton in the Indian subcontinent dates back to the Indus Valley era. Some of the earliest travellers to the region mention cotton. And as the centuries passed, India became one of the centres of a global cotton network. In his monumental *Empire of Cotton*, historian Sven Beckert writes,

> Indian cottons crisscrossed South Asia on the backs of people and bullocks. They crossed the seas in Arab dhows, traversed the great Arabian Desert to Aleppo on the backs of camels, moved down the Nile to the great cotton mart of Cairo, and filled the bottoms of junks on their way to Java ... As an Ottoman official complained in 1647, 'So much cash treasury goes for Indian merchandise that ... the world's wealth accumulates in India.'[11]

On the other end of the world in precolonial America, cotton was the most important manufacturing industry. Mexico, before the Europeans invaded, is said to have produced more than 100 million pounds of cotton annually. And in almost all of these societies across the world, cotton was like a currency. It became a medium of exchange for other goods. Certain kingdoms taxed their populace in cotton; others received tribute in cotton. In comparison, cotton was an exotic import in Europe. And a valuable one. As European powers expanded eastwards, they were consciously infiltrating historical cotton-trading networks dominated by Arab and Muslim merchants.

In the eighteenth century, cotton was the East India Company's major export. When the Company first started trading for cotton, they were happy to integrate with the existing system. Their influence was restricted to ports and hubs where they would contract with a bania to act as their agent. He would, in turn, employ agents of his own who travelled to weaving communities and advanced money to spark off the process. These weavers were usually independent craftsmen with their own access to tools and raw materials. They lived and worked in their own villages. But as the British moved from traders to governors, they dismantled the existing cotton systems and took direct control of as much of the entire supply chain as possible. Slowly, this turned into factory work where the weavers owned nothing. While the pre-existing system was deeply casteist and violent, the British system destroyed what little autonomy these weavers possessed. Historians have calculated that the share of weavers in the revenues of the trade fell from 30 per cent to 6 per cent after the British captured the Indian cotton production industry.[12] This led to sweeping poverty and starvation among communities that were once relatively safe from deprivation.

Meanwhile, England became the new centre of the cotton world. The Industrial Revolution, with its sugary tea breaks, included the mechanical revolution of cotton mills. For the first time, looms were powered not by a torrent of human sweat but by the natural flow of rivers. This meant that spun cotton could now be mass produced – even more cheaply than the cotton from India. European textile manufacturers also organized expeditions to learn specific techniques from Indian artisans, especially around types of weaves and different printing and dyeing techniques. These techniques and the resulting technologies built around them were disseminated across Europe with the other fruits of the Industrial Revolution. The demand for this cheap Indian-like cotton only grew. Between 1780 and 1800, just twenty years, British spinning mills increased their output ten times – from 5 million pounds to 56 million pounds of cotton. Britain came to house two-thirds of the world's spindles. And as all of this cotton was being sold, money was flowing into Britain. It was like they were spinning gold. But for the wheel to keep on turning, they needed the supply of cotton to keep pace.

Cotton followed the trail blazed by sugar. The crop would travel across the Atlantic and dominate the geography of North America. By the beginning of the nineteenth century, the USA were Britain's most important cotton supplier. The planters produced as much as they could, recklessly sucking out as much nutrients and fertility from the lands as possible. Once the soil soured, the plantations just moved westward, onto new tracts. Quickly enough, the American hinterlands were colonized by cotton plantations powered entirely by slave labour. Speaking of cotton and slavery, one nineteenth-century cotton merchant said, 'There is no other product that has had so potent and malign an influence in the past upon the history and institutions of the land; and perhaps no other on which its future material welfare may more depend.'[13] The rise of America in the world stage, as an economic power, was through cotton and, thus, slavery.

In 1807, Britain made trading in slaves illegal. In 1833, they passed a law that would eventually abolish slavery across the entirety of the British empire. But given that this happened after American independence, it did not affect Britain's cotton or sugar supply in the least. They continued to enjoy the benefits of slavery while their own hands were purportedly clean. But as the abolition movement began growing in the USA, cotton manufacturers in Britain began to worry. Abolition would disrupt the smooth functioning of the cotton machine that had been chugging along for decades. Even before the American Civil War broke out (superficially due to the issue of 'state's rights' which was nothing more than a euphemism for slavery), the British cotton industry was sending feelers out across the world. And one of the obvious options was India. Multiple studies were commissioned on how to best use the colony to support the needs of the home country's cotton sector. The results were not overly optimistic. India was a hard country to organize.

But then the civil war broke out and the American South stopped all cotton exports to Britain. This was a power play meant to force their former masters to side with them. But Britain didn't immediately come running to their doorstep, and suddenly, the South was losing money. Money they needed when they were fighting a war. Before they could reverse their decision, the North blockaded all the ports, ensuring that no cotton would be shipped to Britain till the war was over. The immediate effect in Britain was twofold. The mills stopped receiving raw cotton to spin and the thousands of unemployed workers starved and rioted as they were abandoned by their employers. Without fresh supplies, cotton prices skyrocketed. Merchants who had stockpiles in warehouses danced all the way to the bank. But eventually, even their stocks disappeared. The industry needed a new source of raw cotton and so the plans for India roared into action.

This wasn't a minor operation. Laws had to be passed, entire government departments had to be reorganized, and infrastructure had to be built. For cities like Bombay, these processes changed them forever. It also changed whole regions of rural India.

Globalizing Berar

Berar is a region in central India, east of Bombay. Berar was a cotton-producing district where cotton was used to pay land rent to the government. Villages would have a number of weavers to produce cloth for local needs. Most of the surplus raw cotton went to Bengal for the vast handloom industry there. But by the mid nineteenth century, with British cloth becoming so cheap, Bengal's industry was on the decline. Berar cotton started heading to Bombay, in big bulky sacks in caravans of hundreds of bullocks. By the 1870s, Berar was transformed. Now, finished cotton cloth was imported from Britain. And the raw cotton was almost entirely exported. One-third of all the land in Berar grew cotton. This meant that, as Harry Rivett-Carnac, the cotton commissioner of the region who would become the opium agent at Ghazipur, put it cheerfully, the 'population now employed in spinning and weaving would be made available for agricultural labour'.[14]

And the long supply chain of merchants and middlemen that connected Berar to ports like Bombay also disappeared. In their stead, there were firms like the Volkart Brothers. The Switzerland-based trading firm had started out with a branch in Bombay and then moved further and further inland until they directly controlled the cultivators in Berar. The cultivators would take their bundles of raw cotton to Volkart-owned gins where the seeds would be taken out. Then the cotton would be taken to Volkart-owned presses where they would be pressed into bales. They would then be transported to Bombay where Volkart agents would ship them to Britain or Europe as their profit margins dictated. By 1920, this one firm shipped a quarter of all Indian cotton. They had offices in Madras, Cochin, Thelisshery, Thoothikudi, Colombo, Karachi, Calcutta and Bombay, and branches in a dozen countries and on every single continent except Antarctica and Australia.

In this manner, the globalization of Berar was complete. Decisions made on the other side of the world reverberated all the way to this corner of India, affecting the lives of everyone who lived there. As Beckert writes, 'These cultivators understood perfectly well that remote events over which they had no control now determined the most basic conditions of their existence.' Farmers would tell Rivett-Carnac that 'they attributed such volatility to "luck," "a war," the "kindness of a paternal Government," or that "the Queen had given every one in England new clothes" on the occasion of the crown prince's wedding'.[15] This integration wasn't a cause for celebration. Now, Berar, like so many other locales from South America to South East Asia, would experience mass starvation and death because numbers in typewritten reports in Liverpool had changed.

The Coolie Trade

The total estimate of indentured labour exported around the globe in the nineteenth century, also known as the 'coolie trade', is around two million Chinese and Indian men.[16] The first experiment in indentured labour from China was in 1806 where around 200 Chinese men were sent to Trinidad. But it was considered a failure. On the other hand, the translocation of Indians to Mauritius over the next few decades was considered a great success. In 1838, they tried sending both Indian and Chinese men to the Caribbean again – specifically to the colonies of British Guiana, Trinidad and Jamaica. The voyage from China to Cuba or South America was much, much longer than the voyage from West Africa. It usually took four months. Around one in four men died during the trip. This extended period of confinement, surrounded by disease and death, often led to desperate insurrections by the coolies. An 1858 inquiry by the government of British India showed a shocking mortality rate among Indian men and women travelling to the Caribbean. One in ten men and almost one in five women died on the journey. The child mortality was even higher.[17]

Between 1847 and 1874 alone, coolie traders transported around 8000 Chinese men per year – more than 220,000 in total – to plantations in Peru and Cuba.[18] At the time, Cuba was a Spanish colony and Peru was an independent nation. In Peru, slavery was disappearing and would be completely abolished in 1854. But in Cuba, Chinese coolies and African slaves worked side by side. Cuba had continued buying slaves from Africa all the way till the 1860s. As their slave trade disappeared, their coolie trade peaked. It was almost a direct replacement. For most of this time, the 'contract' remained the same. It lasted eight years and the plantation owners paid the Chinese workers 4 pesos a month. In addition, they were given food, some limited clothing and a roof over their heads. While these basic terms were met, the rest of the contract was mostly nonsense. They were promised one day off every week but didn't get it. In some versions, the contract expressly stated that the coolie 'renounces the exercise of all civil rights which are not compatible with the compliance of contract obligations'.[19] According to some estimates, more than half of these Chinese men died before their eight-year contracts were complete – a much higher mortality rate than African slaves.

The laws in Cuba changed in 1860 to force any Chinese workers who completed their contract to either renew their contract or leave the island within two months. As was said about black slaves in America, these workers were 'free, but free only to labour'.[20] Most workers chose to renew their contracts. It's hard to accurately estimate how many ever made it back to China but the number is probably shockingly low.

They were also cheaper than African slaves for plantation owners to acquire. And more profitable for human traffickers. The same multinational banking networks that funded the slave trade were behind the coolie trade. The central figure behind the coolie trade from China to Cuba was a slave trader as well – but his monopoly of the coolie trade ensured that he died the wealthiest man in Spain.[21] The profits of the coolie trade were often two or three times the costs invested.

Before their revolution, the island of Haiti was the largest producer of sugar in the world. After, they were viciously embargoed by their erstwhile customers and the liberated populace weren't keen on the continued existence of the plantations where they had been enslaved. Cuba quickly took their place – eventually producing more than 40 per cent of the world's sugar.[22] Britain, alone consuming about 30 per cent of the entire world's supply, was the major destination.

The Cuban landlords were terrified of another Haiti-style revolution. Just like Haiti, they had a huge slave population. From around 40,000 slaves in 1774, the number was now more than 400,000 – more than 40 per cent of the total population.

So the use of Chinese labour rather than African slaves was one of the ways they tried to limit the risk of a unified revolt. In the racial logic of the Cuban landlords, the Chinese were not black – which meant that they were, at least partially, white. Free Chinese men were recorded as 'white' in the censuses and free black people were banned from 'owning' coolies because a judge felt that that would upset the 'natural order'. It has to be mentioned here that anti-black racism was rife among the Chinese at this time. It has never been the sole domain of whites. Around the 1890s, Cuba's plantation system began to change, relying on less labour-intensive forms of agriculture. But this mechanization depended on wealth and capital that was made possible by the exploitation of slaves for decades. Eventually, revolution did come to Cuba. But even before the one led by Fidel Castro, there was the Ten Years' War, where Cuba fought for independence from the Spanish. A contingent of 500 Chinese men joined as soldiers. After the war, a marble monument was erected in their honour in Havana and can be seen to this day.

Opium and the Coolie Trade

After hearing multiple tragic rumours, the Chinese government commissioned an investigation into the plight of their citizens in Cuba. The Cuba Commission Report came out in 1874 and documented both the underhanded means by which Chinese were convinced to emigrate and the awful conditions in which they lived. It included more than a thousand first-hand accounts. While a small percentage were kidnapped, a similar percentage of people voluntarily chose to emigrate. The vast majority had gotten themselves indebted and then been coerced on to the ships, usually after being misled about the terms of their indenture.

Even before this report, the British had been denouncing the Spanish and others who had been taking coolies to Cuba. In 1855, they banned English traders from taking part. They also closed the Chinese ports that they controlled to the Spanish and French coolie traders. This meant that Macao, where the Portuguese had no such compunctions, became the primary source till 1874. After the report, the Portuguese bowed to diplomatic pressure and ended the trade from Macao as well. The British did not stop the movement of indentured Chinese men to their own colonies in South East Asia, a practice they argued was much more humane.

But while there is consensus that these Chinese workers were abused and treated like slaves, most scholars make a clear distinction between the legal rights they could theoretically enjoy compared to African slaves of the same time period. While they weren't slaves, they were still 'unfree'. Multiple contemporary witnesses described their conditions as virtually the same as slaves. As historian Evelyn Du-Hart writes,

> their long work days, usually starting with roll call at 4:30 in the morning and working until nightfall, lasting 12 or more hours, seven days a week … and most devastating for their moral, physical and emotional well being, was the nightly lockups in the barracks or galpones. These ramshackle, filthy and drafty wooden sheds were locked from the outside and became 'nocturnal prisons'…[23]

The coolies were condemned to 'ceaseless and unremitting toil, without a ray of hope that their condition will ever be better'.[24] In Peru, the coolies were completely isolated from the rest of the world. In many plantations, they were the largest demographic

– sometimes outnumbering whites by 20 to 1. These plantations were referred to as 'Chinese villages'. In this unending cycle of work and sleep, apart from any kind of family or source of entertainment, opium was one of the few pleasures they could access.

Opium was given to them on the ships – to pacify them through the long, dark journey. On the plantation, the owners would ration it out daily, deducting the cost from their salary. But they also withheld it if the workers didn't complete their inhuman quota. The drug was also the most common method of suicide. In just the single year of 1860, there were 900 cases of attempted or actual suicide.[25]

This relationship between drugs and labour has been well documented. In the South African diamond mines, white masters felt of their African workers that 'better work is got out of him if he sees the prospect of a cheering glass at the end of a day's labor'.[26] Alcohol was 'included' in a worker's wages – meaning that it substituted for actual money. This was true even for indentured Indian labourers who were sent to British Guyana.

Ganja (marijuana), which the Indians brought with them, was tolerated (and, to a limited extent, even promoted) as a legitimate 'enhancer' as long as sugar production took place within a loose network of independently owned plantations. But rum, a primary product of the centralized, company-dominated mechanized sugar industry that developed late in the nineteenth century, came to be favored by the authorities, who were as interested in creating a captive consumer class as they were in enhancing the labor of those already working under indenture.[27]

The planters systematically moved to make the production of marijuana by the Indian labourers impossible and replaced it with rum, which as a by-product of the sugar industry was something they could profit from. And alcohol was much more addictive than marijuana – thereby allowing the planters to nudge labourers into drinking themselves into their debt.

Notes

1. Machado, Pedro. *Ocean of Trade: South Asian Merchants, Africa and the Indian Ocean, c. 1750–1850.* Cambridge University Press, 2014, pp. 1–3.
2. Abbott, Elizabeth. *Sugar: A Bittersweet History.* eBook, Harry N. Abrams, 2011.
3. Abbott, Elizabeth. *Sugar: A Bittersweet History.* eBook, Harry N. Abrams, 2011.
4. Abbott, Elizabeth. *Sugar: A Bittersweet History.* eBook, Harry N. Abrams, 2011.
5. Abbott, Elizabeth. *Sugar: A Bittersweet History.* eBook, Harry N. Abrams, 2011.
6. Abbott, Elizabeth. *Sugar: A Bittersweet History.* eBook, Harry N. Abrams, 2011.
7. Abbott, Elizabeth. *Sugar: A Bittersweet History.* eBook, Harry N. Abrams, 2011.
8. Inikori, Joseph E. *Africans and the Industrial Revolution in England: A Study in International Trade and Economic Development.* Cambridge University Press, 2002, pp. 481–82.
9. Beckert, Sven. *Empire of Cotton: A Global History.* eBook, Vintage, 2015.
10. Beckert, Sven. *Empire of Cotton: A Global History.* eBook, Vintage, 2015.
11. Beckert, Sven. *Empire of Cotton: A Global History.* eBook, Vintage, 2015.

12. Beckert, Sven. *Empire of Cotton: A Global History*. eBook, Vintage, 2015.
13. Beckert, Sven. *Empire of Cotton: A Global History*. eBook, Vintage, 2015.
14. Beckert, Sven. *Empire of Cotton: A Global History*. eBook, Vintage, 2015.
15. Beckert, Sven. *Empire of Cotton: A Global History*. eBook, Vintage, 2015.
16. Young, E. 'Chinese Coolies, Universal Rights and the Limits of Liberalism in an Age of Empire.' *Past & Present* 227, no. 1 (1 May 2015): 121–49. https://doi.org/10.1093/pastj/gtv018.
17. Anderson, Clare. 'Convicts and Coolies: Rethinking Indentured Labour in the Nineteenth Century.' *Slavery & Abolition* 30, no. 1 (March 2009): 93–109. doi:10.1080/01440390802673856.
18. Hu-Dehart, Evelyn. 'Opium and Social Control: Coolies on the Plantations of Peru and Cuba.' *Journal of Chinese Overseas* 1, no. 2 (2005): 169–183.
19. Hu-Dehart, Evelyn. 'Opium and Social Control: Coolies on the Plantations of Peru and Cuba.' *Journal of Chinese Overseas* 1, no. 2 (2005): 169–183.
20. Young, E. 'Chinese Coolies, Universal Rights and the Limits of Liberalism in an Age of Empire.' *Past & Present* 227, no. 1 (1 May 2015), p. 124. https://doi.org/10.1093/pastj/gtv018.
21. Yun, Lisa, and Ricardo Rene Laremont. 'Chinese Coolies and African Slaves in Cuba, 1847–74.' *Journal of Asian American Studies* 4, no. 2 (2001): 99–122. https://doi.org/10.1353/jaas.2001.0022.
22. Yun, Lisa, and Ricardo Rene Laremont. 'Chinese Coolies and African Slaves in Cuba, 1847–74.' *Journal of Asian American Studies* 4, no. 2 (2001): 99–122. https://doi.org/10.1353/jaas.2001.0022.
23. Hu-Dehart, Evelyn. 'Opium and Social Control: Coolies on the Plantations of Peru and Cuba.' *Journal of Chinese Overseas* 1, no. 2 (2005): 176.

24. Hu-Dehart, Evelyn. 'Opium and Social Control: Coolies on the Plantations of Peru and Cuba.' *Journal of Chinese Overseas* 1, no. 2 (2005): 176.

25. Hu-Dehart, Evelyn. 'Opium and Social Control: Coolies on the Plantations of Peru and Cuba.' *Journal of Chinese Overseas* 1, no. 2 (2005): 169–183.

26. Jankowiak, William R., and Daniel Bradburd. 'Drugs, Desire, and European Economic Expansion.' In *Drugs, Labor, and Colonial Expansion*, edited by William R. Jankowiak and Daniel Bradburd. University of Arizona Press, 2003, p. 23.

27. Angrosino, Michael V. 'Rum and Ganja: Indenture, Drug Labor Motivation and the Evolution of the Modern Sugar Industry in Trinidad.' In *Drugs, Labor, and Colonial Expansion*, edited by William R. Jankowiak and Daniel Bradburd. University of Arizona Press, 2003, p. 103.

10

Opium Smoke and Mirrors

Opium's many lives in the pages of English language literature shows how the drug transformed. At first, it was a folk medicine and a soporific. The poet Alexander Pope argued that Homer referred to opium when he spoke of nameless drinks that washed away sorrow and brought sleep. This classical imagery of soporific drinks continued into the storytelling lexicon of pre-eighteenth-century writers like Geoffrey Chaucer, Edmund Spenser, William Shakespeare and John Milton. In *Knight's Tale*, Chaucer would write how 'nercotikes and opie' would ensure 'that all that nyght, thogh that men wolde him shake ... he myghte nat awake'.[1] In *Othello*, Shakespeare's titular protagonist is poisoned so that 'Not poppy, nor mandragora, / Nor all the drowsy syrups of the world / Shall ever medicine thee to that sweet sleep.'[2] Milton, again on the theme of searching for peace, would write, 'Sleep hath forsook and giv'n me o're / To deaths benumming Opium as my only cure.'[3]

In 1621, the Oxford don Robert Burton wrote, 'others ... get their knowledge by books, I mine by melancholizing'.[4] But these might not actually be his words because his book, *The Anatomy of Melancholy*, is full of quotes, some real and attributed, some fake or plagiarized. Take a deep breath and consider the book's full title: *The Anatomy of Melancholy, What It Is: With All the Kinds, Causes, Symptomes, Prognostickes, and Several Cures of It. In Three Maine Partitions With Their Several Sections, Members, and Subsections. Philosophically, Medicinally, Historically, Opened and Cut Up*. It's a mouthful. A combination of a medical textbook and virtuoso performance of esoteric classical knowledge, *Anatomy of Melancholy* is a unique work. For those interested in the history of mental health, it's a delightful if slightly impenetrable treasure trove.

To those 'melancholy men' who find themselves unable to sleep due to 'continual cares, fears, sorrows, dry brains', Burton writes that 'sleep by all means procured, which sometimes is a sufficient remedy of itself without any other physic'.[5] For this, the first item on his list is the poppy.[6] He also refers to syrups as 'opiates' – a word that in the seventeenth century would have a very different ring to it.

The Romantics

Despite dying at the early age of twenty-five from tuberculosis, John Keats is remembered as one of the great Romantic poets. Trained as a medical student, Keats secretly dosed himself with opium to fend off pain and the onset of his illness. Though Byron would describe his work as 'a Bedlam vision produced by raw pork and opium',[7] Keats's work references his habit in subtler ways. In 'Sleep and Poetry', he writes of 'Sleep, quiet with his poppy coronet'. Critics have shown how much of the sensual imagery he's remembered for was influenced by his medical knowledge of opium. In 'Ode to Indolence', he would write,

> Ripe was the drowsy hour;
> The blissful cloud of summer-indolence
> Benumb'd my eyes; my pulse grew less and less;
> Pain had no sting, and pleasure's wreath no flower:[8]

Indolence was Keats's word of choice for the soft mood that crept up on him after he took a dose of opium.

Like Lord Byron and Keats, Percy Shelley was another famous Romantic poet who regularly used laudanum to ease both mental anguish and physical pain. Both his friends and detractors remark on his dramatic pronouncements on the drug. In 1814, when he met Mary Godwin (the author of *Frankenstein* and, in many ways, the inventor of science fiction) and fell in love with her, he was still married to his first wife. Mary's parents were understandably less than delighted when they found out. According to Mary's stepmother, Shelley burst into their house and shoved a bottle of laudanum into Mary's hands, saying, 'They wish to separate us, my beloved; but Death shall unite us.'[9] The suicide pact was unnecessary. They eventually eloped. Laudanum makes another appearance in the story of how Mary Shelley first imagined *Frankenstein*. Percy Shelley, Mary, Lord Byron and two others were in a castle in Geneva sharing ghost stories while drinking wine and laudanum. Apparently, they got so intoxicated that Shelley ran out of the room screaming because he imagined Mary Shelley's nipples had turned into demonic eyes.[10]

Scholars have also illustrated how laudanum became a normal domestic item and household medicine, especially among women with chronic pain. In her 'Ode to the Poppy', Henrietta O Neill wrote,

> Hail, lovely blossom! – thou can'st ease,
> The wretched victims of disease;
> Can'st close those weary eyes, in a gentle sleep.
> Which never open but to weep;
> For, oh! thy potent charm,
> Can agonizing pain disarm;[11]

She wrote the poem while she was confined to a bed with illness. Similarly, the poet Maria Logan, who titled a poem 'To Opium', suffered 'seven tedious years of uninterrupted sickness'.[12] The poet Sara Coleridge wrote about the hardship of raising a child while wrestling with cancer and insomnia in her poem 'Poppies'. The poem ends,

> O' then my sweet my happy boy
> Will thank the poppy flow'r
> Which brings the sleep to dear mama
> At midnight's darksome hour.[13]

The opium that these poets described is a banal product – essential but explicable. But at the same time, even as opium was becoming an everyday commodity, it was also being exoticized.

Dreams and Visions

The opening lines of the poem 'Kubla Khan' by the English Romantic poet Samuel Taylor Coleridge are quite famous among literature students and others who indulge in poetry.

In Xanadu did Kubla Khan
A stately pleasure-dome decree:
Where Alph, the sacred river, ran
Through caverns measureless to man
Down to a sunless sea.[14]

The verses drift over a hazy panorama of the descendant of Genghis Khan's palace nestled in a canyon full of forest, rock and ice. But the landscape is tinged with a note of apocalypse and damnation. Famously, Coleridge wrote that the poem came to him in a dream. Feeling sickly, he had retired to a cottage in the country. One day, in 1797, as he was sitting in a chair, drowsy from an opium-based drug and reading a travelogue set far away in Asia, he began to drift into sleep. There, in the grip of a dream, he saw such vivid images of the mythical Xanadu and the legendary Khan that when he woke up, he began to feverishly capture the sensation in verse. But then there was a knock on the door and he rose from his desk; and by the time he came back, an hour or so later, the vision had dissolved and he could remember no more. So the poem was titled 'Kubla Khan: Or, a Vision in a Dream' and described as a 'fragment'. Coleridge didn't even publish the poem till more than a decade later when he was persuaded to do so by another famous literary figure, Lord Byron (who was an opium user himself).

And ever since then, critics have spilled ink and torn shirtsleeves over whether any part of that origin story is true. It has been praised, adored, dismissed and reviled. In 'Kubla Khan', various critics and commentators see a drug-induced fever dream – the stoned imaginings of someone lost in a hallucinogenic fog. They've argued that the poem ends with a direct reference to opium:

Beware! Beware!
His flashing eyes, his floating hair!
Weave a circle round him thrice,
And close your eyes with holy dread,
For he on honey-dew hath fed,
And drunk the milk of Paradise.[15]

Whether the 'milk of Paradise' that so terrified and dazzled the poem's speaker is opium isn't clear. But it's true that Coleridge consumed opium regularly. Ailments and pains had wracked his body from childhood. Opium dulled the pain, allowing him to live his life. A pattern emerges between those who used opium to treat issues of chronic pain and those who took it recreationally. Samuel Johnson, who authored one of the most influential early English dictionaries, also suffered from chronic ailments and relied on opium for relief – albeit unhappily. He grudgingly acknowledged this: 'I need not tell you that opium cures nothing, though by setting the powers of life at ease, I sometimes flatter myself that it may give them time to rectify themselves.'[16]

Wilkie Collins' *Moonstone*, published in 1868, was described by T.S. Eliot as 'the first and the greatest of modern English detective novels'. In the book, an English woman inherits a spectacular diamond stolen from India. It is mysteriously stolen, and in the ensuing investigation, the book morphs into an early example of a 'drug thriller'. Because Collins himself used laudanum regularly, some of the book's observations on drugs predates a lot of later psychological theories on the effects of addiction – including the idea of 'drug dissociation'. Collins celebrated laudanum, saying, 'Who was the man who invented laudanum? I thank him from the bottom of my heart, whoever he was. If all the miserable wretches in pain of body and mind, whose comforter he has been, could meet together to sing his praises, what a chorus it would be.'[17]

De Quincey's *Confessions*

If a single person is to be blamed for nineteenth-century Britain's popular understanding of drug addiction, it would probably be Thomas De Quincey, who invented the genre of 'addiction narrative' with *Confessions of an English Opium-Eater*. De Quincey cemented a reputation as a proto-psychonaut, nobly experimenting on himself so that he could report back to 'normal society' from the distant shores he visited. But the book only had such power because Victorian morality was taking hold of the British upper classes. Before this, opium wasn't very remarkable. But in the nineteenth century, it was assuming its now familiar place as a degenerate vice that degraded body and soul. In an attempt to provide a more correct accounting, Quincey discussed both the pleasures and the pains of opium. But as the pains were much less exciting, it was the pleasures – notably the idea of opium as the key that unlocked his creativity – that made the largest impression. Describing opium's effect on his dreams, he said that 'a theatre seemed suddenly opened and lighted up within my brain, which presented nightly spectacles of more than earthly splendour'.[18] But this wouldn't happen to just anybody. Oh, no. Quincey was a philosopher and so his dreams were much deeper than the ordinary man's. He wrote, 'If a man whose talk is of oxen should become an opium-eater, the probability is, that (if he is not too dull to dream at all) he will dream about oxen.'[19]

Quincey's *Confessions* caused a scandal in British society when it was published anonymously in 1821. It was an ironic defence of opium that, in the end, exoticized it for the sake of scandal. As one scholar puts it, the book was the 'locus classicus of narcotic experience'.[20] Quincey was a journalist with empty pockets and an expensive addiction. His provocative writings made him famous, though they didn't help too much with his debtors. At one point, he allegedly racked up bills of more than £1000 or one lakh rupees a week in today's currency to fuel his laudanum habit.[21]

After Quincey, there was a series of famous opium users. Jean Cocteau, the French literary icon, was addicted to opium for twenty-five years. It was almost a divine experience for a man who felt existentially bored and isolated. He would write, 'Everything one does in life, even love, occurs in an express train racing toward death. To smoke opium is to get out of the train while it is still moving. It is to concern oneself with something other than life or death.'[22]

Now American literature abounds with books that illustrate the experience of addiction. Early classics include *Diary of a Drug Fiend* by occultist Aleister Crowley and *Junkie* by the Beat generation icon, William S. Burroughs.

The Opium Den

While *Confessions'* influence was wide and multifaceted, by the end of the century, opium mixed with nationalism and xenophobia had become the site of question of cultural identity. The sinister 'opium den' became a metaphor for a disappearing, nostalgic British way of life. It became a kind of meme – reproduced in fiction, quickly escaping any ties to real life.

In Oscar Wilde's seminal 1890 novel, *The Picture of Dorian Gray*, the corrupted protagonist visits opium dens 'where one could buy oblivion, dens of horror where the memory of old sins could be destroyed by the madness of sins that were new'.

As the 'hunger for opium' gnaws at him, his throat burns and his 'delicate hands' twitch nervously. When Gray reaches the den, Wilde treats us to a fanciful description.

> Shrill flaring gas-jets, dulled and distorted in the fly-blown mirrors that faced them, were ranged round the walls. Greasy reflectors of ribbed tin backed them, making quivering disks of light. The floor was covered with ochre-coloured sawdust, trampled here and there into mud, and stained with dark rings of spilled liquor. Some Malays were crouching by a little charcoal stove, playing with bone counters and showing their white teeth as they chattered.[23]

In another corner, a terrified old man brushes his sleeves, imagining that they're covered with red ants. The other residents of the den simply laugh at his suffering.

In the 1891 Sherlock Holmes' story, *The Man with the Twisted Lip*, Doctor Watson visits an opium den to look for a man who has been missing for days. The den is 'between a slop-shop and a gin-shop, approached by a steep flight of steps leading down to a black gap like the mouth of a cave'. From there, Watson enters:

> a long, low room, thick and heavy with the brown opium smoke, and terraced with wooden berths, like the forecastle of an emigrant ship. Through the gloom one could dimly catch a glimpse of bodies lying in strange fantastic poses, bowed shoulders, bent knees, heads thrown back, and chins pointing upward, with here and there a dark, lack-lustre eye turned upon the newcomer. Out of the black shadows there glimmered little red circles of light, now bright, now faint, as the burning poison waxed or waned in the bowls of the metal pipes. The most lay silent, but some muttered

to themselves, and others talked together in a strange, low, monotonous voice, their conversation coming in gushes, and then suddenly tailing off into silence, each mumbling out his own thoughts and paying little heed to the words of his neighbour.[24]

In the room crowded like an 'emigrant ship', strange men in 'fantastic poses' mutter to themselves senselessly while they smoke from pipes.

In 1884, Rudyard Kipling's first published story, *The Gate of the Hundred Sorrows*, tells the tale of a person in India with an addiction to opium. When he wrote this, Kipling was just nineteen years old but the story adopts an air of worldly maturity – a sentiment that anybody who was ever a young writer will sympathize with. It isn't clear how much of the story is fictional and how much was based on an actual conversation with a person with an addiction. On a street so narrow that 'a loaded donkey couldn't pass between the walls', there was a *'pukka*, respectable opium-house ... not one of those stifling, sweltering *chando o-khanas* that you can find all over the City'.[25] The den is populated with government servants, Anglo-Indians, women, Afghans, etc. Kipling's character shares the tragic stories of these denizens with a nonchalant attitude. He acknowledges that he's going to die from the drug and couldn't care less. Despite being well received at the time, it reads today as the sensationalized tale of a young writer trying to make a name for himself – which was more or less what it was. In fact, Kipling's next story, which was never published, featured another opium den in Lahore run by an old Irish woman. While Kipling describes opium as hallucinogenic, he knew better. When he was eighteen and suffering from an intense fever, his servant, called Baksh, brought him opium and a pipe to help. Maybe it did because he survived. He secretly continued taking opium and bhang for many years after that (usually recreationally), though he did his best to hide it from other Europeans.

In *The Mystery of Edwin Drood*, Charles Dickens's unfinished final novel, British society's horror of 'racial mixing' and homosexuality is made painfully apparent through a description of an opium den. The main character finds himself waking up 'in the meanest and closest of small rooms' on a bed with a Chinese man, a lascar and a haggard English woman. Before his eyes, the woman, as she smokes opium, 'transforms into a strange likeness of the Chinaman'. The Chinese man 'convulsively wrestles with one of his many Gods or Devils, perhaps, and snarls horribly. The Lascar laughs and dribbles at the mouth.' With the transformation of the woman, Dickens is leveraging the racist horror of his readers as they imagined the woman's whiteness literally disappearing because she might be in some kind of sexual relationship with the two Asians. This idea of good Western blood being 'infected' with 'foreign degeneracy' is an old idea that's never really gone away – as is obvious from present-day far-right white supremacist groups in America and elsewhere.

The opium den outside of Western fiction looks very different. Chinese sources describe large, well-lit rooms, ornately decorated. In Jeet Thayil's *Narcopolis*, the opium den is free of the racial hysteria but it's not a cheerful space of simple pleasures either.

Bombay as a Narcopolis

In *Narcopolis*, Thayil dreams (or remembers a dream) of Bombay in the 1970s where opium still haunts the city. It's a postmodern

222 \ Opium Inc.

narrative written in a steady stream of consciousness that actively dismantles the 'maximum city' that lives in our heads. The city isn't beautiful or slick; it's pulpy – like a fruit that's burst open in your hands. Shuklaji Street where Thayil used to smoke opium is described in the book as 'a fever grid of rooms, boom-boom rooms, family rooms, god rooms, secret rooms that contracted in the daytime and expanded at night. It wasn't much of a street … and to walk along it was to tour the city's fleshiest parts, the long rooms of sex and nasha.'[26] As this Bombay 'progresses' into the 1990s, the street transforms. Things change. The old opium den becomes a fancy office space. But the drug itself hasn't gone away. It, like the city's murky history, is still there – it just got a touch of paint and an agent.

Narcopolis is a book of juxtapositions and reversals. The very first line reads: 'Bombay, which obliterated its own history by changing its name and surgically altering its face, is the hero or heroin of this story.'[27] Bombay is the hero of the story. It's the first and last word of the book – literally bookending the narrative. But Thayil isn't being inclusive with language when he says 'hero or heroin' there. The line mirrors De Quincey's *Confessions* that refers to opium as 'the true hero of the tale'. In *Narcopolis*, Bombay is both central character and drug of choice. Thayil makes the allusion clearer later in the prologue when he writes, 'I found Bombay and opium, the drug and the city, the city of opium and the drug Bombay.' This is a technique he uses repeatedly to disorient conventional images. For example, he conjures up the depravity of his characters but then immediately undercuts any moral judgement by pointing out the greater depravity of everything else.

Then there are the addicts, the hunger addicts, the rage addicts, the poverty addicts, and power addicts, and the pure addicts who are addicted not to substances but to the oblivion and the tenderness the substances engender. An addict, if you don't mind me saying so, is like a saint. What is a saint but someone who has cut himself off, voluntarily, from the world's traffic and currency.[28]

The Epic Journey of the *Ibis*

Amitav Ghosh's Ibis trilogy contains three books: *Sea of Poppies*, *River of Smoke* and *Flood of Fire*. The name itself comes from a ship, the *Ibis*, a silent but ever-present figure in all three books. *Sea of Poppies* begins with a vision of the *Ibis*, a former slave trading ship pulling into Calcutta on the behest of an opium trader. The person seeing this vision is in Ghazipur, where the opium factory dominates the physical and emotional landscape. She is a petty farmer, grinding poppy husk for the factory, where her husband works. By the end of the book, she is an indentured labourer on her way from India to Mauritius. In *River of Smoke*, the *Ibis* sails into Canton, carrying a cargo full of opium, right at the start of Commissioner Lin's assault on opium smuggling. Like the other books, there are multiple threads but the central one is a Parsi merchant from Bombay whose fortune is too intertwined with opium for his own good. In *Flood of Fire*, the *Ibis* is a part of the naval fleet that fights the First Opium War. A central thread is an Indian soldier through the war as he wrestles with his complicated relationship with his British commanding officer. The *Ibis* carries migrant labour, fortunes, goods of trade, drugs, weapons of war – it is a literal vehicle of the British empire.

As a metaphor, the *Ibis* has space for a lot of cargo. Ghosh employs it in a dozen ways. One example is its use to highlight the British link between the Atlantic slave trade and the subsequent coolie trade. The opium trader and masochist Burnham, in *Sea of Poppies*, says, 'Have you not heard that when God closes one door he opens another? When the doors of freedom were closed to the African, the Lord opened them to a tribe that was yet more needful of it – the Asiatick.' Later, he adds, 'A hold that was designed to carry slaves will serve just as well to carry coolies and convicts.'[29] He says this to Zachary Reid, a descendant of a freed African slave who passes for a white man. Two disparate systems of subjugation are tied neatly together in the twin metaphors of Reid on the deck of the ship and the dark, claustrophobic hold lurking below. As Gaurav Desai, who co-edited a book on teaching Ghosh's works in college classrooms, puts it,

> Whether it be the traumas of the delinking of Bangladesh from India in *The Shadow Lines*, or the links between Gulf petrochemicals and Indian migrant labor in *The Circle of Reason*, or those between Burma and India in *The Glass Palace*, Egypt and India in *In an Antique Land*, subaltern knowledges and official histories of science in *The Calcutta Chromosome*, or the human, the animal, and the environmental in *The Hungry Tide*, Ghosh has been our master linkister for some time now.[30]

Rightly praised for its attention to historical detail, the Ibis trilogy is a remarkable exercise in bringing a lost historical movement to life. A feat that's more impressive because of the sweeping nature of its canvas. It's clear that one of Ghosh's objectives with the book is to provide a guided, enlivened tour of a dusty history. His inspiration is too systematic to be otherwise. In *River of Smoke*, a character reports on 'the greatest of Canton's suburbs': the river boats. He writes in a letter:

Their boats are moored along the water's edge, on either side, and they are so numerous you cannot see the water beneath. At first this floating city looks like a vast shanty town made of driftwood, bamboo and thatch; the boats are so tightly packed that if not for the rolls and tremors that shake them from time to time you would take them for oddly-shaped huts ... The occupants are all so busy that you would imagine the floating city to be a waterborne hive: here in this boat someone is making bean-curd; in another, joss-sticks; in that one noodles, and over there something else – and all to the accompaniment of a great cacophony of clucking, grunting and barking, for every floating manufactory is also a farmyard! And between them there are little watery lanes and galis, just wide enough to allow a shop-boat to pass ... all barricking their wares with bells, gongs and shouts.[31]

This is a rare feast of description – one that generously renders both waterscape and soundscape in high fidelity.

There is a fundamental challenge in telling the histories of cultures and societies that did not leave behind reams of written records. Even where such sources existed, myriad factors have meant that much of it simply didn't survive to the modern day. Humidity kills paper, time wears away rock, colonialism warps even memory. As various historians have stated, there is a colossal act of imagination needed to conjure up the historical worlds that have been lost to us. This process of imagination is inherently speculative as every archive is imperfect. When they spin narratives from their fractured sources, historians engage in a process that's similar to a novelist. As Ghosh himself puts it, 'history and storytelling are so closely joined together that it is impossible to pick apart their roots: they are like two trees grafted upon each other as seedlings ... the storyteller's dependence on the past is so inescapable as to be apparent also in the rhetorical form that fiction most commonly employs: the past tense.'[32] Of course, novelists, unlike historians, can leverage poetic license. Which means that if they are so inclined, they can springboard off existing historical research, and like Ghosh, create a version of worlds and peoples whose records have been structurally erased.

The weight of the historical record is transferred to opium which, like a planet, exerts its own gravitational pull on the destiny of its characters. In *Sea of Poppies*, one of the characters holds the tiny poppy seed in her hand and ponders about its giant effect on their lives.

> On any other night she would have scanned the sky for the planet she had always thought to be the arbiter of her fate – but tonight her eyes dropped instead to the tiny sphere she was holding between her thumb and forefinger. She looked at the seed as if she had never seen one before, and suddenly she knew that it was not the planet above that governed her life: it was this minuscule orb – at once bountiful and all-devouring, merciful and destructive, sustaining and vengeful.[33]

But despite a recurring theme of how the drug degrades and destroys those that it sinks its claws into, Ghosh's books seem fundamentally optimistic and cheerful. Another writer had once called a trafficking ship 'a Dantean dream' which had 'the lid of Hades, and the damned were below'.[34] But Ghosh's characters aren't doomed – even when they pass into Hades. There is always a sense of romantic hope. That the world gets better – somewhere just past the horizon.

Notes

1. Cox, Octavia. 'Historicising Keats' Opium Imagery Through Neoclassical Medical and Literary Discourses.' In *Psychopharmacology in British Literature and Culture, 1780–1900*, edited by Natalie Roxburgh and Jennifer S. Henke. Springer, 2020, pp. 26–27.

2. As cited in: Cox, Octavia. 'Historicising Keats: Opium Imagery Through Neoclassical Medical and Literary Discourses.' In *Psychopharmacology in British Literature and Culture, 1780–1900*, edited by Natalie Roxburgh and Jennifer S. Henke. Springer, 2020, p. 27.

3. As cited in: Cox, Octavia. 'Historicising Keats: Opium Imagery Through Neoclassical Medical and Literary Discourses.' In *Psychopharmacology in British Literature and Culture, 1780–1900*, edited by Natalie Roxburgh and Jennifer S. Henke. Springer, 2020, p. 27.

4. Burton, Robert. *The Anatomy of Melancholy*. eBook, Project Gutenberg, 2004. Retrieved 25 May 2021 from https://www.gutenberg.org/ebooks/10800

5. Burton, Robert. *The Anatomy of Melancholy*. eBook, Project Gutenberg, 2004. Retrieved 25 May 2021 from https://www.gutenberg.org/ebooks/10800

6. Along with 'nymphea, violets, roses, lettuce, mandrake, henbane, nightshade or solanum, saffron, hemp-seed, nutmegs, willows'.

7. Cox, Octavia. 'Historicising Keats: Opium Imagery Through Neoclassical Medical and Literary Discourses.' *Psychopharmacology in British Literature and Culture, 1780–1900*, edited by Natalie Roxburgh and Jennifer S. Henke. Springer, 2020, pp. 23–46.

8. Keats, John. 'Ode to Indolence.' Poetry Foundation, 1819. https://www.poetryfoundation.org/poems/52995/ode-on-indolence. Accessed on 25 May 2021.

9. Hayter, Alethea. '"The Laudanum Bottle Loomed Large": Opium in the English Literary World in the Nineteenth Century.' *Ariel: A Review of International English Literature* 11, no. 4 (1980): 37–51.

10. Vincent, Alice. 'Ghost Stories, Opium and Relentless Rain: The Story of Literature's Worst – and Most Pivotal - Holiday.' Penguin Random House, 23 June 2020. https://www.penguin.co.uk/articles/2020/june/geneva-holiday-frankenstein-mary-shelley.html.

11. O'Neill, Henrietta. 'Ode to the Poppy.' All Poetry, 1792. https://allpoetry.com/poem/8574257-Ode-To-The-Poppy-by-Henrietta-O-Neill. Accessed on 25 May 2021.

12. Logan, Maria. 'To Opium.' All Poetry, 1793. https://allpoetry.com/To-Opium. Accessed on 25 May 2021.

13. Coleridge, Sara. 'Poppies.' Black Cat Poems, 1835. http://www.blackcatpoems.com/c/poppies.html. Accessed on 25 May 2021.

14. Coleridge, Samuel Taylor. 'Kubla Khan.' Poetry Foundation, 1816. https://www.poetryfoundation.org/poems/43991/kubla-khan. Accessed on 25 May 2021.

15. Coleridge, Samuel Taylor. 'Kubla Khan.' Poetry Foundation, 1816. https://www.poetryfoundation.org/poems/43991/kubla-khan. Accessed on 25 May 2021.

16. Hubble, Douglas. 'Opium Addiction and English Literature.' *Medical History* 1, no. 4 (October 1957): 325. https://doi.org/10.1017/S0025727300021505.

17. Siegel, Shepard. 'Wilkie Collins: Victorian Novelist as Psychopharmacologist.' *Journal of the History of Medicine and Allied Sciences* 38, no. 2 (1983): 166. https://doi.org/10.1093/jhmas/38.2.161.

18. De Quincey, Thomas. *Confessions of an English Opium-Eater*. eBook, Project Gutenberg, 2000. Retrieved 25 May 2021 from https://www.gutenberg.org/ebooks/2040

19. De Quincey, Thomas. *Confessions of an English Opium-Eater*. eBook, Project Gutenberg, 2000. Retrieved 25 May 2021 from https://www.gutenberg.org/ebooks/2040

20. Cox, Octavia. 'Historicising Keats' Opium Imagery Through Neoclassical Medical and Literary Discourses.' In *Psychopharmacology in British Literature and Culture, 1780–1900*, edited by Natalie Roxburgh and Jennifer S. Henke. Springer, 2020, p. 28.

21. Dormandy, Thomas. *Opium: Reality's Dark Dream*. Yale University Press, 2012, p. 94.

22. Inglis, Lucy. 'How Did So Many Writers Get Access to Opiates?' Literary Hub, February 2019. https://lithub.com/how-did-so-many-writers-get-access-to-opiates/.

23. Wilde, Oscar. *The Picture of Dorian Gray*. eBook, Project Gutenberg, 1994. Retrieved 25 May 2021 from https://www.gutenberg.org/ebooks/174

24. Doyle, Arthur Conan. 'The Man with the Twisted Lip.' *The Adventures of Sherlock Holmes*. eBook, Project Gutenberg, 1999. Retrieved 25 May 2021 from https://www.gutenberg.org/ebooks/1661

25. Kipling, Rudyard. 'The Gate of the Hundred Sorrows.' *Plain Tales from the Hills*. MacMillan and Co, 1920, p. 278.

26. Thayil, Jeet. *Narcopolis*. eBook, Faber & Faber, 2012.

27. Thayil, Jeet. *Narcopolis*. eBook, Faber & Faber, 2012.

28. Thayil, Jeet. *Narcopolis*. eBook, Faber & Faber, 2012.

29. Ghosh, Amitav. *Sea of Poppies*. eBook, Penguin Random House, 2015.

30. Desai, Gaurav. 'The Novelist as Linkister.' *The American Historical Review* 121, no. 5 (December 2016): 1531–36.

31. Ghosh, Amitav. *River of Smoke*. eBook, Penguin Random House India, 2015.

32. Ghosh, Amitav. 'Storytelling and the Spectrum of the Past.' *The American Historical Review* 121, no. 5 (December 2016): 1552.

33. Ghosh, Amitav. *Sea of Poppies*. eBook, Penguin Random House, 2015.
34. Yun, Lisa, and Ricardo Rene Laremont. 'Chinese Coolies and African Slaves in Cuba, 1847–74.' *Journal of Asian American Studies* 4, no. 2 (2001), p. 112. https://doi.org/10.1353/jaas.2001.0022.

11

Opium Today

The Era of International Drug Law

After the 1925 meeting in Geneva, the international gatherings didn't stop. In 1931, another convention was drafted that focused on morphine and cocaine. There was a conference in Bangkok the same year where the USA essentially forced Turkey to ratify the drug conventions if they wanted to continue supplying opium to the American pharmaceutical industry. There was a sense (in the USA at least) that American moral pressure could change the world for the better. Domestically, America had a burgeoning anti-drug infrastructure that was a breeding ground for a new kind of individual: the ambitious narco-crat. Numerous charismatic narco-crats used anti-drug hysteria to concoct schemes to build and consolidate their own political powers – and these schemes affected the whole world.

One American scheme was the post-Second World War campaign to launch an International Opium Monopoly. It would be a central agency that would coordinate between all of the world's opium producers and pharmaceutical companies. This agency would ensure that only the opium needed for legal manufacturing would be produced, and thus, according to its proponents, end all illegal production and smuggling. But the other countries on the Commission on Narcotic Drugs, the anti-drug body convened under the United Nations, didn't seem too excited. Like all such policy discussions, it's hard to disentangle substantive criticism from venal power politics. There were two kinds of countries that had a direct stake in opium control: manufacturing countries (where the big pharmaceutical companies were based) and producing countries (where large-scale opium production was taking place). These two camps tussled over potential control of the International Opium Monopoly, refusing to cede power to the other camp. There was a brief moment where it seemed like the agency would be born, but ultimately, the nations of the world shied away from a centralized agency and elected to proceed with the existing treaty formula. In the early 1950s, the United Nations began the development of the 'Single Convention' that would replace the existing morass of conventions and treaties. It was a much-needed streamlining but they dragged their feet.

In the meantime, led by France, the Commission on Narcotic Drugs began discussing a whole new set of resolutions called the 1953 Opium Protocol. Given the existing morass of treaties, there should've been no stomach for another new code at this time but the French delegate at the head of the Commission 'ruled legitimate amendments out of order, forced votes on problematic and confusing provisions before delegations could examine them, and ran roughshod over opponents'. He 'apparently understood the likelihood of stalemate if he allowed delegations to dissect the draft article-by-article'.[1] The whole treaty was ready before anyone knew it. And it was extremely strict. Too strict for many parties. While some ratified it, most decided to wait for the Single Convention. Eventually, after three drafts and a thirteen-year gestation period, the nations of the world arrived at a version of the United Nation's Single Convention that they deemed worth debating. While large sections were the same as the 1953 Opium Protocol, the Single Convention was much less demanding.

Because the intention was to design a treaty to replace ten other existing treaties, the Single Convention needed mass support. This meant that smaller producing countries were able to band together and effectively push back against provisions they didn't like. Manufacturing countries also ensured that psychotropic drugs (which would come to be forever associated with the 1960s in America) were not included; the pharmaceutical industry had a large financial interest in these new drugs. In the same way, the American government made sure there was enough wiggle room for Coca-Cola to keep importing coca leaves (the raw material in the production of cocaine) as a flavouring agent. Eventually, after typically furious debate, the Single Convention was accepted and ratified. It forms the basis for international drug law till today.

The CIA and America's Other Side

But even as these grand schemes were deliberated under the hallowed arches of the United Nations, another arm of the American government was actively aiding drug smugglers: the CIA. The Central Intelligence Agency was born out of the twisted worldview that America (and thus the very idea of

'Western democracy') was threatened by powerful outside forces (originally 'communism' and now 'Islam'). Therefore, with the stakes being this high, the shadowy organization was empowered to break international laws if that was what it took to 'keep the world safe'. This included the promotion of one of America's most dangerous opioids: heroin. According to Professor Alfred McCoy, American media have popularized this image of:

> the international heroin traffic as a medieval morality play: the traffickers are portrayed as the basest criminals, continually on the run from the minions of law and order; and American diplomats and law enforcement personnel are depicted as modern-day knights errant staunchly committed to the total, immediate eradication of heroin trafficking. Unfortunately, the characters in this drama cannot be so easily stereotyped.[2]

The Second World War almost inadvertently ended a heroin epidemic in the USA. The increased naval security shut down the regular smuggling routes. Anyone with an addiction was forced to survive without the drug as supply dried up. The entire illicit drug trafficking ecosystem had been disrupted. With the right interventions, it could've been destroyed completely. In Italy, the mafia had been decimated by Mussolini's Fascist Party, allegedly because one member had insulted him personally when he was on vacation. But because an 'enemy of my enemy is a friend', the CIA's predecessor, the Office of Strategic Services or OSS, had allied with the mafia to aid American troops in their invasion of southern Italy during the Second World War. The mafia sold them information, helped them avoid enemy traps, and procured supplies for them. As the American Army liberated towns from fascist control, local mafia bosses were appointed mayors to maintain law and order. This alliance of convenience was brokered by one of the American mafia's top bosses who was languishing in prison after his prostitution racket was busted. After the war, he was released and deported to Italy as a reward. On returning to Italy, the same boss would restart heroin smuggling to the USA.

This wouldn't be the only deal between the American intelligence agencies and organized crime in Europe. To tackle the rise of the Communist Party in France, the CIA funded any opponent they could find – including the Socialist Party. In the late 1940s in Marseille, where a massive strike by dock workers was perceived as a gambit to take over the government, the CIA funded the mafia to act as strike breakers. They were successful – too successful. With the CIA's funds, the mafia consolidated power in Marseille and turned it into the premier laboratory for heroin production. Soon, the bulk of American heroin was smuggled through Marseille.[3]

The Golden Triangle and the Golden Crescent

The source of most of the world's illicit opium from 1950 to 1990 was a dense swathe of mountainous jungle in South East Asia called the Golden Triangle lying across parts of Laos, Thailand and Myanmar. Coined in the 1970s by the US government, the 'golden' prefix was chosen to conjure up images of the vast sums of money the opium producers were allegedly enjoying. While opium had been grown in the region from the nineteenth century, political events of the mid twentieth century changed the destiny of this tiny area. In China, the Communist Party came to power in a military coup against the ruling Kuomintang. The country under Chairman Mao ruthlessly shut down opium production and smuggling into the country. Meanwhile, the CIA tried to reorganize the fractured remnants of the Kuomintang army that had fled into the mountains south of China. They hoped that these ragtag troops would form the base for an insurgency into China that would take back the country – or at least, destabilize the communist government. To raise funds for weapons, they coerced the indigenous population of the region into large-scale opium farming and their CIA contact in Thailand, a military general, helped them sell the drug to organized crime syndicates like the American mafia. Which meant that the CIA had contributed to illegal drugs smuggled into the USA. Ironically, in 1951, the Boggs Act was passed in the USA, greatly increasing sentencing and other penalties for drug crimes because of the rise of 'communist opium'.[4] Today, after multiple kinds of domestic and international intervention, most of the opium farms in Thailand and Laos have disappeared; whatever remains of the Golden Triangle is in north Myanmar.

These tactics weren't unique to the CIA. At the time this was happening, there is evidence that French intelligence agencies used similar stratagems in their battle against the Viet Cong in Vietnam. To raise funding for guerrilla armies in the 1940s and 1950s, French intelligence restarted the opium monopoly that the French government had officially ended. They usurped former official channels and ran a clandestine drug operation for years in a secret programme referred to as 'Operation X'.[5] Many have pointed out that the definition of narco-terrorists used by the Drug Enforcement Administration – 'an organized group that is complicit in the activities of drug trafficking in order to further, or fund, premeditated, politically motivated violence perpetrated against non-combatant targets with the intention to influence (that is, to influence a government or group of people)'[6]– fits these state-sanctioned intelligence organizations perfectly.

The Golden Crescent is another amorphous geographic area from Iran to Afghanistan that was a hub of illegal opium production. The name mimics the nomenclature of the Golden Triangle but the 'crescent' isn't about shape as much as a reference to the predominantly Muslim population of the region. When large-scale opium cultivation first emerged in the region, the international community wasn't particularly bothered. Most of the resulting opium was headed to Iran, where addiction reached epidemic levels. As long as it wasn't affecting Europe or America, they were happy to ignore it. Iran still has one of the highest rates of opiate and opioid addiction in the world. Eventually, foreign intervention and domestic prohibition slowly turned the region, specifically Afghanistan, into the largest supplier of heroin in the world today.[7] Over the 1980s, Pakistan became a major producer and consumer of opium. In 1989, the Pakistan Narcotics Control Board estimated that the country had 1.2 million people who were dependent on opioids in some way. In the same year, when Benazir Bhutto lost power in a no-confidence motion, she accused the country's drug oligarchs of spending almost 9 crore Pakistani rupees on a coordinated campaign against her.[8]

In the 1980s, the CIA funded militant groups in Afghanistan to counteract Soviet influence on the Soviet–Afghan War. While they enjoyed lavish support from their American allies, these groups (referred to as the mujahedeen) didn't need any other source of money. But after the war, when the CIA withdrew support, opium farms became the base of a new source of wealth. The existing agricultural economy had been destroyed during the war. Millions had died and been displaced. When these displaced farmers returned to their shattered villages, militant groups coerced them into producing opium rather than traditional crops, like wheat. Since the 1990s, opium production in Afghanistan has boomed. It went from around 3500 tons in 1994 to 8200 tons in 2007 and is now estimated to be 93 per cent of global production.[9]

While the disastrous drug-related schemes of the CIA might seem far-fetched or salacious, there are many more. When the Sandinista rebellion overthrew the ruling dictator in the small South American country of Nicaragua in 1979, the CIA funded a counter-insurgency group known as the Contras. Despite wide evidence that the Sandinistas had broad democratic support, the CIA supported and trained the Contras as they committed a series of military atrocities to 'take back' Nicaragua. While the facts of the case are still disputed, American journalists have documented that as a part of this support, the CIA enabled drug traffickers to smuggle crack cocaine into America to raise money for the Contras.[10] These reports accused the agency of contributing to the crack cocaine epidemic that ravaged the USA, primarily affecting poor African-American households. These allegations might seem unbelievable – especially given that multiple federal investigations have partially or completely exonerated the CIA. But they are only a few controversial examples of what can be seen as standard long-running American foreign policy in South America. Even if they are not true, the international legacy of America's War on Drugs is damning. In her book, journalist Dawn Paley calls this legacy 'Drug War Capitalism'.

Paley describes how the War on Drugs was used by American corporations – banks, arms dealers, oil and mining companies – to expand into and then exploit South America. To Paley, it's not drugs that are important – it's war. A militarized, terrorized atmosphere in South America has facilitated exactly the kind of extraction that multinational conglomerates desired. It has expanded markets for their goods, allowed them to displace citizens from valuable lands, and reframe exploitation as 'investment'.[11] The form this process took in South America might be unique – but its effects are all too common. It is the same process as the one instigated by the East India Company.

The War on Drugs

In 1971, the American President Richard Nixon officially declared a 'War on Drugs', naming drug abuse as 'public enemy number one'. 'If we cannot destroy the drug menace in America, then it will surely in time destroy us,' he said later.[12] But while there was a legitimate drug crisis, the entire campaign was essentially manufactured to boost Nixon's political profile, especially among young white Americans. It also gave him weapons to use against communities that supported his political opponents. Decades later, a journalist published an interview with one of Nixon's aides where the aide declared,

> We knew we couldn't make it illegal to be either against the war or black, but by getting the public to associate the hippies with marijuana and blacks with heroin, and then criminalizing both heavily, we could disrupt those communities. We could arrest their leaders, raid their homes, break up their meetings, and vilify them night after night on the evening news. Did we know we were lying about the drugs? Of course, we did.[13]

These deplorable tactics worked for Nixon and they would work again for Ronald Reagan when he became President a decade later. He did away with Nixon's lip service to medical treatment and rehabilitation. This was now solely an issue of 'law and order' and 'public morality' because that was what was going to rally his base. The Republican Party's voters didn't seem to care about rehabilitation. Reagan would call the War on Drugs a 'national crusade'. 'In this crusade, let us not forget who we are,' Reagan said. He added, 'Drug abuse is a repudiation of everything America is. The destructiveness and human wreckage mock our heritage.'[14]

This messaging was designed to appeal to white voters who already held biases against minorities specifically African Americans as being perpetrators of crime. The legacy of Reagan's policies is apparent in the massively skewed incarceration rates for African American men in the USA today. They make up only 13 per cent of drug users but count for 70 per cent of drug-related incarcerations.[15] This disparity is also made explicit in the laws themselves. Powdered cocaine, which is most commonly used by white men, attracts a sentence of five years in prison for possession of 500 grams. For crack cocaine, which is predominantly used by black men, the same prison term is applicable for possession of just 5 grams. Combine this with the disenfranchisement laws that take away voting rights from convicts (sometimes permanently) and the discrimination of the War on Drugs is revealed to be a feature and not a bug. According to the American Civil Liberties Union, 'Across the nation, 13% of all adult black men have lost their right to vote, with rates reaching a staggering 40% of adult black men in some states.'[16] As African Americans predominantly vote for Democratic candidates, the stripping of rights from every such voter directly increases the odds of victory for Republican candidates. As one scholar put it,

> the Black community was targeted by a vicious three-pronged assault; a drug epidemic with all of the attendant social, health and economic costs; a draconian prosecution-centered drug policy that did not stop the flow of illegal drugs and exacerbated the Black community's social and economic

problems; and the callous exploitation of the African American community's misery to advance the government's larger geo-political ends.[17]

Within the USA, the War on Drugs had led to a generalized militarization of the police and a resulting boom in police violence and police killings. But even beyond their borders, the politically motivated war on drugs has affected the lives of millions across the world because of the USA's outsized international influence. In 1971, the United Nations instituted the UN Fund for Drug Abuse Control, which was meant to monetarily incentivize countries to implement good (that is, USA-approved) drug policies and programmes. The USA contributed the bulk of the money to set up the fund and essentially used it as an extension of their foreign policy for years. There are roughly two types of anti-drug strategies: those that focus on the supply side (drug production and transport) and those that focus on the demand for drugs. The USA's policies have emphasized measures to limit the supply. This meant targeting regions where illegal opium was produced and intervening at the source in military-style operations. And where they did engage in reducing demand, they didn't advocate for large-scale rehabilitation and medical treatment centres or cutting-edge epidemiological strategies. Instead, their primary technique has been to encourage visibility of law enforcement, increase the length of jail times, and promote capital punishment for offenders.

Opium in Independent India

After independence, India's drug policies were caught between opposing forces. On one side, there was the pressure from international bodies like the United Nations. On the other side, there were the endless budgetary needs of a nascent nation. The result was a series of confused policies – either poorly drafted or weakly implemented.

During the Constituent Assembly Debates, prohibition seemed to have the sympathy of the majority of the assembly. Those who tried to argue against the idea on the grounds of personal liberty were drowned out by those who declared that they had 'pledged in front of Gandhiji' [18] to enact prohibition. Eventually, a draft article on public health and nutrition was amended to include a call for prohibition. This became Article 47 of the final Constitution:

> The State shall regard the raising of the level of nutrition and the standard of living of its people and the improvement of public health as among its primary duties and, in particular, the State shall endeavour to bring about prohibition of the consumption except for medicinal purposes of intoxicating drinks and of drugs which are injurious to health.

But such a vague directive meant that states were free to enact conflicting policies. While some like Madras and Bombay enforced full prohibition, others implemented little to no restrictions. In most states, opium could still be purchased at state-licensed retail stores though the amount available for sale gradually decreased as per India's international commitments to the United Nations. Cognizant of the chaotic nature of these piecemeal laws, the Planning Commission formed a Prohibition Enquiry Committee in 1954 ahead of the Second Five Year Plan. The Committee was tasked with formulating how to implement the objective of Article 47 on a national level. While the primary focus was always on alcohol, the Committee noted that opium was already 'marching to its doom slowly but surely'.[19] After fifty days and more than 250 witnesses, the Committee recommended a roadmap for total prohibition by 1958. This cold efficiency was too much for the Congress government who ignored their recommendations completely.

Even by the time of the Third Five Year Plan, prohibition was far from taken for granted. The entire problem of substance abuse was branded as 'essentially a social welfare movement' that was the prerogative of NGOs and other welfare organizations. For the government, the revenue from it was now officially the priority.[20] Indian opium exports were becoming a vital source of foreign exchange for a country that had precious little to balance its imports at the time. Even as domestic opium was strictly reduced, the export of raw opium tripled between 1947 and 1951. This was still only a fraction of what it had been under the British less than fifty years ago. This was only possibly because India was one of the seven countries that could commercially produce opium for medical purposes legally via the 1953 Opium Protocol. While initially most of the opium went to pharmaceutical industries in Britain, the USA quickly became the country's most important customer. Where once poppy was grown for Canton, now it was grown for New York. Over the course of the 1960s and 1970s, India became the largest global supplier of raw opium, responsible for almost 90 per cent of the entire market.[21]

This was derailed when pharmaceutical giants like Johnson and Johnson and Glaxo began producing opium in Tasmania in Australia. The tiny island quickly became the home of a highly sophisticated opium industry. India's export sales plummeted, even as production continued. Eventually, India approached the United Nations and pleaded for help. Indian opium was quoted at half the price of Australian opium but the country was still not able to maintain their exports. The Indian government had amassed 2600 tons of unsold opium. The USA came to their aid, formulating a policy that required their companies to buy 80 per cent of their raw opium stock from either Turkey or India – the 'traditional suppliers'. This actually worked, and with the help of the United Nations, India managed to temporarily halt Australian exports and successfully unloaded all excess stock by 1994.[22]

But during this period of turmoil for India's legal trade, illegal trade took root. While estimates varied, international bodies calculated that 10–50 per cent of legal opium production was being diverted into the hands of illegal drug traffickers. This might have been as high as 200 tons every year. The system in India required that every farmer with an opium license hand over a minimum statutory amount. This was fixed at around 40 kilos per hectare. In practice, if a farmer did produce more, they could dispose of the surplus in the black market for a much more lucrative price. A black market that was, in all probability, run by criminals with political connections. These political connections ensured the minimum statutory production amount remained low despite numerous attempts to raise the threshold value. Historian Emdad-ul Haq writes that an 'unholy nexus amongst poppy cultivators, politicians and drug traffickers' ensures that 'a large quantity of the official opium in India ends up with black marketers who offer a higher price to the poppy farmers to sell their unaccounted daily reserve of opium'.[23] The black market prices could be up to thirty times higher than government prices.

Prior to the 1980s, international agencies believed that whatever opium was pilfered from the legal production system was consumed in India and thus wasn't a problem for the global community. But as the decade passed, they discovered that large quantities were being smuggled to other countries in South Asia, Africa, Europe or the USA. There have been multiple instances of international drug authorities intercepting smuggled drugs that originated in India. As their biggest rival in the legal production of opium, Australia led the charge in international meetings to highlight India's lax security. At the same time, the final deadline to abolish all non-medicinal use of opium had arrived. So in India, the 1980s saw two sweeping anti-drug laws come into effect: the Narcotic Drugs and Psychotropic Substances Act 1985 (NDPS Act) and the Prevention of Illicit Traffic in Narcotic Drugs and Psychotropic Substances Act 1988 (PITNDPS Act). These replaced most of the anti-drug laws that had existed before, including the old opium Acts.

The NDPS Act primarily lays down punishments for any illegal handling of drugs like cannabis, cocaine, LSD and opium. It also allows for the death penalty in case a person is caught committing repeat offences. One of the many anachronisms of the now-dated NDPS Act is that it allows for legal opium users; they can be registered under the Act and receive quantities of opium required for their medical treatment. While this provision is hardly used any more, there are about a thousand people still registered under the legacy system. The PITNDPS Act allows for preventative detention of suspected drug traffickers. Both Acts are extremely harsh laws in terms of penalties. They have led to numerous instances of people caught with milligrams of an illegal drug spending decades in prison. In India, 70 per cent of all prison inmates are 'under trials', that is, they haven't been convicted of their crime. Many suffer for years behind bars and are later proved innocent. Sometimes, the evidence that justifies an arrest is nil. Despite these exaggerated powers, these laws have been fundamentally unsuccessful in ending organized drug traffic in India and keeping behind bars the drug lords who direct the trade.

By the 2000s, opium wasn't a money-spinner any more. Almost all the money earned from exports was being spent on expensive anti-smuggling operations that the country was bound to maintain. At the same time, companies in Australia had produced a genetically modified poppy that didn't contain any morphine at all, making it unusable for heroin production but still useful for pharmaceutical companies. India's opium exports shrank drastically. Regardless, in 2017 and 2018, there were still more than 50,000 farmers with opium licenses.[24] Most of these farmers are concentrated in five districts in Rajasthan and Madhya Pradesh. Just one district in Madhya Pradesh, Mandsaur, is home to about the quarter of the license holders and has produced more than 100 tons of opium in a single year.

Mandsaur has a historical connection to the opium trade. It was central to the Malwa trade during the early nineteenth century under the Scindia dynasty. But that legacy isn't positive. Farmers in Mandsaur tend to grow multiple crops, but because they cultivate opium, they're often automatically assumed to be criminals by local police. 'We grow more than 40 different crops. My village supplies thousands of litres of milk every day to dairies ... but when officials visit our village and see a nicely built house, they chuckle and say, your wealth is due to taskari (illegal trade),' said one farmer to a reporter.[25] Research has shown that districts like Mandsaur where opium was produced historically have suffered from under-development, even as other districts around them have progressed. According to economist Jonathan Lehne, 'areas with a high likelihood of historical opium production continue to have lower literacy, fewer schools and fewer health centres'. His study argues that areas in Bihar, Jharkhand, and Uttar Pradesh where opium was cultivated under the British 'lag behind much of India in terms of income, literacy, and access to public goods'.[26] The colonial opium administration's focus in these areas was irrigation and policing; social welfare was ignored.

In terms of illegal production, the bulk (which is still a relatively small amount) happens in Himachal Pradesh, Kashmir, Uttarakhand and Arunachal Pradesh. According to a 2010 survey by an anti-drug NGO, there were more than 150 square kilometres of illegal poppy crops in just two districts of Arunachal Pradesh. In Anjaw district, opium was cultivated by every household in almost every village. The former Narcotics Commissioner of India, Romesh Bhattacharji, has claimed that legalization was the only way forward in the region as leaders from every political party were involved in the trade.[27]

The Punjab Opioid Crisis

In 2019, a report published by the Ministry of Social Justice estimated that there were around 77 lakh people in the country who needed treatment for opioid dependency. This is more than the entire population of Scotland. This report, *Magnitude of Substance Use in India*, looked at substance abuse in general, not just opioids. It is the result of a mammoth effort, involving more than twenty different organizations and 1500 people across every state in the country. There were two parts to the data collection: a general household survey where the researchers spoke to more than 450,000 people and a targeted survey of around 70,000 people with addictions. One of the report's many shocking conclusions is that around 2.1 per cent of the country use opioids. Of these, heroin is the most common, though pharmaceutical opioids, opium pills, bhukki (which is made from poppy husk) and doda (powdered poppy husk) aren't far behind. From this survey, the report extrapolates that 77 lakh people are engaged in harmful drug use. But to put this number in context, the report estimates that the number of people needing treatment for alcohol dependency is about ten times larger. The majority of those who need treatment for their dependency are concentrated in states like Uttar Pradesh, Punjab, Haryana, Delhi, Maharashtra, Rajasthan and Gujarat. In terms of the rates of addiction, the sparsely populated northeastern states, Punjab, Haryana and Delhi are the worst affected.

Historically, the highest numbers of opioid users have been found in border states where smuggling is easier. India sits in between the Golden Triangle and the Golden Crescent. On the northwestern border, there is smuggling from Afghanistan through Pakistan and on the northeastern border, from Burma. These borders stretch for hundreds of kilometres and have always been porous. In villages that exist right on the border with Pakistan, many farmers cultivate land that falls in the cracks between the two countries: no man's land. When they go out to their fields, the farmers are rigorously searched by border guards. According to the BBC, they sometimes find packets of heroin just lying on the ground, having been thrown over the Pakistan border. If the farmers pick them up (and successfully sneak them past the border guards when they're searched again on returning), a courier comes to their home and collects the drugs after paying a small fee.[28] This 'spray-and-pray' system allegedly sits alongside sophisticated syndicates that smuggle hundreds of kilograms of drugs through Delhi's airport.

In 2015, the Society for Promotion of Youth and Masses and the All-India Institute of Medical Sciences in Delhi conducted the first large-scale survey of addiction in Punjab.[29] The study estimated that there were more than 850,000 drug users across the whole state, most of whom were young men. Of these, more than 200,000 were dependent. Out of all the opioids used, heroin was the most common. It was also the most expensive.

The survey calculated that the 'opioid industry' in Punjab was worth Rs 7500 crores, of which heroin accounted for Rs 6000 crores. According to the study, people with heroin addictions might be spending as much as Rs 1400 a day to source the drug.

After 2015, there have been several other small-scale studies. According to one in 2019, while heroin remained the most commonly used opioid, the prescription drug tramadol was also becoming extremely common. The study, agreeing with previous estimates from other sources, concluded that there were around 270,000 people who could be considered 'opioid dependent'. This is about 2.5 per cent of the total population of Punjab. From their sample of 6600 people, less than 15 per cent had visited a medical treatment centre. The Ministry of Social Justice's all-India report calculated that of those who need medical care for their drug dependency, only one out of every four receive any kind of treatment. But this is predominantly outpatient care: even a single consultation would count for the sake of the survey. The availability of full-time or part-time rehabilitation in a medical treatment centre is much lower: only one out of every twenty are lucky enough to access that kind of treatment.

The political leaders of the state and central governments seem content to focus on the crisis as a series of individual failings. In an episode of his radio programme, *Mann ki Baat*, Prime Minister Narendra Modi asked young people to just 'say no to drugs' – a phrase popularized by Nancy Reagan during her husband's racist anti-drug campaign in the 1980s. Whenever there is a discussion of broader systemic issues, the Indian government remains fixated on 'external threats' – narco-terrorists from Pakistan and so on. Narco-terrorist is another artifact from the Reagan era of world politics. Reagan used it to describe a conspiracy between communists and drug smugglers – a conspiracy that has been proven to be completely fictional.

In Punjab, the law enforcement agencies have stepped up arrests but most of these are of minor flunkies or individual consumers. According to P.S. Verma, a professor of political science, 'As many as 11,715 persons were arrested in 2012 which was almost double the number in 2011. The total number of arrests made in three years (2012–14) soared to 45,558.'[30] In the years 2012–14, the average number of arrests almost quadrupled from the rates in the 2000s. But these have had almost no effect on the broader drug ecosystem. Speaking to a reporter, a lawmaker from the Aam Aadmi Party asked,

> Where has the supply chain been broken? (Habit forming) tablets, poppy husk, smack, heroin and other drugs are easily available. Nothing has changed in three years … They say that drugs are making their way to Punjab from places like Madhya Pradesh, Delhi, Haryana, Rajasthan and Afghanistan. Have they arrested any supplier of these drugs from those places? The Punjab police–politicians–drug smugglers nexus continues. There is no change.[31]

An Appraisal of Fifty Years of Drug Policy

After more than fifty years of drug regulation, the 'drug-free world' imagined by the 1961 Single Convention is further away than ever. According to the United Nations data, there were an estimated 269 million drug users in 2018 – which is roughly 5 per cent of the world population (counting people between 15 and 64). Out of these, about 60 million were opioid users – accounting for around 1 per cent of the world population.[32] All of these statistics are much higher than for the previous decade.

Drug use is only growing. The illicit drug trade is now estimated to be the second largest industry in the world – only lagging behind the gargantuan oil industry.

In 2003, the British government's premier policy think tank produced a report that weighed the success of half a century of supply-side drug control policies driven by the USA. According to the report, 'despite interventions at every point in the supply chain, cocaine and heroin consumption has been rising, prices falling and drugs have continued to reach users'.[33] The report also claimed that if reducing harm to citizens was the goal of drug policy, supply-side measures have fundamentally failed. There is no evidence that they work. Initially, the British government tried to suppress the report but it was leaked to the public. As psychopharmacologist David Nutt puts it, 'anything that tries to measure or evaluate the success of the War on Drugs inevitably finds that it has failed, so evaluation and measurement are either suppressed, or not carried out in the first place'.[34]

Nutt is one of the foremost voices in the movement for more rational and pragmatic drug policies. He was an official advisor to the British government but was fired for publishing research and airing contrarian views to official government drug policy. In a famous 2010 study, Nutt along with a team of other experts drafted a comprehensive framework for analysing drug-related harm.[35] The framework lists sixteen types of harm: nine that affected the drug user, seven that affected other people. The nine harms that affected the user ranged from increased risk of death to loss of relationships. The other seven harms included increased rates of crime, economic costs, impact on family members, and so on. Using these criteria, they compared twenty different drugs – including legal ones like alcohol and tobacco (yes, they are drugs by any meaningful definition of the word). The results were completely at odds with prevailing

British policy. The drugs that caused the highest overall harm (to the user and to society) were alcohol, followed by heroin and crack cocaine. At the opposite end of the spectrum, the drugs that caused the least harm were LSD and mushrooms. While the study isn't perfect, there is broad consensus that their findings point in the right direction. It's undoubtedly on better scientific footing than the current drug laws which classify drugs according to completely arbitrary schedules. The US Drug Enforcement Administration classifies LSD and marijuana in the same category as heroin.

Criticism of drug policy often elicits a kneejerk response. Like every attempt at pointing out the violence and harm and fundamental failure of law enforcement agencies is often met with moral panic. Reforming drug laws isn't the same as legalizing all drugs; they will not lead to heroin being sold in supermarkets to children or something equally absurd. The hysteria is unfounded. The policies proposed by drug law reformers almost always start with decriminalization of small-scale drug possession. This doesn't affect the sale and manufacture of drugs – or the violent crimes associated with trafficking. It only ensures that drug use and addiction is removed from the criminal justice system and integrated into the healthcare system. For all the harm that drugs can cause the people who use them, imprisonment is almost universally more damaging. This is not a radical proposal. It has been tried and tested. In 2001, Portugal decriminalized the use and possession of all drugs. In 2020, the American state of Oregon did the same. Both times these initiatives were combined with measures for treatment and harm reduction. Hopefully, these are signs that the War on Drugs is slowly coming to an end.

Notes

1. McAllister, William B. *Drug Diplomacy in the Twentieth Century.* Routledge, 2000, p. 180.
2. McCoy, Alfred W. *The Politics of Heroin: CIA Complicity in the Global Drug Trade.* eBook, Lawrence Hill Books, 2003.
3. McCoy, Alfred W. *The Politics of Heroin: CIA Complicity in the Global Drug Trade.* eBook, Lawrence Hill Books, 2003.
4. Gunja, Fatima. *Race and the War on Drugs.* ACLU Drug Policy Litigation Project, 2003. https://www.aclu.org/other/race-war-drugs.
5. McCoy, Alfred W. *The Politics of Heroin: CIA Complicity in the Global Drug Trade.* eBook, Lawrence Hill Books, 2003.
6. Chouvy, Pierre-Arnaud. *Opium: Uncovering the Politics of the Poppy.* Harvard University Press, 2010, p. 117.
7. McCoy, Alfred W. *The Politics of Heroin: CIA Complicity in the Global Drug Trade.* eBook, Lawrence Hill Books, 2003.
8. Khan, Waseem, Jahanzeb Khalil and Manzoor Ahmad. 'History of Opium Cultivation in Pakistan: Socio-Economic Significance and Politics of Opium Eradication.' *Science International* 28, no. 2 (2016): 6.
9. Chouvy, Pierre-Arnaud. *Opium: Uncovering the Politics of the Poppy.* Harvard University Press, 2010, p. xiii.
10. For more info, see: Webb, Gary. *Dark Alliance: The CIA, the Contras, and the Crack Cocaine Explosion.* Seven Stories Press, 1998.
11. For more information, see: Paley, Dawn. *Drug War Capitalism.* AK Press, 2014.
12. Lopez, German. 'The War on Drugs, Explained.' *Vox*, 8 May 2016, https://www.vox.com/2016/5/8/18089368/war-on-drugs-marijuana-cocaine-heroin-meth.
13. This has been disputed by the aide's family. The aide himself couldn't speak one way or another since he had passed

away. For the full story, read: Baum, Dan. 'Legalize It All.' *Harper's Magazine*, April 2016. https://harpers.org/archive/2016/04/legalize-it-all/.

14. Boyd, Gerald M. 'Reagans Advocate "Crusade" On Drugs.' *New York Times*, 15 September 1986. https://www.nytimes.com/1986/09/15/us/reagans-advocate-crusade-on-drugs.html.

15. Block, Judge Frederic. 'Racism's Hidden History in the War on Drugs.' HuffPost, 1 March 2013. https://www.huffpost.com/entry/war-on-drugs_b_2384624.

16. Gunja, Fatima. *Race and the War on Drugs*. ACLU Drug Policy Litigation Project, 2003. https://www.aclu.org/other/race-war-drugs.

17. Nunn, Kenneth. 'Race, Crime and the Pool of Surplus Criminality: Or Why the "War on Drugs" Was a "War on Blacks".' *Journal of Gender Race & Justice* 6, no. 381 (January 2002): 427, https://scholarship.law.ufl.edu/facultypub/107.

18. Article 47, Directive Principles of State Policy, Constitution of India, 1950. https://www.constitutionofindia.net/constitution_of_india/directive_principles_of_state_policy/articles/Article%2047.

19. *Report of the Prohibition Enquiry Committee (1954–55)*. Government of India, 1955, p. 53.

20. Haq, M. *Drugs in South Asia: From the Opium Trade to the Present Day*. Springer, 2000, p. 112.

21. Haq, M. *Drugs in South Asia: From the Opium Trade to the Present Day*. Springer, 2000, p. 130.

22. Haq, M. *Drugs in South Asia: From the Opium Trade to the Present Day*. Springer, 2000, p. 136.

23. Haq, M. *Drugs in South Asia: From the Opium Trade to the Present Day*. Springer, 2000, pp. 140–41.

24. As per the data published by the Central Bureau of Narcotics available at http://cbn.nic.in/html/operationscbn.htm.

25. Bera, Sayantan. 'The Opium Trap.' LiveMint, 8 September 2017. https://www.livemint.com/Politics/6goxa4WRLKwlfonpAIFntM/The-opium-trap.html.

26. Lehne, Jonathan. 'Irrigation vs Education: The Long-Run Effects of Opium Cultivation in British India.' https://sites.google.com/view/jonathan-lehne/research. Working Paper.

27. Kh, Nivedita. 'Between Tradition and Trafficking: Opium in Arunachal Pradesh.' *Third Pole*, 28 December 2019. https://www.thethirdpole.net/en/2019/12/28/best-of-2019-between-tradition-and-trafficking-opium-in-arunachal-pradesh/.

28. Chhabra, Arvind. 'Punjab's Drug Menace: "I Wanted My Son to Die."' BBC News, 23 November 2018. www.bbc.com, https://www.bbc.com/news/world-asia-india-46218646.

29. *The Punjab Opioid Dependent Survey (PODS)*. Society for the Promotion of the Youth and Masses and the National Drug Dependence Treatment Centre, AIIMS New Delhi, 2015.

30. Verma, P.S. 'Punjab's Drug Problem: Contours and Characteristics.' *Economic & Political Weekly*, vol. LII, no. 3 (2017): 41.

31. Gopal, Navjeevan. 'The Never Ending War on Drugs.' *Indian Express*, 18 March 2020, https://indianexpress.com/article/cities/chandigarh/drug-menace-punjab-amarinder-singh-narcotics-drugs-and-psychotropic-substances-ndps-act-6319664/.

32. *World Drug Report 2020*. United Nations, Sales No. E.20.XI.6.

33. Nutt, David J. *Drugs – without the Hot Air: Minimizing the Harms of Legal and Illegal Drugs*. UIT Cambridge, 2012, p. 271.

34. Nutt, David J. *Drugs – without the Hot Air: Minimizing the Harms of Legal and Illegal Drugs.* UIT Cambridge, 2012, p. 273.

35. Nutt, David J., et al. 'Drug Harms in the UK: A Multicriteria Decision Analysis.' *Lancet* (London) 376, no. 9752 (November 2010): 1558–65.

Index

About the Author

Thomas Manuel is a journalist and award-winning playwright whose work revolves around history, science, education, or the intersection of all three. His words can be found in *Lapham's Quarterly*, Nib, Wire, *The Hindu*, among other publications. In 2016, he won The Hindu Playwright Award for his play *Hamlet and Angad*. He currently works at India Ink, a public history project where he makes videos about how the past continues to affect us today.

For the writing of his book *Opium Inc.* the author would like to acknowledge the support of the International Centre Goa (IGC) and its Scholars-in-Residence programme.

Website: thomasmanuel.com